Paul's Message and Ministry in Covenant Perspective

Paul's Message and Ministry in Covenant Perspective

Selected Essays

Scott J. Hafemann

CASCADE *Books* • Eugene, Oregon

PAUL'S MESSAGE AND MINISTRY IN COVENANT PERSPECTIVE
Selected Essays

Copyright © 2015 Scott J. Hafemann. All rights reserved. Except for brief quotations in critical publications or reviews, no part of this book may be reproduced in any manner without prior written permission from the publisher. Write: Permissions. Wipf and Stock Publishers, 199 W. 8th Ave., Suite 3, Eugene, OR 97401.

Cascade Books
An Imprint of Wipf and Stock Publishers
199 W. 8th Ave., Suite 3
Eugene, OR 97401

www.wipfandstock.com

ISBN 13: 978-1-62564-666-8

Cataloguing-in-Publication Data

Hafemann, Scott J.

Paul's message and ministry in covenant perspective : selected essays / Scott J. Hafemann

xx + 208 p. ; 23 cm. Includes bibliographical references.

ISBN 13: 978-1-62564-666-8

1. Paul, the Apostle, Saint. 2. Bible. Epistles of Paul—Theology. 3. Bible. Epistles of Paul—Criticism, interpretation, etc. I. Title.

BS2650.52 H33 2015

Manufactured in the U.S.A.   01/21/2015

To Dorington G. Little III

A pastor who can say with Paul the words of 1 Corinthians 11:1

Contents

Preface | ix
Abbreviations | xiv
Abbreviations of Ancient Sources | xviii

PART ONE

Paul's Message

1 Paul and His Interpreters since F. C. Baur | 3

2 Reading Paul's ΔIKAIO-Language: A Response to Douglas Campbell's "Rereading Paul's ΔIKAIO-Language" | 29

3 Paul's "History-of-Redemption" Use of the Old Testament in 2 Corinthians | 48

4 The Comfort and Power of the Gospel: The Argument of 2 Corinthians 1–3 | 62

5 The Glory and Veil of Moses in 2 Corinthians 3:7–14: An Example of Paul's Contextual Exegesis of the Old Testament | 85

6 The Sum of the Matter: Paul's Understanding of Perseverance | 100

PART TWO

Paul's Ministry

7 Paul's "Jeremiah" Ministry in Reverse and the Reality of the New Covenant | 107

8 "Because of Weakness" (Gal 4:13): The Role of Suffering in the Mission of Paul | 116

9 Pastoral Suffering: Recovering Paul's Model of Ministry in 2 Corinthians | 133

10 The "Temple of the Spirit" as the Inaugural Fulfillment of the New Covenant | 150

11 Paul's Concern for the Unity of the Church: An Embodiment of His New Covenant Theology | 167

12 Divine Judgment and the Completion of the Missionary Task: Paul's Motivation for Ministry in 1–2 Thessalonians | 185

13 The Sum of the Ministry: Challenges to Paul's Exclusive Gospel | 195

Bibliography | 201

Preface

This collection of thematically related, exegetical essays owes its existence to the encouragement of three people. Robin Parry, the respected editor of Cascade Books, invited me to put these articles together into a whole that has become greater than the sum of its parts. Robin's own work as a serious biblical-theological scholar made this invitation all the more encouraging. Tim Fox, one of my research students here at St. Andrews, did the hard work of organizing and reformatting all of the articles. It was only Tim's diligent, timely, and meticulous work, together with his cheerful attitude through all of the tedium of such labor, that made the completion of this project "doable." Finally, Mark Elliott, our Head of School, helped to make the project possible by providing monies through our Deas Fund to support Tim's efforts. Mark's collegiality, commitment to what is important, and striking erudition play a significant role both in my life and in the work of St. Mary's College. Thank you to all three. I know how fortunate I am for these gifts (1 Cor 4:7).

All of the essays presented here have been published previously. I am thankful for the permission granted in each case to reproduce them in this new context. Their current arrangement under the two rubrics of "message" and "ministry," and in this order, is intentional. For the driving force of these articles, taken as a whole, is to demonstrate that Paul's message of "the gospel of Christ" (cf. 1 Thess 3:2; Gal 1:7; 1 Cor 9:12; 2 Cor 2:12; 10:14; Phil 1:27; Rom 15:19) was determinative for the character of his ministry (1 Cor 2:1–5; 4:9–13; 2 Cor 2:14; 4:7–11; 6:3–10; 12:7–10). To imitate Paul was therefore to imitate Christ (1 Cor 11:1). The "stumbling block" and "foolishness" of the crucified Messiah that Paul proclaimed (i.e., the central content of his kerygma: 1 Cor 1:21–23) was embodied in the "weakness" that characterized his proclamation (i.e., the essential manner of his kerygma: 1 Cor 2:3–5), all of which took it shape from the contours of the history of redemption as expressed in the dawning of the new covenant (1 Cor 11:23-26).

Given their common themes, some overlap in the articles here collected is thus inevitable. Part of the reason for this as well is that many of the essays are "Corinthians-centric," especially 2 Corinthians. Though 1-2 Corinthians too often live in the shadow of Galatians and Romans, it is important to keep in view that Paul most likely wrote the Corinthian correspondence against the backdrop of what he had learned in Galatia and that he wrote Romans against the backdrop of what he had experienced in Corinth, having written his letter to the Romans from Corinth itself before returning to Jerusalem with the collection. Second Corinthians in particular consequently offers a central vantage point for examining the development of Paul's thinking at a crucial turning point in his life and ministry.

The articles also interrelate because Paul's message and ministry emerge from a history-of-redemption framework that fueled his theology. Indeed, as A. M. Hunter observed in 1943, the concept that best describes "the manifold wisdom of God" displayed both in the gospel of the kingdom and in the church it creates (Eph 3:8-12) must be borrowed from the Germans—namely, "the *Heilsgeschichte*" that "treats of a Saviour, a Saved (and saving) People, and the means of Salvation. . . . For the 'story' is of the consummation of God's saving purpose for his People (Ecclesiology) through the sending of his Messiah (Christology) and of the means of Salvation (Soteriology) . . . all of these are so closely connected that one implies the other—and all lead to the one centre, the *Heilsgeschichte*."[1] In a related word, one could say that Paul's thinking takes place within a historically oriented "eschatology." More specifically, Paul's theology centers on the salvific and ecclesiological implications of the dawning of the new age (Gal 1:4) of the new creation (Gal 6:15; 2 Cor 5:17) of the new covenant (1 Cor 11:25; 2 Cor 3:6; cf. Gal 4:24) in the midst of this evil age.

By the "covenant perspective" of Paul's message and ministry I therefore intend three interrelated realities, depending on the context. First, "covenant" can refer to God's overarching promise(s) as that which determines his actions. In this sense, for example, Paul talks about God's "promise to Abraham" in Rom 4:13, 20, which in view of the passages quoted in the context from Gen 15:6 and 17:5 makes it clear that he is referring to the Abrahamic "covenant" (cf. Rom 4:9, 17, 18, 22; for the same use, see

---

1. *Unity of the New Testament*, 9, 19. For the still-programmatic development of the concept, see Cullmann, *Heil als Geschichte*. For the history of this minority, but significantly persistent, school of thought, see Yarbrough, *The Salvation Historical Fallacy?* and my review of it in *TJ* 29 (2008) 153-56. For what this perspective looks like in practice, see Stuhlmacher, *Biblische Theologie des Neuen Testaments: Grundlegung*.

Rom 9:4, 7–9 [Gen 21:12; 18:10, 14;]; Rom 15:8; 2 Cor 7:1; Gal 3:14, 16; etc.). Second, in view of these promises, "covenant" can refer to Paul's understanding of a linear, promise-fulfillment relationship between the history of Israel as the "old covenant" and the history of the church under the Lordship of Jesus Christ as that of the "new covenant" (2 Cor 3:6, 14; cf. 2 Cor 1:20; Rom 9:7–8; 11:1; Gal 3:19, 29; 4:28; Eph 2:12; 3:6; etc.). Third, by "covenant" I also refer to my understanding of the implicit substructure of the relationship that exists between God and his people throughout the history of redemption. This relationship is determined by and consists of 1) God's covenant-creating redemption via acts of unconditional grace, 2) the covenant-defining stipulations that inextricably express this redemption, and 3) God's covenant-consummating promises of blessing and curse that fulfill redemption in relationship to the covenant stipulations.[2]

Though implicit, this threefold covenant structure, which Paul inherited from the Scriptures, can be detected throughout his writings. The first two senses of "covenant" have often been treated in Paul's writings and are minor themes in the essays that follow. It is Paul's elaboration of the covenant relationship, though often implied in his argumentation and in my treatment of it, that is the primary frame of reference for what follows. This threefold covenant relationship can be summarized and outlined as follows:

The Threefold Covenant Structure

Covenant Prologue
(The Past Indicatives of Redemption)

Covenant Stipulations
(The Present Expression of Redemption in Imperatives)

Covenant Blessings or Curses
(The Promised Future Indicatives of Redemption and Judgment)

This threefold covenant structure may be outlined as follows:

God's Unconditional Acts of Provision
by which he establishes the covenant relationship
(The Redemptive Foundation of the Covenant,
given as an act of grace in the past)

---

2. For an explication of this threefold covenant relationship throughout the canon, see my essay, "The Covenant Relationship."

which entails

The "Conditional" Stipulations
through which the covenant relationship is expressed
(The Commands of the Covenant
to be kept in the present)

which entails

The "Conditional" Promises or Curses
by which the covenant is consummated,
in regard to keeping or not keeping the covenant
(The Consummation of the Covenant,
to be fulfilled in the future)

It is my hope that in the following essays the tightly woven web of Paul's "covenant" perspective might become more apparent. In republishing these essays I have taken the liberty only to clarify their grammar and syntax and on occasion to add a small bit of information or to make more explicit the flow of the argument. My one regret in presenting this work, however, is its lack of interaction with more recent developments in scholarship, which would sharpen and refine my arguments in various important ways.[3] My review of Pauline scholarship in chapter 1 stops short of the latest debates. It especially lacks an awareness of the contemporary emphasis on Paul and the Roman Empire.[4] And most of the other essays were written before the current fissure opened up between those who emphasize an apocalyptic, participatory interpretation of Paul's theology and those who stress its historical, covenantal framework.

At the same time, this limitation also has a positive side. One value in looking at these "older" essays from the perspective of the present-day debates is to be able to see the ways in which current issues in Pauline scholarship are yet another instantiation of the fundamental difference between the "new perspective(s)" on the one hand and the understanding of the law/gospel contrast inherited from F. C. Baur on the other (see chapter 1). While the former began with a strong emphasis on the rediscovery of Schweitzer's

---

3. Of special interest is the recent work on Paul's hermeneutics in the Corinthian correspondence and its impact on early Christian exegetes by Mitchell, *Paul, the Corinthians and the Birth of Christian Hermeneutics*, as well as the recent commentaries and specialized studies of 2 Corinthians.

4. For a programmatic example of this emphasis, see Harrison, *Paul and the Imperial Authorities*.

"Christ-mysticism" as the center of Paul's theology, it eventually became broadly "covenantal" in its approach.[5] Conversely, the latter, though once strongly based on a two-covenant, law/gospel reading of Paul, has ironically now fostered a participatory reading of Paul's "gospel" that is taken to be a radical, apocalyptic break with the "law."[6] As my response to Doug Campbell's recent reading of justification suggests (chapter 2), such polarities are unfortunate, especially since Paul's understanding of the eschatological new covenant inaugurated with the coming of the Messiah may not include "participation in Christ" in the sense so often assumed to be at the heart of Paul's "in Christ" terminology.[7]

Lastly, in looking back over the span of time represented by these essays, I am much aware of the "covenant" relationships that, under God in Christ, sustain me and determine who I am: with my wife, Debara (still the definition of "partner"), with our family (now including Levi and Johanna!) and friends (N.B. Paul, as ever), and with my *Doktorvater*, Prof. Dr. Peter Stuhlmacher—more gifts from God not to be taken for granted. And inasmuch as this book focuses on the relationship between the apostle Paul's message and ministry, it is only fitting that the book be dedicated to my longtime friend and pastor, Dori Little. I am honored to be able to say "thanks" in this way for his faithfulness to God's call, his example of Christ-like perseverance, his profound prayers and expository preaching (always applicable!), his dedication to his family, and for the countless, unnoticed hours he spends in the long-lost, pastoral ministry of "visitation," even to me, though we are now an ocean apart.

---

5. For the former, see the programmatic work of Stendahl and Sanders surveyed in chapter 1. For the latter, see now Dunn's helpful summary, "The New Perspective on Paul."

6. See now, e.g., de Boer, *Galatians*, based on the earlier work of Martyn, esp. his collected essays, *Theological Issues*.

7. For one influential, participatory reading of Paul, see Gorman, *Inhabiting the Cruciform God*. Over against this polarization, N. T. Wright's *magnum opus*, *Paul and the Faithfulness of God* (esp. vol. 2), seeks to integrate a broadly covenantal reading of Paul's eschatology and ecclesiology with a strongly participatory reading of Paul's soteriology. For the beginning of a reexamination of the "in Christ" conceptuality in Paul's thinking, which I think points in the right direction, see now Novenson, *Christ among the Messiahs*, 119–26, and my review of it, "From Christ to Christ," in *ExpTim* 125 (2014) 179–81. In my view, when Paul speaks of "in Christ" (ἐν Χριστῷ [Ἰησοῦ]) with verbs of "being" he is referring to life within the sphere of the Messiah's rule as Lord; when he uses "in Christ" with statements of action he is referring to the Messiah's agency in bringing them about, i.e., "by means of the Messiah." This corresponds to the way in which ἐν + dative normally works; see Porter, *Idioms of the Greek New Testament*, 157, 159.

Abbreviations

AB	Anchor Bible
ABD	*Anchor Bible Dictionary.* 6 vols. Edited by D. N. Freedman. New York: Doubleday, 1992.
AnBib	Analecta biblica
ANRW	*Aufstieg und Niedergang der römischen Welt: Geschichte und Kultur Roms im Spiegel der neueren Forschung.* Part 2, *Principat,* 33.1. Edited by Hildegard Temporini and Wolfgang Haase. New York: de Gruyter, 1989.
BDAG	Walter Bauer, Frederick W. Danker, W. F. Arndt, and F. W. Gingrich. *Greek-English Lexicon of the New Testament and Other Early Christian Literature.* 3rd ed. Chicago: University of Chicago Press, 2000.
BDF	Friedrich Blass and Albert Debrunner. *A Greek Grammar of the New Testament* and *Other Early Christian Literature.* Translated and revised by Robert W. Funk. Chicago: University of Chicago Press, 1961.
BECNT	Baker Exegetical Commentary on the New Testament
BETL	Bibliotheca ephemeridum theologicarum lovaniensium
BJRL	*Bulletin of the John Rylands University Library of Manchester*
ca.	circa
CBQ	*Catholic Biblical Quarterly*
cent.	century
cf.	compare
ch./chs.	chapter/chapters
DJD	Discoveries in the Judaean Desert

DTJ	*Doon Theological Journal*
e.g.	for example
esp.	especially
ET	English translation
EvQ	*Evangelical Quarterly*
EvT	*Evangelische Theologie*
ExAud	*Ex Auditu*
ExpTim	*Expository Times*
GTJ	*Grace Theological Journal*
HNTC	Harper's New Testament Commentaries
HUCA	*Hebrew Union College Annual*
ibid.	in the same source as just cited
ICC	International Critical Commentary
i.e.	that is
Int	*Interpretation*
JBL	*Journal of Biblical Literature*
JETS	*Journal of the Evangelical Theological Society*
JSNT	*Journal for the Study of the New Testament*
JSNTSup	Journal for the Study of the New Testament: Supplement Series
JSOTSup	Journal for the Study of the Old Testament: Supplement Series
KEK	Kritisch-exegetischer Kommentar über das Neue Testament
LSJ	Henry George Liddell, Robert Scott, and Henry Stuart Jones. *A Greek-English Lexicon*. 9th ed. Oxford: Clarendon, 1996.
LXX	Septuagint
MT	Masoretic Text
n/nn	note/notes
NIBC	New International Biblical Commentary
NICNT	New International Commentary on the New Testament
NIGTC	New International Greek Testament Commentary
NIVAC	NIV Application Commentary
NovT	*Novum Testamentum*

NovTSup	Novum Testamentum Supplements
NSBT	New Studies in Biblical Theology
NT	New Testament
NTD	Das Neue Testament Deutsch
NTS	*New Testament Studies*
OT	Old Testament
OTL	Old Testament Library
SBJT	*Southern Baptist Journal of Theology*
SEÅ	*Svensk exegetisk årsbok*
SemeiaSt	Semeia Studies
SJT	*Scottish Journal of Theology*
SMT	*Swedish Missiological Themes*
SNTSMS	Society for New Testament Studies Monograph Series
ST	*Studia theologica*
s.v.	*sub verbo*; under the word
TANTZ	Texte und Arbeiten zum neutestamentlichen Zeitalter
TBei	*Theologische Beiträge*
TDNT	*Theological Dictionary of the New Testament*. 10 vols. Edited by Gerhard Kittel and Gerhard Friedrich. Translated by Geoffrey W. Bromiley. Grand Rapids: Eerdmans, 1964–76.
ThTo	*Theology Today*
TJ	*Trinity Journal*
TLG	*Thesaurus Linguae Graecae Digital Library of Greek Literature*. Irvine, CA: University of California, Irvine. Online: https://www.tlg.uci.edu.
TynB	*Tyndale Bulletin*
TZT	*Tübinger Zeitschrift für Theologie*
v./vv.	verse/verses
WBC	Word Biblical Commentary
WUNT	Wissenschaftliche Untersuchungen zum Neuen Testament
ZAW	*Zeitschrift für die alttestamentliche Wissenschaft*

ZNW	*Zeitschrift für die neutestamentliche Wissenschaft und die Kunde der älteren Kirche*
ZTK	*Zeitschrift für Theologie und Kirche*

Abbreviations of Ancient Sources

Aem.	Plutarch, *Aemilius Paullus*
Ant.	Plutarch, *Antonius*
Ant. Rom.	Dionysius of Halicarnassus, *Antiquitates romanae*
b. Ned.	Babylonian Nedarim
Bar.	Baruch
Exod. Rab.	Rabbah Exodus
1 En.	*1 Enoch*
4 Macc	4 Maccabees
Jub.	*Jubilees*
J.W.	Josephus, *Jewish War*
L.A.B.	Pseudo-Philo, *Liber antiquitatum biblicarum*
Lev. Rab.	Leviticus Rabbah
Liv. Pro.	Lives of the Prophets
m. Ker.	Mishnah Kerrithot
m. Mak.	Mishnah Makkot
Mart. Ascen. Isa.	*Martyrdom and Ascension of Isaiah*
Mith.	Appian, *Mithridatic Wars*
Num. Rab.	Numbers Rabbah
1QH	*Thanksgiving Hymns*
1QS	*Rule of the Community*
Pirqe R. El.	*Pirqe Rabbi Eliezer*

Praep. ev.	Eusebius, *Praeparatio evangelica* (*Preparation for the Gospel*)
QE	Philo, *Quaestiones et solutiones in Exodum* (*Questions and Answers on Exodus*)
Rom.	Plutarch, *Romulus*
Sat.	Horace, *Satires*
2 Bar.	*2 Baruch*
2 Macc	2 Maccabees
Sir	Sirach
T. Jos.	*Testament of Joseph*
T. Levi	*Testament of Levi*
T. Sol.	*Testament of Solomon*
Tg. Hos.	*Targum Hosea*
Tg. Ps.-J.	*Targum Pseudo-Jonathan*
Thes.	Plutarch, *Theseus*

PART ONE

Paul's Message

1

Paul and His Interpreters since F. C. Baur[1]

The history of Paul's significant interpreters stretches from his contemporaries (cf. 2 Pet 3:15–16!) to the present and includes such notable figures as Augustine, Luther, Calvin, and Wesley. Our focus here is on the way in which Pauline scholarship since the mid-nineteenth century has taken its cues from F. C. Baur and the "Tübingen school" that grew up around him. For despite the exponentially burgeoning volume of studies in the last 150 years, the basic perspectives of the Tübingen school have continued to provide both the structure and presuppositions for the modern study of Paul's writings. As a result of the agenda set by Baur's work, Pauline research in the twentieth century has focused predominantly on the interrelated questions of the center of Paul's thinking, Paul's view of the law, and the nature of Paul's opponents. Moreover, the questions raised by Baur concerning the place of Paul's theology in the history of the early church still remain unresolved.

F. C. BAUR AND THE TÜBINGEN SCHOOL

Ferdinand Christian Baur was professor of NT at the University of Tübingen from 1826 until his death in 1860. At the heart of Baur's work was his conviction that modernity could no longer accept the traditional Christian view of a transcendent, personal God. The concept of revelation as the disclosure of God's will, and of miracles as the act of a personal God in history,

---

1. From Scott J. Hafemann, "Paul and His Interpreters since F. C. Baur." In *Dictionary of Paul and His Letters*, edited by Ralph P. Martin et al., 666–79. Downers Grove, IL: InterVarsity, 1993.

must therefore also be rejected. By midcareer Baur became convinced that the traditional Christian view must be replaced by the new speculative philosophy of Hegel, which to Baur's mind offered the most coherent and comprehensive explanation of history and of the nature of reality. But in the final fifteen years of his life Baur came to reject Hegel's abstract view of God as infinite Spirit or eternal Idea, which in the evolving process of history was emerging from its own previous finite manifestations. In its place Baur returned to a simpler rationalism that emphasized universal ethical principles as the meaning of life. The value of Christianity lay in the fact that it taught such principles. Nevertheless, it was the Hegelian orientation of Baur's earlier and formative understanding of Paul and early Christianity that became determinative for subsequent scholarship.

Baur's Paradigm

In 1831 Baur published his seminal essay, "Die Christuspartei in der korinthischen Gemeinde, der Gegensatz des petrinischen und paulinischen Christenthums in der ältesten Kirche, der Apostel Petrus in Rom."[2] In it he laid out the foundation for his understanding of Paul and the history of the early church by applying the dialectical, evolutionary approach of Hegel's philosophy to 1 Cor 1:11–12. Based on this text Baur posited a *fundamental opposition* between Gentile Christianity, represented by Paul and the party of Apollos, with its universal, law-free, Hellenistically determined gospel, and Jewish Christianity, represented by Cephas and the "Christ-party," with its particular, law-orientated, Jewish-bound interpretation of the significance of Jesus. According to Baur, the "Christ-Party" was a Jewish-Christian faction that followed Peter and emphasized its own direct relationship to the historical Jesus through the original apostles whom Christ had appointed.

First Corinthians 1:11–12 thus provided a basic framework for understanding the conflict within early Christianity that provided the inner dynamic of Paul's writings. Paul's law/gospel contrast was seen to reflect the opposition within early Christianity between Paul and Gentile Christianity on the one side, and the Jewish Christianity supported by Peter, James, and the rest of the Jerusalem apostles on the other. It was to fend off the continual attacks by his Jewish-Christian opponents that Paul consequently developed his doctrine of justification by faith as the center of his theology. Moreover, according to Baur, this bitter conflict between Peter and Paul not

---

2. "The Christ-party in the Corinthian Church, the Conflict between Petrine and Pauline Christianity in the Early Church, the Apostle Peter in Rome." *TZT* 4 (1831) 61–206.

only dominated the rest of the writings of the NT, it also drove the historical development of the early church until the end of the second century, when it was eventually resolved by the emerging unity of the hierarchical Catholic church.

The height of the Tübingen school was reached in 1845 with the publication of Baur's *Paulus, der Apostel Jesu Christi: Sein Leben und Wirken, seine Briefe und seine Lehre* (published in English in 1875 in two volumes as *Paul, the Apostle of Jesus Christ, His Life and Work, His Epistles and His Doctrine*). As the capstone of his work on Paul, Baur now argued that the authentic Paul could only be found where the conflict between Jewish (Petrine) and Gentile (Pauline) Christianity was evident *and* where Paul's doctrine of a law-free justification by faith was explicitly presented in response. Those writings attributed to Paul that evince an attempt to mediate this conflict by finding a middle ground were regarded as a second stage in the development of the early church. Furthermore, any documents that reflected an authoritarian or ecclesiological attempt to resolve this conflict were considered part of the eventual Catholic resolution of the Jewish-Gentile Christian conflict around A.D. 200, which came about only in response to the common threat of Gnosticism.

Armed with this paradigm, Baur concluded that only Romans, Galatians, and the Corinthian letters could be considered authentic. On the other extreme, the Pastorals were clearly inauthentic, late second-century documents written against gnostics and Marcionites. The Prison Epistles and Philemon, although sometimes disputed in terms of authorship and theology, were also in reality aimed at gnostic opponents, being written between A.D. 120 and 140 as late examples of the Pauline school. First and Second Thessalonians were written in the generation after Paul (A.D. 70–75), but were of no particular significance, since they were of inferior quality theologically. They had no trace of the Pauline doctrine of justification by faith, nor of the conflict between Peter and Paul, and their eschatology conflicted with 1 Cor 15. Following his lead, Baur's students and followers then applied this basic scheme to the rest of the NT writings by categorizing them according to their theological "tendency" (*Tendenz*) as either Pauline (e.g., Hebrews; 1 Peter), Petrine-judaizing (e.g., James; Matthew; Revelation), mediating and conciliatory (e.g., Luke-Acts; Mark), or catholicizing (2 Peter; Jude; John).

Baur's Impact

As time went on scholars rejected the Tübingen school's evaluation of the late date and character of the majority of the Pauline letters. Its analysis of the rest of the NT and of the second century as a continuation of a conflict between Gentile and Jewish Christianity has also proved unconvincing, since it was based on the groundless identification of Simon the Magician in *Pseudo-Clementines* with Paul! Many, if not most, NT scholars have also rejected Baur's historical skepticism and philosophical rationalism, which as a matter of principle excluded the supernatural from history. Nor has the Tübingen school's complete skepticism concerning the historical Jesus gained wide acceptance, beginning as it did with D. F. Strauss's *Life of Jesus* in 1835 and positing as a result a decisive break between the life and teaching of Jesus and the Jerusalem apostles on the one hand, and that of Paul on the other.

But in spite of the weakness of his historical and theological judgments, Baur's consistent attempt to provide a comprehensive and coherent understanding of the history of the early church on the basis of historical reasoning alone, without recourse to supernatural interventions or to explanations based on the miraculous, did propel biblical scholarship into the modern world. Moreover, Baur's work also set the stage for the debate in the twentieth century over the relationship between the life and teaching of the historical Jesus and the theology of Paul. Most importantly, Baur's treatment of Paul raised the three interrelated, interpretative questions with which all subsequent students of Paul have had to wrestle in attempting to work out a comprehensive picture of Paul's life and theology: (1) the identity and perspective of Paul's opposition as a key to his own life and thought, (2) Paul's view of the law and its relationship to his own understanding of the gospel, and (3) the search for the generating center of Paul's theology (if indeed it is possible to talk about one such generative principle within Paul's varied writings).

It is these three questions, above all, which have determined the interpretation of Paul and his place within the history of the early church for the last 150 years. How one answers any one of them will greatly influence, and be greatly influenced by, one's understanding of the others. But for the sake of clarity, the three issues will be treated separately, inasmuch as the interpreters of Paul since Baur have usually entered the debate by one of these three avenues.

THE IDENTITY AND THEOLOGY OF PAUL'S OPPONENTS

No aspect of Pauline studies has received more attention in the twentieth century than the identity and arguments of Paul's opponents. And nowhere has the disagreement been more far reaching. Beginning with the work of Baur there have been at least eight major theories proposed for Galatians, and in the more difficult cases such as 2 Corinthians and Philippians, scholars have proposed no less than thirteen and eighteen different proposals respectively.[3] Despite the multitude of proposals, the debate concerning the identity of Paul's opponents in his various letters still centers on the validity of Baur's understanding of the conflict between Jewish and Gentile Christianity during Paul's day and on its *extent* within the Pauline corpus, since Baur was the first modem scholar to make Paul's opponents the key to interpreting the whole of Paul's writings.

The Polarization of Views in the Nineteenth Century

Of course, Baur's view was not new, nor was it uncontested. Ever since the Reformation most Protestant exegetes have held that Paul's opponents were "Judaizers" who advocated the necessity for Gentile Christians to be circumcised and to keep the Mosaic law. But already in the seventeenth century some scholars argued, in contrast, that Paul's opponents were gnostics, while others maintained that Paul's opponents were not comprised simply of Judaizers or gnostics, but included those whose teaching mixed legalistic, gnostic and/or enthusiastic elements. Indeed, just prior to Baur's work, Edward Burton offered in 1829 the most thoroughgoing presentation to date of the thesis that Paul's opponents were gnostics. The debate in the first half of the twentieth century thus had its immediate roots in the polarization that took place during the previous century between those who presented Paul's opponents as gnostics and those who, following Baur, saw them as Judaizers. Moreover, the debate centered primarily on the identity of Paul's opponents in Corinth because of the difference in subject matter between 1 and 2 Corinthians and the other Pauline letters. If Baur's thesis was to stand, it must be able to account for Paul's theology and opposition in 1 and 2 Corinthians, where the issue of the law does not appear to be central, even though, especially in 2 Corinthians, the focus of Paul's apologetic is still on his own legitimacy as an apostle.

---

3. See Gunther, *Opponents*, 1–5.

Lightfoot, Lütgert, and the History of Religions School

In nineteenth-century Germany the overwhelming majority of scholars thought that Baur was right, even in regard to the issues at stake in the Corinthian correspondence. But outside of Germany the reaction to Baur was significantly different. This was especially true in England, where J. B. Lightfoot led the way with his critique of Baur, entitled "St. Paul and the Three" (in his *St. Paul's Epistle to the Galatians*, 5th ed., 1884, 292–374), in which he maintained that Paul did not stand in opposition to the chief "apostles of the circumcision," James, Peter, and John, and that the opponents of Paul were not rival Christians associated with the "Pillar" apostles (Gal 2:9). Rather, the opponents behind Colossians, Romans, 1 Corinthians, and the Pastorals were part of a "Christian Essene" movement that was more gnostic in orientation than the traditional Pharisaic Judaizers whom Paul opposed in Galatians, 2 Corinthians, and Philippians. In contrast to the situation in Germany, Lightfoot's influence in the English-speaking world consequently mitigated Baur's impact by keeping scholars from interpreting Paul's letters as reflecting only one type of judaizing heresy.

Within Germany the first significant break with Baur did not come until the beginning of the twentieth century with the publication in 1908 of W. Lütgert's work, *Freiheitspredigt und Schwärmgeister in Korinth*. In Lütgert's view, Paul's opponents in his various writings could all be subsumed under the overarching rubric of "gnostics," or "pneumatics," whose background was a liberal, Alexandrian Judaism that taught a gnosis in the form of a haggadic exposition and expansion of Scripture. Only in Galatians could Paul's opponents clearly be identified as Christian, Pharisaic Judaizers. But even in Galatia a pneumatic opposition still existed, so that in his letter to the Galatians Paul was fighting against two fronts at once.

It was the rise of the *religionsgeschichtliche* ("history of religions") school, however, with its emphasis on a gnostic, mystery religion backdrop to early Christianity, that appeared to deal the deathblow to the reign of Baur's position. The history of religions school crystallized around the scholarship of W. Bousset, especially his 1913 work, *Kyrios Christos: Geschichte des Christusglaubens von den Anfängen des Christentums bis Irenaeus* (ET *Kyrios Christos: A History of the Belief in Christ from the Beginnings of Christianity to Irenaeus*, 1970), and R. Reitzenstein's study of the ancient mystery religions, *Die hellenistischen Mysterienreligionen* (1927, 3rd ed.; ET *Hellenistic Mystery-Religions: Their Basic Ideas and Significance*, 1977). As a result of these works, the attention of NT scholars was now forcefully directed to the conceptual world of Hellenism. In addition, the history of religions school offered for the first time a reconstruction of the development of early

Christianity that was just as comprehensive and extensive as that of Baur's. Prior to this time, the concept of "Gnosticism" had been used merely as a general description for certain theological tendencies. With the rise of the history-of-religions approach, this formerly vague term was now given the concrete and well-defined content needed to compete with the Tübingen school's ability to define the precise nature of Jewish-Christian legalism.

Yet, ironically, it was precisely the well-defined nature of Gnosticism offered by the history of religions school that brought about its own demise. In fact, the last serious attempt to argue that Paul's opponents in 2 Corinthians were gnostics was R. Bultmann's 1947 essay, *Exegetische Probleme des Zweiten Korintherbriefes zu 2 Kor 5:1–5; 5:11—6:10; 10–13; 12:21*, written in response to E. Käsemann's influential article, "Die Legitimität des Apostels: Eine Untersuchung zu II Korinther 10–13" (*ZNW* 41 [1942] 33–71). Käsemann had concluded that Paul's opponents in Corinth were simply pneumatics who, as part of an association of Palestinians in the Diaspora, emphasized in their preaching their own spiritual exploits and accomplishments. In Käsemann's view, to say more than this, especially to understand them as gnostics, was to go beyond the evidence of the text. In response, Bultmann argued that Paul's opponents in 2 Corinthians were in fact the same Christian gnostics whom Paul had opposed in 1 Cor 15. But what is most evident in Bultmann's response is his determination to maintain at all costs the existence of a pre-Christian Gnosticism. Bultmann's desperate attempt eventually failed, taking with it the entire program of interpreting early Christianity against the backdrop of the gnostic mystery religions, which had been a central tenant of the history of religions school. There was simply no evidence to justify their extension of the incipient gnostic tendencies apparent in some parts of the NT into a reconstruction of a full-blown pre-Christian Gnosticism like that first attested only in the second and third centuries.

The Bornkamm-Georgi Hypothesis

The collapse of the Bousset-Reitzenstein-Bultmann hypothesis thus freed scholarship from the burden of its past bias toward Gnosticism as the key to Paul's thought, while at the same time allowing it to retain the history of religions school's sound insight that early Christianity must be interpreted in the light of its surrounding religious context. Ultimately this continuing interest in Paul's religious environment and his opponents in Corinth culminated in the massive work of Dieter Georgi, *Die Gegner des Paulus im 2. Korintherbrief* (1964; ET *The Opponents of Paul in Second Corinthians*,

1986). Georgi's work was an extension and substantiation of the position of his mentor, Günther Bornkamm, whose overall understanding of Paul's life and thought was summarized in his now classic study, *Paul* (original German ed., 1969; ET 1971).

Georgi concluded that Baur's earlier adversaries had not been able to offer an adequate alternative because they had not taken seriously enough the Jewish origins and aspects of Paul's opposition. Georgi's extensive study of the missionary activities of Hellenistic Jews therefore sought to provide the history-of-religions foundation Lütgert and Bultmann had failed to produce in order to combat Baur's extensive depiction of Palestinian Judaism and Judaizers. Against this backdrop, Georgi's own study of the terminology in 2 Cor 10–13 led him to the conclusion that Paul's opponents were Jewish-Christian missionaries of Palestinian origin who utilized the propaganda methods of Hellenistic Jewish apologists. The result of Georgi's surveys of the Hellenistic-Jewish sources is a picture of Paul's opponents as Hellenistic-Jewish pneumatic missionaries whose self-understanding was based on the "divine man" (θεῖος ἀνήρ) tradition within Hellenistic Judaism.

The publication of Georgi's work finally confronted Baur's thesis with an equally systematic and comprehensive antithesis. If Lütgert had ended the *dominance* of Baur's position, Georgi appeared to have called into question its very *legitimacy*! Baur's traditional picture now seemed to be a thing of the past. The only task remaining, apparently, was to refine Georgi's position, which many scholars since then have attempted to do.

Oostendorp, Barrett, and the Revival of F. C. Baur

This new surge of optimism was premature. Not only was Georgi's work severely criticized for his methodology and use of sources, but the position of Baur itself still remained very much alive, despite the rise of the history of religions school. In a reversal of roles, however, it was now two scholars from outside Germany, D. W. Oostendorp and C. K. Barrett, who rose up to defend Baur's classic thesis, albeit with certain significant modifications.

Oostendorp modified Baur's Judaistic hypothesis by incorporating within it the central significance of the Spirit, which Baur had excluded and which had repeatedly become the basis upon which he was attacked. According to Oostendorp (*Another Jesus: A Gospel of Jewish Christian Superiority in II Corinthians*, 1967), the Judaizers in Corinth, as in Galatia, had connected the work of the Spirit with the observance of the law (cf. Gal 5:13–26), so that Paul's purpose was to contrast the law and the Spirit in such a way as to contradict their teaching (cf. Gal 3:1–5; 2 Cor 3:6). Oostendorp was able to integrate the reception and role of the Spirit with the issue of obedience to the law, both in the theology of Paul's opponents and in Paul's own understanding. Oostendorp thus brought together what, in the more traditional approach to Paul's opponents, had always been kept apart: the Spirit and the law.

Of even greater significance for the history of the debate is the fact that Baur's position has been strongly represented by one of the most influential of the recent interpreters of Paul in the English-speaking world, C. K. Barrett. In 1953 Barrett laid the foundation for his future work in his article, "Paul and the 'Pillar' Apostles" (in *Studia Paulina* [ed. J. N. Sevenster and W. C. Van Unnik; 1953], 1–19). Ten years later Barrett built upon this foundational study with a reexamination of the references and possible allusions to Peter in 1 and 2 Corinthians entitled "Cephas and Corinth" (in *Abraham unser Vater: Juden und Christen im Gespräch über die Bibel*; [ed. Otto Betz et al., 1963], 1–12). In this study Barrett concluded not only that it was probable that Cephas had visited Corinth, but also that the "man" who was building on Paul's foundation in 1 Cor 3:10–17 was either Peter himself or someone acting in Peter's name. Like Baur before him, Barrett thus posited the existence in Corinth of a Jewish-Christian "Cephas Party" in opposition to Paul.

If that were true, why then was Peter not mentioned in 2 Corinthians? Because, according to Barrett, and contrary to Baur's view, Paul still retained some respect for the original Jerusalem apostles. For this reason, rather than attack Peter directly, Paul released all of his "vigorous antipathy" on the "other agents" at work in Corinth under the guise of the authority of Peter—that is, the "false apostles" of 2 Cor 11:13–15. Thus for Barrett, as for Käsemann before him, a distinction must be made between the "false apostles" and the eminent Jerusalem apostles of 2 Cor 11:5 and Gal 2:9. Furthermore, the key to the situation in 2 Corinthians is the same as that in Gal 2:12: Peter's heart was in the right place, but he was easily frightened and used by others! At Corinth Peter had once again become an easily manipulated figurehead whose name and authority were being used by impostors. As in Gal 2, Paul was therefore once again in the uncomfortable position of not being able to repudiate Peter, while at the same time having to deal with those who wanted to destroy his work in Peter's name. From this point on, Barrett's subsequent work was aimed at strengthening this basic position.

The Deadlock in Recent Scholarship

After more than 150 years of scholarship the result of Barrett's extensive work was to destroy any notion that a general consensus had been reached concerning the identity and theology of Paul's opponents. By the mid-1970s the camps were equally divided. The very fact that Barrett could argue for Baur's position so persuasively in the face of its most serious challenge made it clear that scholarship was at a stalemate. The two basic positions were now both firmly entrenched and well fortified with a strong supply of documented arguments and counterarguments.

Equally devastating to the modern debate has been the serious doubt raised concerning the historical reality that is said to undergird both of these positions. Georgi's evidence for the existence of a "divine man" persona in Judaism as the key to Paul's opponents' self-understanding has been seriously called into question. Others have criticized Georgi's attempt to interpret "servants of Christ" in 2 Cor 11:23 in the sense of "envoys," while still others have rejected his entire enterprise by maintaining that Jewish parallels to the missionary motives and methods of Paul do not exist. On the other hand, those who want to maintain that Paul's opponents were in some sense "Judaizers" must now contend with the various challenges raised by the "new perspective on Paul" (see below). Indeed, some from this perspective doubt if Paul's polemics had anything to do with the real position of his opponents at all! Hence, like the gnostic hypothesis of a previous generation, both of the basic, remaining hypotheses now stand under the shadow of serious questions concerning their historical reliability.

Central to these questions is the realization that the current stalemate is a direct and natural result of the methodology employed in attempting to determine the nature of Paul's opposition. The inconclusive and internally contradictory history of Pauline studies since Baur has demonstrated that scholars must resist the temptation to reconstruct a grand hypothesis based on isolated fragments and "catchwords" from Paul's letters, which are then filled out by recourse to distant parallels. The simple fact is that there is no direct evidence from any of Paul's opponents themselves, unless James is read as an anti-Pauline polemic, which is itself certainly questionable.

Sumney's proposal of a "minimalist approach" to identifying Paul's opponents is therefore to be welcomed for its emphasis on the priority of exegesis in a "text-focused method," for its insistence upon a sound evaluation and use of proper sources, together with a "stringently" limited application of the "mirror technique" (i.e., reading the position of Paul's opponents directly out of Paul's own assertions as their opposite), and for its rejection of the attempt to approach the text with a previously determined, externally based reconstruction. It is also significant in view of the history of research that when Sumney himself applies his method to 2 Corinthians he offers no new insights into the identity of Paul's opponents. As Sumney's work thus illustrates, if progress is to be made in breaking the current deadlock, it will come about only when such a text-oriented approach to the problem is combined with a renewed analysis of Paul's own view of the law and the center of his thinking as they impinge upon the opposition that he faced, not only in Corinth, but also in Galatia, Antioch, and Jerusalem. Essential to such a renewed study is the recognition that in countering his opponents Paul drove a wedge between the "pillar apostles" and those who worked in their name by underscoring his essential unity with the Jerusalem apostles while at the same time opposing those who claimed to represent them (cf. Gal 2:1–10; 1 Cor 15:1–11; 2 Cor 11:5–6).

PAUL'S VIEW OF THE LAW

Baur's understanding of the conflict in the early church between a law-free, Pauline, Gentile Christianity and its judaizing, Petrine, Jewish-Christian counterpart was wedded to his acceptance of the Reformation understanding of Paul's law/gospel contrast. But as Douglas Moo observed in 1987, following the insight of Robert Jewett, "scholarship on Paul and the law in the last ten years has witnessed a 'paradigm shift.'"[4] All of the traditional "assured results" concerning Paul's law/gospel contrast are now being so seriously called into question that, after a long period of dormancy characterized by only minor refinements of the reigning paradigm, Paul's understanding of the law is currently the most debated topic among Pauline scholars.

Antecedents to the Paradigm Shift in Recent Scholarship

The recent destruction of the modern consensus concerning Paul's law/gospel contrast corresponds to the largely unheeded dissatisfaction earlier in the twentieth century with the traditional Reformation understanding of the centrality of justification by faith in Paul's theology (see below). It also picks up Johannes Munck's explicit and sustained critique of the continuing influence of Baur on modern scholarship.[5] To argue as Munck did, however, that the only substantive difference between Paul and the Jerusalem apostles was over mission strategy, based on Paul's conviction that the Gentiles must

---

4. Moo, "Paul and the Law," 287.
5. See his *Paul and the Salvation of Mankind*, 1959 (German, 1954).

be won to Christ *first* as a prelude to the salvation of Israel, did not seem to account for Paul's critique of the law itself. Moreover, Munck's contention that Paul was convinced that the arrival of the messianic age depended upon his own ministry, so that Paul himself becomes the central figure in salvation history, was viewed both as an overstatement of the case and as an untenable denial of the centrality of Christ in Paul's eschatology. Munck's supporting thesis that Paul's opponents were *Gentile* Judaizers has also garnered little support. Nevertheless, Munck's strong rejection of Baur's conflict theory concerning the relationship between Paul and the rest of the primitive church, based upon a supposed difference in their fundamental perspectives concerning Jesus and the law, is a lasting contribution of his work. For Munck, there was no essential theological conflict between Paul and Jewish Christianity.

On the other hand, H. J. Schoeps, *Paul: The Theology of the Apostle in the Light of Jewish Religious History* (1961; German, 1959), and W. D. Davies, *Paul and Rabbinic Judaism* (1948; see now the revised 4th ed., 1980), sought in different ways to challenge the traditionally negative view of Judaism and the supposed antagonism between Paul and the Jewish-Christian apostles against which Paul had been interpreted since Baur. Schoeps did not deny the basic Reformation understanding of Paul's view of the law. He merely sought to show its irrelevance to the "mainstream" Judaism of Paul's day, since, in Schoeps's view, Paul was in essence attacking only a distortion of Judaism represented by the Hellenistic Jews of the Diaspora. Conversely, Davies discounted Paul's critique of the law as mere polemic, and therefore as not essential to Paul's otherwise normal "rabbinic" views. As a result, Schoeps's "Paul" was not Jewish enough to win the day, and Davies's "Paul" was too Jewish to be accepted.

The modern consensus was significantly attacked again in 1964 in C. E. B. Cranfield's now programmatic article, "St. Paul and the Law" (*SJT* 17 [1964] 43–68). Cranfield did not deny the centrality of justification by faith for Paul's theology or the Reformation understanding of Paul's opponents. Rather, he redefined the focus of Paul's criticism of the "law" not to be on the Torah itself, but on its *perversion* into legalism as represented by the unique Pauline phrase, "works of the law" (cf. Rom 3:20, 28; Gal 3:2, 19, etc.). According to Cranfield, Paul coined this new terminology because there was no designation available in Greek to represent "legalism." Hence, when Paul speaks negatively of the "works of the law," or simply the "law," he is not opposing the law itself, but its perversion into works-righteousness. In 2 Cor 3:6 it is thus the "legalistic misunderstanding and perversion of the law," not the law itself, which kills. Conversely, Paul's positive statements concerning the law refer to the law freed from this legalistic misuse.

In arguing this, Cranfield's overall intention was to counter the axiom of the modern consensus that, for Paul, Christ had abolished the law. In stark contrast, though he abolished all forms of "legalism," Christ was the "goal" (τέλος) of the law itself (Rom 10:4).

Cranfield's view has won many followers and has been refined in many directions (see now his two-volume commentary on Romans, and the studies of C. F. D. Moule [1976], Ragnar Bring [1971], and, most importantly, D. P. Fuller [1980; 1992].) But this position has also been severely criticized for its reliance on what appears to many to be a self-confirming hypothesis in which Paul's negative statements concerning the law are simply taken to be about legalism, even when the full phrase "works of the law" is not used (see, e.g., Gal 3:10–12, 17–19). Others have pointed to its apparent failure to incorporate adequately some of Paul's statements concerning the abolition of the law itself (e.g., Gal 3:12, 15–20; Rom 6:14; 7:4). And now, after the advent of E. P. Sanders's work, NT scholars increasingly regard the historical basis for Cranfield's view to be a phantom.[6]

Finally, from a very different perspective on Paul's theology as a whole, a revitalized interest in biblical theology has led Hartmut Gese and Peter Stuhlmacher to reject the traditional Reformation understanding of the law/gospel contrast as a theological distinction between two competing ways of salvation (see P. Stuhlmacher, "Paul's View of the Law in the Letter to the Romans," *SEÅ* 50 [1985] 87–104; his *Reconciliation, Law, and Righteousness* [1986]; and his commentary on Romans [1989]). Instead, the law and the gospel are seen to represent an eschatological contrast between two periods in God's salvation history. Though still retaining the Reformation emphasis on the centrality of justification by faith in Paul's theology and on his corresponding critique of the law apart from faith, this approach views the law itself as also in need of "redemption" from its flesh-dominated role within the old covenant as the "Sinai Torah." Through the atonement of Christ and by the power of the Spirit, God has therefore redeemed not only humanity from the power of sin, but also the law. As the freed, eschatological "Zion Torah," God gives back to the law its original function of giving life which it had in paradise.

To date, although its contours are clear, this approach has not yet been fully developed. In addition, the refinement it offers with its emphasis on an eschatologically redeemed law either goes too far for the traditional view, or not far enough for those seeking to replace the old perspective with a new one. For in maintaining the centrality of justification by faith in Paul's thinking its criticism of the more traditional view does not strike at its essence.

---

6. But see his self-defense: Cranfield, "Works of the Law."

The "New Perspective" on Paul

Though substantial critiques of the reigning paradigm could certainly be found prior to 1977, these attacks were primarily aimed at the Reformation understanding of Paul's theology, rather than launching an assault on its perception of Paul's judaizing opponents. But as long as the traditional view of Paul's opponents remained substantially in place, the attempt to rethink Paul's own view could be dismissed not only as theologically or exegetically unsound, but also as historically misguided. Moo is therefore right in dating the destruction of the modern consensus to the advent of Sanders's contribution to the debate, beginning with his *Paul and Palestinian Judaism* in 1977. Sanders's view of Paul is, of course, in and of itself worthy of note. But this is not what turned the tide in Pauline studies.

Sanders changed the course of scholarship on Paul because he succeeded in forcing scholars to rethink *fundamentally* the nature of the opposition Paul faced in his churches, and consequently the character and content of the criticism he raised against it. He accomplished this feat by presenting his own portrayal of Paul against the backdrop of a comprehensive and polemically forceful understanding of Palestinian Judaism as a religion of nonlegalistic "covenantal nomism." According to Sanders, rather than demanding a perfect "works-righteousness" as the prerequisite for entering into the covenant, the "covenantal nomism" pervasively found throughout Palestinian Judaism "is the view that one's place in God's plan is established on the basis of the covenant and that the covenant requires as the proper response of man his obedience to its commandments, while providing means of atonement for transgression."[7] Thus, for Palestinian Judaism at the time of Paul, "the intention and effort to be obedient constitute the *condition for remaining in the covenant*, but they do not *earn* it."[8] Sanders's conclusions concerning Palestinian Judaism, though certainly not new (cf., e.g., the work of G. F. Moore before him), and not without their critics, could therefore not be ignored, combined as they were with a corresponding reinterpretation of Paul's polemic against the law.

For the majority of scholars, Paul's world had suddenly changed, and with this change came the need to rethink Paul's view of the "problem" or "plight" of the law itself, which for Sanders came about for Paul not in response to Judaism *per se*, but only in view of the "solution" now offered in Christ. For if Sanders and his followers are right about the nature of Palestinian Judaism in Paul's day and the impetus for Paul's critique of the "law,"

---

7. Sanders, *Paul and Palestinian Judaism*, 75.
8. Ibid., 180 (emphasis his).

then the traditional Reformation view of "Paul's polemic is left hanging in midair, and it is necessary either to accuse Paul of misunderstanding (or misrepresenting) his opponents, or to find new opponents for him to be criticizing."[9] The effects of the paradigm shift regarding Judaism precipitated by Sanders, now widely accepted, have thus been both far-reaching and decisive for the way in which Paul has been read in the decades after Sanders's work.

As is always the case, it is easier to tear down than to build up. Since the early 1980s the study of Paul's view of the law has been marked by a flood of studies seeking to work out the implications of Sanders's paradigm for "the new perspective on Paul," to quote the title of the 1983 article written by J. D. G. Dunn, one of the leading voices of this radical reorientation. In addition to Dunn's many studies (see, e.g., his collection of essays, *Jesus, Paul, and the Law: Studies in Mark and Galatians*, 1990; his two-volume commentary, *Romans*, 1988; and now his volume, *The New Perspective on Paul: Collected Essays*, 2005) and Sanders's own subsequent works on Paul and Judaism (see especially his *Paul, the Law, and the Jewish People*, 1983; *Judaism: Practice and Belief, 63 BCE–66 CE*, 1992; and *Paul*, 1991), most important among these new voices have been the works of Heikki Räisänen in Scandinavia, especially his *Paul and the Law* (1983), and, in Germany, the study of Reinhold Liebers, *Das Gesetz als Evangelium: Untersuchungen zur Gesetzeskritik des Paulus* (1989). Pride of place in terms of widespread influence goes of course to the voluminous body of work created by the British scholar, N. T. Wright, earlier marked out by his *Climax of the Covenant* (1991) and *What Saint Paul Really Said* (1997), and now culminating in his two-volume magnum opus, *Paul and the Faithfulness of God* (2013). Often at odds with one another on individual points of history and exegesis small and large, these studies are unified by their common conviction concerning the nonlegalistic nature of first-century Judaism and their corresponding rejection of the traditional Reformation understanding of the law/gospel antithesis as the key to Paul's view of the law and the theology of his opponents.

The Current Diversity of Proposals

Dating from Sanders's initial work in 1977 a forceful and, in part, successful attack has thus been mounted on the traditional understanding of Paul's view of the law. The plethora of new proposals spawned by this paradigm shift, however, suffers as much from internal dissent as from external

---

9. Moo, "Paul and the Law," 293.

critique, since no new consensus has yet emerged among them concerning the reason(s) why Paul actually rejected the "works of the law," nor concerning the actual referent of "works of the law" in Paul's writings. Moreover, the earlier positions represented by Cranfield and Stuhlmacher continue to win adherents, while the early studies of Charles H. Cosgrove, *The Cross and the Spirit: A Study in the Argument and Theology of Galatians* (1988); Roman Heiligenthal, *Werke als Zeichen, Untersuchungen zur Bedeutung der menschlichen Taten im Frühjudentum, Neuen Testament und Frühchristentum* (1983); Frank Thielman, *From Plight to Solution: A Jewish Framework for Understanding Paul's View of the Law in Galatians and Romans* (1989); and Peter J. Tomson, *Paul and the Jewish Law: Halakha in the Letters of the Apostle to the Gentiles* (1990), have signaled a new way forward due to their recognition of the positive role that obedience to the law plays in the soteriological structures of both Judaism and Paul. At the same time, although the pendulum of opinion is now swinging toward the new perspective, proponents of the more traditional view, such as Seyoon Kim, Gerd Lüdemann (who has once again picked up and argued extensively and explicitly for the validity of the Tübingen school's perspective), Otfried Hofius, Martin Hengel, Robert H. Gundry, Thomas R. Schreiner, Brice L. Martin, Stephen Westerholm, together with a growing number of more recent, often nuanced studies (e.g., Roland Deines, John Barclay, Francis Watson, Michael Bird, Preston Sprinkle, Simon Gathercole), continue to argue that the "paradigm shift" in Pauline studies has been misguided and that "there is more of Paul in Luther than many twentieth-century scholars are inclined to allow."[10]

As with the question of the identity and nature of Paul's opponents, the positive result of this great diversity among contemporary scholars is that it drives interpreters back to the text itself. Students of Paul are now approaching his writings with a healthy skepticism concerning *all* paradigms as they search for fresh insight into passages that suddenly look new again. To that end, Paul's emphasis on his essential unity with the Jerusalem apostles as the conduits of the teaching of Jesus and on the positive role that the law played "in Christ" and under the power of the Spirit must once again play a decisive part in the forging of a new consensus (cf. 1 Cor 11:23-26; 15:1-7; Rom 1:1-4; Gal 5:1—6:16; Rom 8:1-8; and the use of the law in Pauline ethics). Furthermore, the centrality of Paul's eschatological conviction that Christ has initiated the beginning of the new creation and the establishment of the new covenant in fulfillment of Jer 31:31-34 and Ezek 36:26-27 needs to be taken seriously as a key to Paul's understanding of the law. As Peter Stuhlmacher has stressed, it is against this eschatological backdrop that the

---

10. Westerholm, *Israel's Law*, 173.

question must be raised regarding the exact locus of the "problem" with the law as it functioned under the old covenant, as well as its role in the new. To raise the question of the impact of Paul's eschatology on his view of the law is also to call attention to the larger question of the center of Paul's theology as such, which is the last and most important question raised by Baur's work.

THE CENTER OF PAUL'S THEOLOGY

Until the mid-1970s most German scholarship maintained an inextricable link between its traditional Reformation understanding of Paul's law/gospel contrast and the overriding conviction that the center of Paul's thinking was the concept of the righteousness of God as encountered in the doctrine of justification. This view was bolstered by the corresponding understanding of Paul's opponents as predominantly Judaistic legalists who insisted that, in addition to faith in Christ, adherence to the law was necessary for gaining and/or maintaining a righteous standing before God.

As with the other pillars of Baur's perspective, this too was not without its challengers within Germany (see below), while Anglo-Saxon scholarship was never dominated by this position or directed in the same way by the search for the center of Paul's theology. Instead, some of the leading scholars outside of Germany sought to understand Paul's doctrine of justification as merely one aspect within a larger panorama of theological themes. The various themes of Paul's theology were therefore not organized as derivatives of this one, generating center of Paul's thought. Rather, Paul's theology was analyzed either according to the traditional structure of systematic theology (e.g., creation, anthropology, sin, redemption, christology, eschatology, etc; for prime examples of this approach, see D. E. H. Whiteley, *The Theology of St. Paul*, 1964; and Herman Ridderbos, *Paul: An Outline of His Theology*, 1975 [original Dutch ed., 1966]), or within the structure of some other organizational principle (see, e.g., Richard N. Longenecker, *Paul: Apostle of Liberty*, 1964, who took the broader issue of "legality-liberty" as the organizational framework for displaying Paul's thought; and F. F. Bruce, *Paul: Apostle of the Heart Set Free*, 1977, who presented Paul's theology within the historical outline of Paul's missionary travels). And yet, due to the influence of the Reformation's questions on the study of Paul and as a result of the leading role that German scholarship played for the first seventy years of the twentieth century, the dominant question within Pauline studies has remained whether justification by faith is the conceptual center of Paul's thought.

Challenges to the Traditional View

Already in 1904 William Wrede had argued in his book, *Paulus*, that the doctrine of justification was not the generating principle of Paul's thinking but merely a polemical doctrine (*Kampfeslehre*) aimed at the Judaism of his day. The generating principle of Paul's theology, Wrede maintained, was his eschatological conviction that Christ had ushered in the proleptic beginning of the kingdom of God. But it was left to Albert Schweitzer to take Wrede's emphasis on eschatology and employ it as the *framework* of Paul's thought in his influential book, *Die Mystik des Apostels Paulus* (1930; ET *The Mysticism of Paul the Apostle*, 1931), which was to date the most convincing and thoroughgoing alternative to the traditional view. Schweitzer combined Wrede's emphasis on eschatology with Adolf Deissmann's earlier development of Paul's "Christ-mysticism," which Deissmann had argued was "the characteristic expression of [Paul's] Christianity," as evidenced by the 164 times that the formula "in Christ" appears in Paul's writings.[11] Hence, for Schweitzer, being "in Christ" was not merely a cultic reality as Deissmann had emphasized, but an eschatological reality that was experienced physically and sacramentally, having been brought about by the inaugurated kingdom of God now present with the turn of the ages. Viewed in this way, "mysticism" was the key to Paul's thinking. The title of Schweitzer's book is thus misleading, since for Schweitzer this mysticism was not the result of some immediate and timeless "oneness" with Christ. Nevertheless, Schweitzer relegated the doctrine of justification by faith to a mere "subsidiary crater" (*Nebenkrater*) of Paul's thought, since it was found only in certain letters (predominantly in Galatians and Romans) and then only in reference to the specific problem of the law as raised by Paul's controversy with the Judaizers.

Despite their programmatic nature, the work of Wrede, Deissmann, and Schweitzer did not win the day in the German-speaking world. Nor did W. D. Davies's rejection of the centrality of the law/gospel contrast and the doctrine of justification in Paul's thought, argued in his *Paul and Rabbinic Judaism* (1950), gain a hearing outside of England and America. It was not until the seminal writings of Krister Stendahl and E. P. Sanders that these earlier protests found a foothold in scholarship. For ever since the work of Stendahl and Sanders the traditional understanding of the center of Paul's thought has been increasingly called into question.

Stendahl's essays, "The Apostle Paul and the Introspective Conscience of the West" (1960) and "Paul among Jews and Gentiles" (1963), were

---

11. See his *Paulus*, 1911 and 1926; ET *Paul: A Study in Social and Religious History*, 1912, p. 140, for the quote and evidence.

originally written in Swedish and were published in English in his *Paul among Jews and Gentiles and other Essays* (1976). Stendahl's reinterpretation of Paul's theology grew out of his conviction that, due to Reformation theology and the grid of Luther's own conversion experience, Paul's teaching concerning justification by faith had been removed from its original setting regarding the relationship between Jews and Gentiles and transposed into the very center of his teaching about salvation. Rather than addressing the status of Gentiles within God's plan for the world, as it does in Paul's writings, the doctrine of justification by faith was now seen to be the abstract, doctrinal response to the despair of humanity brought about by the failed attempt to live up to the moral demands of the law or by the pride caused by humanity's attempt to justify itself by the law. When the original focus of justification is lost, the Pauline problem of the relationship between Jews and Gentiles becomes captive to the Western problem of the introspective conscience. As a corollary to this misunderstanding of the role of justification in Paul's thought, Paul's Damascus Road experience has been wrongly universalized as an experience of conversion, rather than rightly understood as Paul's specific call to be the apostle to the Gentiles.

Hence, for Stendahl, "Paul's argument about justification by faith neither grows out of his 'dissatisfaction' with Judaism, nor is intended as a frontal attack on 'legalism,'" but instead was "hammered out by Paul for the very specific and limited purpose of defending the rights of Gentile converts to be full and genuine heirs to the promises of God to Israel. Their rights were based solely on faith in Jesus Christ."[12] For Stendahl, therefore, Paul's view of justification by faith served merely as an apologetic doctrine that "'justified' the status of Gentile Christians as honorary Jews."[13] As such, the doctrine of justification by faith can lay no claim to being the pervasive or organizing principle of Paul's thought.

In much the same way, E. P. Sanders's reexamination of the religious pattern of Judaism in light of the central issue in Paul's thinking of the relationship between Jews and Gentiles led him as well to reevaluate the driving force of Paul's theology. Just as Paul's opponents can no longer be understood as legalistic Jews who held to a form of works-righteousness, so too justification by faith must be given up as the clue to Paul's thought.[14] Instead, following Schweitzer, the dominant conception of salvation in Paul's letters is the transfer from one sphere of lordship (sin, death, the law) to another (righteousness, life, the gospel), so that being saved both entails

12. Stendahl, *Paul*, 127, 2.
13. Ibid., 5, cf. 130.
14. Sanders, *Paul and Palestinian Judaism*, 438.

and is brought about by becoming "one" with Christ. If the religious pattern of Judaism in Paul's day can be called "covenantal nomism," the pattern of Paul's religion can thus be described as "participationist eschatology."[15]

There have also been those who, like H. Räisänen, have stressed that due to the occasional nature of Paul's theology it is asking too much to seek the center to Paul's thinking in the first place. Indeed, the fact that Paul was not a systematic theologian in his approach to doctrine, or in his mode of presentation, is widely acknowledged today. But for Räisänen, not only is Paul not systematic in his framework, his thinking itself is characterized by internal contradictions concerning the relationship between the law and his gospel, from hostility and mutual exclusion in Galatians, to compatibility and inclusion in Romans. Räisänen's understanding of Paul as fundamentally inconsistent has not carried the day, nor should it. It is one thing to recognize the occasional nature of Paul's letters, but quite another to conclude that Paul's thinking lacks an internal coherence or conceptual focus.

The Debate within and against the Traditional View

The traditional interpretation of justification by faith as the center of Paul's theology has undergone a significant development of its own in the last fifty years. The internal debate has focused on the meaning of the "righteousness of God" in Paul's thought (cf. Rom 1:17; 3:21–22, 26; 10:3; 2 Cor 5:21; Phil 3:9) and on the relationship of Paul's doctrine of justification to his other central affirmations. Above all, scholars have sought to understand more precisely the interplay between justification by faith and the new creation, the role of the Spirit, the expectation of moral transformation in Christ, the coming judgment by works, and Paul's hope for the future consummation and vindication at Christ's return (cf., e.g., Rom 2:13; 3:24; 4:25; 5:9; 10:4; 1 Cor 6:11; 2 Cor 5:17; Gal 6:15; Titus 3:7).

The starting point for the modern debate is the work of Rudolf Bultmann, no doubt the most influential NT scholar of the twentieth century. As an extension of Luther's basic position, Bultmann argued in §§28–30 of his *Theology of the New Testament* (2 vols.; 1948, 1953; ET 1951, 1955) that for Paul the righteousness of God, which is granted to the *individual* upon his or her justification by *faith*, was a forensic concept. As such, it does not refer to an ethical change brought about in a person as a result of one's obedience to the law, but to an eschatological reality, which, although originally related to the end times, is now experienced by the believer as a pure gift of God's grace.

15. Ibid., 552.

Bultmann's view was based on his reinterpretation of Paul's theological categories in existential terms in which God was viewed not as an external subject in himself, but only from the perspective of his relationship to humanity, while humanity was equally viewed only in relationship to God. For Bultmann, history thus becomes the arena in which God encounters humanity directly and individually in order to call for a decision in response to the preaching of the gospel, rather than being the working out of God's redemptive plan on the way toward an ultimate consummation at the return of Christ.

The legitimacy for this reinterpretation of Paul's view of history and eschatology was found in Paul himself, who had continued the process of demythologizing the Jewish, apocalyptic gospel of Jesus as the messianic Son of Man originally preached by the early church into a kerygma concerning Jesus as the divine Son of God which could be preached and understood in a Hellenistic context. For Bultmann, this explains why Paul's letters show hardly a trace of the historical Jesus or of the Jewish and Palestinian tradition of the early Christians, since Paul received the Christian tradition after it had already been passed through the filter of the Hellenistic church. In line with this reconstruction, Bultmann saw Paul's opposition to be a Judaistic legalism based on the law's own teaching, which not only could not be kept perfectly, but also *itself* brought about sinful boasting as a result of the very demand for obedience. So Paul opposed the law and those Jewish Christians who held to it for both quantitative reasons (no one can keep the law perfectly) *and* qualitative reasons (the very attempt *itself* to keep the law is already sin). Luther's law/gospel contrast therefore reaches its apex in Bultmann's reading of Paul.

In stark contrast, Ernst Käsemann argued in his paradigmatic 1961 article, "Gottesgerechtigkeit bei Paulus" (*ZTK* 58 [1961] 367–78; ET "The Righteousness of God in Paul," in *New Testament Questions of Today*, 1969, 168–82), that for Paul the righteousness of God was not primarily a *gift* for the *individual* as a consequence of encountering God, but a cosmic and creative *power* under which the *corporate* people of God are brought to live as a result of having been freed in baptism from the power of sin and death. Rather than referring to a righteousness that *comes* from God as a gift, as Bultmann argued, for Käsemann the righteousness of God is God's *own* righteous behavior, expressed in his saving activity as an outworking of his covenantal faithfulness to his creation and to his people. Hence, for Käsemann, Paul's thought must not be interpreted primarily in existential terms, but in apocalyptic categories. The content of the righteousness of God is the rule of Christ over the world and his people in anticipation of God's final cosmic triumph. Salvation is not fundamentally the experience of receiving

God's righteousness, but of being brought back into obedience to the righteousness of God manifest in Christ.

The most important contribution to this ongoing debate has been the further development of Käsemann's basic perspective in the work of Peter Stuhlmacher, beginning with the 1966 revised form of his dissertation, *Gerechtigkeit Gottes bei Paulus* (*The Righteousness of God in Paul*). Against the backdrop of the OT and Jewish, apocalyptic understandings of the righteousness of God, Stuhlmacher has argued that decisive for Paul's thought was his conviction that the new age of the righteousness of God has already broken in with Christ, so that God's people are now living in the overlapping of the ages. The present experience of the righteousness of God does not refer, therefore, primarily to a forensic transaction in heaven that transcends time. Instead, Paul spoke of the present reality of the righteousness of God precisely because God's power to save and to vindicate, in accordance with his faithfulness to his covenant, was already being poured out in the world through Christ. The righteousness of God is thus first and foremost the power of God that brings one into the new world of the kingdom of God. In turn, the believer's experience of God's righteousness is made possible by the "forensic situation" brought about by the cross of Christ and realized in the world through participation in the body of Christ.

Stuhlmacher then addresses the tension between the theological categories of imputed and effective or real righteousness by emphasizing that the Spirit is the ontological bridge that makes possible the Pauline assertions concerning one's real participation in the righteousness of God. In contrast to the view of Schweitzer and those who follow him, by virtue of the presence of the Spirit mystic union with Christ and justification are bound together in one reality for Paul, rather than being in conflict or distinct from one another. For according to Stuhlmacher, being justified includes, in Paul's perspective, being put into the realm and experiencing the reality of the Spirit as a proleptic realization of the future new creation (cf. Rom 8:2–17; 1 Cor 12:13).

In the English-speaking context Käsemann's fundamental paradigm, based on the conviction that apocalyptic thinking is the "mother" of all Christian theology, was further developed and applied consistently to all of Paul's thought in J. Christiaan Beker's, *Paul the Apostle: The Triumph of God in Life and Thought* (1980). Beker too recognized with the majority of modern scholars that Paul's thought is not systematically developed or presented. Beker's distinct contribution was to argue, however, that for Paul the apocalyptic triumph of God that has now been brought about proleptically in the Christ-event, but will only reach its final victory in the imminent future triumph of God, is nevertheless the coherent and *symbolic* (not doctrinal!) center of Paul's gospel. The center of Paul's thought is thus neither an abstract doctrine nor a life-changing experience. According to Beker, it is "a mistake to define Paul's coherent center *either* in terms of a too-narrow conceptual definition—that is, in a petrified conceptuality ('justification by faith,' 'sacramental participation,' etc.)—*or* in terms of a too-general characterization ('being in Christ,' 'the Lordship of Christ')."[16] Instead, "Paul's coherent center must be viewed as a symbolic structure in which a primordial experience (Paul's call) is brought into language in a particular way.... That language is, for Paul, the apocalyptic language of Judaism, in which he lived and thought."[17]

In Beker's view, the genius of Paul is his corresponding ability to correlate and apply this overarching and consistent apocalyptic theme to various, distinct situations without dissolving the coherence of the gospel. Beker argues that for Paul "in nearly all cases the contingent interpretation of the gospel points—whether implicitly or explicitly—to the imminent cosmic triumph of God."[18] Hence, Beker too rejects Bultmann's attempt to remove the apocalyptic elements from Paul's gospel by demythologizing them into an existential self-understanding as an attempt to remove the very content of the gospel itself. But unlike Käsemann and Stuhlmacher, Beker rejects the conclusion that the theme of the righteousness of God is the central theme of Paul's writings. For Beker, it too is merely one of the many expressions of the underlying symbolic theme of the coming triumph of God. "Thus, righteousness must be viewed as *one* symbol *among* others and not as *the* center of Paul's thought."[19]

As the history of scholarship from Wrede to Beker demonstrates, the challenge from the end of the twentieth century is to rethink Paul's theology in such a way that the implicit centrality of eschatology is brought together with Paul's actual assertions on a doctrinal and personal level concerning what *God through the Christ* has accomplished in history and for the believer. At the same time, to pursue the question of the center of Paul's theology is also to ask what it means for the *believer* to be living in the kingdom of God, which, although *already* inaugurated, has *not yet* been established in all its fullness. Within this context, and in anticipation of the coming triumph and judgment of God, the need to delineate the meaning of the righteousness of

---

16. Beker, *Paul the Apostle* (preface to the 1984 ed.), xvii. See too the review of Beker's work by R. P. Martin, *JBL* 101 (1982) 463–66.

17. Ibid., 15–16.

18. Ibid., 19.

19. Ibid., 17.

God and the means of the justification of God's people, both now and in the future, still remains the crux for interpreting Paul's letters.

PROSPECTS FOR THE FUTURE

The history of Pauline research since F. C. Baur has highlighted the crucial importance of determining the historical context within which Paul's thought was developed and expressed. As a consequence, recent studies of Paul have increasingly focused on the study and classification of Paul's rhetoric (programmatically in this regard, H. D. Betz's *Galatians*, 1979; and his earlier work, *Der Apostel Paulus und die sokratische Tradition: Eine exegetische Untersuchung zu einer 'Apologie' 2 Korinther 10–13*, 1972) and on the sociology of Paul's communities (programmatically, Wayne A. Meeks, *The First Urban Christians: The Social World of the Apostle Paul*, 1983; and the many works of Gerd Theissen, especially *The Social Setting of Pauline Christianity*, 1982). Nevertheless, such studies remain subsidiary "craters" in service of the main task of interpreting the *content* of Paul's *own* thought as it was expressed in response to the needs of his communities and the opposition that he faced.

The history of Pauline research since Baur has also made it clear that one's picture of Paul will be determined, above all, by whether one interprets his letters primarily and predominantly against the Greco-Roman philosophical and religious world of Paul's day, as Bultmann argued (to which we must now add "political"!), or in light of the Hellenistic-Jewish subculture of the first century and its Scriptures, as Adolf Schlatter proposed. This is the great watershed among students of Paul. It remains true despite the fact that modem scholarship has shown the great degree to which the Judaism of Paul's day had already become Hellenized, so that it is both a historical and categorical mistake to view Paul as *either* Jewish *or* Hellenistic in his thought. Paul was clearly a Hellenistic Jew. Nevertheless, the fundamental issue in Pauline studies remains the determination of the *primary* religious and theological context within which Paul's thought is to be understood.

How one decides this issue will determine how one reads Paul. And how one reads Paul will determine how one evaluates the relationship between Jesus and Paul on the one hand, and the place of Paul in the development of the early church on the other. Baur saw Paul as the great "Hellenizer of Christianity," so that Paul's opponents became the other apostles themselves. Those who likewise look first to the religions and philosophies (and now politics) of the Greco-Roman world to explain Paul's thought must also posit a gap, if not hostility, between Paul and the early church in Jerusalem.

Against the backdrop of this decision, it is worth remembering the words of Ritschl. Already in 1856 he recognized that the enduring value of Baur and the Tübingen school would be in the counter-reactions that it would evoke: "The Tübingen school has fallen to pieces and its initiative will only deserve recognition in the measure that it leads to opposition against the system of early Church history as presented by Baur and Schwegler, and as it furthers the cultivation of biblical theology more than has been the case up to now."[20]

After one hundred fifty years of Pauline studies the need still exists for a developmental, rather than conflict model of Paul's apostolic life within the history of the early church, and for the corresponding cultivation of a biblical theology that incorporates Paul's theology not only within that history, but also within the Old Testament and Jewish *Traditionsgeschichte* that created it. This need has been underscored in the twentieth century by the study of Paul from an explicitly Jewish perspective (in addition to the work by Schoeps, see Samuel Sandmel, *The Genius of Paul: A Study in History*, 1958; Schalom Ben-Chorin, *Paulus: Der Völkerapostel in jüdischer Sicht*, 1970; and now Alan F. Segal, *Paul the Convert: The Apostolate and Apostasy of Saul the Pharisee*, 1990). Even adherents to the "new perspective" on Paul, who have worked hard to renew our understanding of Paul within the Judaism of his day, have often not taken the Jewish matrix of Paul's own thinking seriously enough as the decisive conceptual source for Paul's thinking. Moreover, the debate concerning the law and the role of justification in Paul's thought hinges on the question of Paul's understanding of redemptive history (cf. Gal 3–4; 2 Cor 3:7–18; Rom 3:21–26; 9–11), which itself can only be answered by a renewed study of Paul's "use" of the OT. This, in turn, raises the still larger question of the relationship of Paul as the "apostle to the Gentiles" to Israel as the old covenant people of God. Such studies have all received decisive beginnings at the end of the twentieth century (see, e.g., the works of Dietrich-Alex Koch, *Die Schrift als Zeuge des Evangeliums: Untersuchungen zur Verwendung und zum Verständnis der Schrift bei Paulus*, 1986; Richard B. Hays, *Echoes of Scripture in the Letters of Paul*, 1989; N. T. Wright, *The Climax of the Covenant: Christ and the Law in Pauline Theology*, 1991; and the various motif studies and treatments of particular key passages in which Paul quotes, alludes to, or relies upon the OT implicitly for his self-understanding and theology, such as Seyoon Kim, *The Origin of Paul's Gospel*, 1981; James M. Scott, *Adoption as Sons of God*, 1992; and Karl Olav Sandnes, *Paul—One of the Prophets?* 1991). The future of Pauline studies at this juncture in its history is dependent upon just these

---

20. Quoted by Harris, *Tübingen School*, 108–9.

kinds of studies if we are to move forward in our understanding of Paul as he understood himself: the Jewish apostle to the Gentiles, whose message came from the history of his people, their Scriptures, and the history of Israel's Messiah.[21]

---

21. For further reference, see Becker, *Paulus*; Bring, "Paul and the Old Testament"; Colpe, *Die religionsgeschichtliche Schule*; Cranfield, *Epistle to the Romans*; Cranfield, "Works of the Law"; Davies, *Paul and Rabbinic Judaism*; Dunn, "New Perspective on Paul"; Ellis, *Paul and His Recent Interpreters*; Ellis, "Paul and His Opponents: Trends in Research"; Epp and MacRae, eds., *New Testament and Its Modern Interpreters*; Fuller, *Gospel and Law*; Fuller, *Unity of the Bible*; Gunther, *St. Paul's Opponents and Their Background*; Harris, *Tübingen School*; Hübner, "Paulusforschung seit 1945"; Kümmel, *New Testament*; Moo, "Paul and the Law"; Moule, "Obligation in the Ethic of Paul"; S. Neill and N. T. Wright, *Interpretation of the New Testament 1861–1986*; Sanders, *Paul and Palestinian Judaism*; Schweitzer, *Paul and His Interpreters*; Schweitzer, *Mysticism of Paul the Apostle*; Stendahl, *Paul among Jews and Gentiles*; Sumney, *Identifying Paul's Opponents*; Gundry Volf, *Paul and Perseverance*; Way, *Lordship of Christ*; Westerholm, *Israel's Law and the Church's Faith*; Wright, *Climax of the Covenant*; Wright, *What Saint Paul Really Said*; Wright, *Paul and the Faithfulness of God*.

2

Reading Paul's ΔIKAIO-Language

A Response to Douglas Campbell's "Rereading Paul's ΔIKAIO-Language"[1]

Theologically, in understanding our relationship with God we ought to agree with Douglas Campbell's concern to combat all "Western contractualism," which is so "congenial to modern thought and culture" (196). Contrary to Paul's perspective, such a worldview entails "a fundamentally rationalistic and moralistic, and invariably quite individualizing, anthropology" based on "a conception of the human person that primarily governs itself . . ." (196). Campbell is right to reject any anthropology in which "an essentially autonomous individual sets off on a quest for salvation driven and governed by her own conceptions" (196).

Campbell's own resistance to such a construct is based on his conviction that this "Western contractualism" can be countered once we reject "a forward construal of the argument in Rom 1–3" and resist its "virulent conditionality . . . within Paul . . ." (196). This rejection of Rom 1–3 as the foundation to Paul's own thought must include a rejection of any "conditional account of Paul's discussions of faith" (197) and its corresponding

---

1. From Scott J. Hafemann, "Reading Paul's ΔIKAIO-Language: A Response to Douglas Campbell's 'Rereading Paul's ΔIKAIO-Language.'" In *Beyond Old and New Perspectives on Paul: Reflections on the Work of Douglas Campbell*, edited by Chris Tilling, 214–33. Eugene, OR: Cascade, 2014. All in-text citations refer to Douglas Campbell, "Rereading Paul's ΔIKAIO-Language," in *Beyond Old and New Perspectives on Paul: Reflections on the Work of Douglas Campbell*, edited by Chris Tilling, 196–213 Eugene, OR: Cascade, 2014.

retributive-justice reading of Paul's δικαιο-terms (197). Concerning the latter, Campbell rightly points out that inasmuch as δικαιοσύνη θεοῦ is a subset of all descriptions of being, it too is "fundamentally active and dynamic," since we should resist any dichotomy between "being and act or activity" (198, following Gunton). A "dynamic understanding of ontology" further underscores an essentially subjective reading of the genitive θεοῦ, since "any reference to a divine attribute or aspect of being *must* be a reference simultaneously to divine activity and hence to something both inherent in and proceeding from God..." (198). The same holds true for the "ontological dynamism" of human δικαιοσύνη, which "*must* be an ongoing, dynamic state of right behavior and activity..." (198).

In turning to the Pauline texts regarding the righteousness of God themselves, a proper emphasis on the decisive role of internal, contextual evidence in order to overcome the lexical fallacy of etymologizing (199) leads Campbell to conclude that "δικαιοσύνη θεοῦ is an event; it is singular; it is saving, it is liberating; it is life-giving; and it is eschatological or resurrecting" (199–200).[2] This description aligns with Käsemann's conclusion in *Paulinische Perspektiven* that the righteousness of God is "God's sovereignty over the world revealing itself eschatologically in Jesus' leading to a saving gift with the characteristics also of a power..." (200).

THE ACTIVITY OF BEING

At this point, a small, but eventually significant observation needs to be made about Campbell's adaptation of Käsemann's work: given Campbell's own emphasis on "ontological dynamism," it is equally important not to collapse being *into* activity (e.g., indicating that the righteousness of God *is* an event or power) lest the dynamism itself be destroyed or replaced with a beingless monism. Käsemann's definition exhibits this danger. The righteousness of God is not the activity *per se*, but an inextricable, organic *expression* of God's character in saving, life-giving, eschatological acts of deliverance that express both God's sovereignty and his power, which in turn can be evaluated or described as a characteristic of God in view of God's right actions (i.e., in the abstraction δικαιοσύνη θεοῦ). As Campbell himself points out, the use of δικαιοσύνη in reference to God "often seems to have a connotation of 'rightness'" (201). God is righteous because, as the expression of his being, he does what is right. This becomes significant in view of the scriptural contexts of the Pauline affirmations dealing with the righteousness of God, to which Campbell then turns.

2. See Campbell, *Deliverance*, 683–88.

Romans 1:16-17 is the *locus classicus* in any treatment of the righteousness of God in Paul's theology. Campbell's treatment of this passage is incisive in its focus on Ps 98/97:2-3LXX as an essential backdrop to Paul's argument in this passage. In this regard it is important to note that Paul's use of Ps 98/97:2-3LXX in Rom 1:17 points to the significance of the organic unity of, but at the same time distinction between, divine being and activity. For as Campbell helpfully points out, Paul is relying on this psalm of divine kingship for his understanding of God's righteousness, in which God *displays* his sovereignty as king by delivering his people. However, this is only half of the story. The same *distinction between*—albeit at the same time *unity of*—God's character as king and the expression thereof also makes it possible and necessary to link the expression of God's righteous kingship not only to his rescue of the righteous, but also to God's judgment of the wicked. Cremer's classic study pointed in the right direction, but it failed to incorporate the entire scope of God's being-action. This led to the one-sided interpretation of God's righteousness only in terms of its salvific action that has been typical of German scholarship.[3] Indeed, as Campbell observes, "it is 'right' for a king to save his people when they are in extremity" (202). But there is a strong, albeit secondary emphasis in the biblical tradition that it is also right for the king to judge those in rebellion against his rightful authority.[4] Both are equally "ethical action," and both are demanded by the "underlying relationship" with his people that exists in accord with the king's responsibilities (quotes from 202; the point is mine). This dual focus is reflected in Psalm 98/97LXX itself. There the *inclusio* to the revelation of God's righteousness in saving his people in Ps 98/97:2-3LXX is the affirmation in Ps 98/97:9LXX that the Lord comes to judge (κρίνω) the inhabited world ἐν δικαιοσύνῃ and the peoples "in justice" (ἐν εὐθύτητι).

It does not seem possible to limit the divine judgment in view in Ps 98/97LXX only to his salvific actions on behalf of his people; rather, in order to deliver his people, God must judge the nations, an action that is equally righteous and just. This has important implications for reading Paul's argument in Rom 1:16-32. In view of the organic unity that exists between God's righteous character and the entirety of his actions within the biblical narrative in general, and against the specific scriptural backdrop of Ps 98/97LXX in particular, no wedge need be driven between Rom 1:17 and 18. Instead, it is possible to take the γάρ of Rom 1:18 seriously as a ground

---

3. For the German tradition and its subsequent adaptation to include God's *Richtergerechtigkeit*, see my "'Righteousness of God,'" xv-xli.

4. Cf. Isa 5:16; 10:22; Lam 1:18; Neh 9:33; Dan 9:14; cf. Rev 19:11; and in relationship to God's "righteousness," see Deut 33:21; Judg 5:11; 1 Sam 12:7; Pss 31:1-3; 51:14; 89:15-17; 103:16; 143:1-2, 11-12; Isa 26:8-10; Dan 9:7, 13-19.

for the argument of the revelation of God's righteousness in 1:16–17. Indeed, is Paul following the flow of the argument from Ps 98/97:2 to 97:9LXX in his own move from Rom 1:16–17 to 1:18?

KINGSHIP AND COVENANT

Campbell derives God's right action from God's underlying identity as a king "*qua* king" and from the "nature of the underlying relationship" with God's people that this entails, which he can then parallel in part with the role of a contemporary business executive (202). As he summarizes it, "The story of divine kingship that (Paul) evokes establishes the rightness of God's saving action *in its own terms*" (202, emphasis mine). It must be asked, however, whether biblically, and especially in Psalm 98/97LXX as a backdrop to Rom 1:17, this relationship between God as king and his people is presented as intrinsic to God by virtue of his being a (divine) king, or whether it is established with Israel as a contingent consequence of God's particular covenant actions on her behalf.[5] In *Deliverance*, Campbell could affirm in regard to divine kingship in general that covenantal associations of divine faithfulness "are clearly not far away, and any such reading is not far from the truth," so that "covenantal associations" are "*possibly*" found also in relation to the "righteousness of God"; nevertheless, such "covenantal connotations are consequently *possible* but not *necessary* semantic resonances of the phrase δικαιοσύνη Θεοῦ."[6] In fact, Campbell asserts, "In the immediate location of 1:16–17, and its particular allusion to Ps 98, I see nothing that activates such specific resonances explicitly."[7]

However, in Ps 97:3LXX God makes his righteousness known by mightily saving his people, not because he is a "king," but as a result of the fact that God "remembered his mercy to Jacob and his truth to the house of Israel" (ἐμνήσθη τοῦ ἐλέους αὐτοῦ τῷ Ιακωβ καὶ τῆς ἀληθείας αὐτοῦ τῷ οἴκῳ Ισραηλ). Far from being merely "possible," the collocation of the motifs of "remembrance," "mercy and truth" (cf. the typical covenant formula for describing God, חסד ואמונה[8]), "Jacob," and "the house of Israel"

---

5. Cf., e.g., Ps 98:2LXX, where the God who rules as the one sitting amidst the cherubim on high is the great God who is exalted by all peoples as the God "in Zion" on earth, his characteristically covenant location.

6. *Deliverance*, 700, emphasis his.

7. Ibid., 701.

8. Contra Campbell, the reference to "his steadfast love and faithfulness" (חסדו ואמונתו) in Ps 98:3 is a reference to God's response to his covenant commitments or promises; cf. Gen 24:27 (covenant promise to Abraham); Gen 32:10 (covenant promises to Jacob over Esau); Exod 34:6 (basic covenant declaration); 2 Sam 2:6; Isa

is overwhelmingly covenantal. What obligates God is not the fact that he is a king *per se*, but the fact that he is king *over Israel* as a result of his own covenant-creating and covenant-sustaining actions in fulfillment of his promises to the patriarchs. It is not kingship *qua* kingship, but the king's role in the covenant that provides the key explanatory concept canonically for Paul's understanding of righteousness. God is not simply a divine king, he is *Israel's* king because of the covenant he has enacted based on his acts of deliverance as recounted in the historical prologues of the covenant texts. It is this covenant-commitment that is the ground for Israel's appeal to YHWH for help.

The biblical material is unique in this regard. The Scriptures are the only ancient texts in which the concept of covenant was applied directly to a deity in relationship to his people; everywhere else it is used only of earthly kings.[9] To look to God as king within this context is thus itself an inherently covenantal act. Campbell rightly observes that this ancient covenant framework also explains why in Israel's world the role of king and judge were united in one person. A covenantal notion of righteousness, with its forensic

---

16:5 (steadfast love, faithfulness, righteousness as coordinate concepts); Mic 7:20 (in reverse order, with reference in context both to Exod 34:6 and to God's faithfulness and steadfast love to Jacob and Abraham); Ps 25:10 (the Lord shows steadfast love and faithfulness to those who keep his covenant!); Ps 40:10-11 (God's righteousness, faithfulness, salvation, steadfast love [LXX: ἔλεος!], and truthfulness are all used synonymously in the context of keeping the covenant Torah); Ps 88:11 (they are not found in the grave or Abbadon!); Ps 89:2-3 [ET: 89:1-2] (in the context of an explicit reference to God's covenant with David); Ps 89:25, 34, 50 [ET: 89:24, 33, 49] (in the context of God's keeping his steadfast love in 89:29 [ET: 89:28], used synonymously with keeping the covenant to David); Ps 92:3 [ET: 92:2] (in a song for the Sabbath); Ps 100:5 (to his covenant people as his "sheep," cf. Num 27:17; 2 Sam 24:17//1 Chr 21:17, with King David, the former sheepherder now watching over the people); 1 Kgs 22:17//2 Chr 18:16; Pss 74:1; 78:52; 95:7; 119:176; Isa 53:6; Jer 23:1; 50:6; Ezek 34:2-31; Mic 2:12; Zech 10:2; 11:7, 11; Mark 6:34//Matt 9:36; John 10:4-27; 21:16-17; Heb 13:20; 1 Pet 2:25. Cf. חסד in the context of keeping the covenant in references to Exod 34:6 in Num 14:18; Deut 5:9-10; Jer 32:18; Joel 2:13; Jonah 4:2; Pss 103:8; 145:8; Neh 9:17; and חסד used alone in Deut 7:9, 12; 1 Kgs 8:23; Ps 106:45; Dan 9:4; Neh 1:5; 9:32; 2 Chr 6:14; 2 Sam 22:51, with its reference to praise among the nations for God's salvation of the king, David, and all his descendants (cf. Ps 18:50); 1 Kgs 3:6; Isa 54:10; 55:3, used with an explicit reference to covenant; Isa 63:7, with reference to the house of Israel; Jer 9:24, in the context of God's righteousness to those of the circumcision, with uncircumcised hearts; Jer 33:11, with its contextual reference to keeping the promises of the covenant to David; and note esp. that Ps 61:7 speaks of the enthronement of God's king, with a prayer for God's steadfast love and truthfulness over him; cf. Ps 89:15.

9. For a most helpful discussion of the comparative nature and function of covenant in the ancient Near East and within the Pentateuch, see now Walton, *Ancient Near Eastern Thought*, 287-301, esp. his corresponding emphasis on the differences between the abstraction "law" within a legal system and the Torah of covenant stipulations.

implications, is therefore integral to the righteousness of God expressed in his apocalyptic acts of deliverance as "king." As Ps 98/97LXX declares, God acts covenantally as king in accord with his righteous judgments in regard both to his people and to those who oppress them. In view of God's covenant promise to Abraham to bless those who, like Abraham, honor him by placing their faith in the Lord (Gen 12:1–3, etc.), God may even decide that those called to be his people may not always be his people; likewise, the Gentiles who formerly oppressed God's people may be incorporated into them (cf. Rom 2:23–29 in relationship to Rom 4:11–12, 16–17 and Rom 9:24–26; 10:11–13).

THE (UN)CONDITIONALITY OF THE COVENANT

The diminishing of covenant as a key explanatory concept for Paul's theology of divine kingship and, hence, for Paul's understanding of the righteousness of God, seems to lead Campbell to lapse into the same kind of natural theology that he rightly rejects as part of the traditional justification paradigm. The sinner and the sinful nation do not appeal to God's righteousness for help because they are sinners *qua* sinners and because God is a king *per se*, banking on the fact that it is naturally "right" for God, as such, to help (202). Biblically speaking, and by definition, people have no inherent claim on God's mercy. This is made clear by Ps 143/142:2LXX, which Campbell again helpfully points out is quoted in Gal 2:16 and Rom 3:20 (203). Here too the sinner's appeal for mercy is based on the fact that God's specific covenant acts and concomitant commitments (the "promises" of God) make the God of Abraham the king of this *particular* sinful nation, so that, unlike all others, God's reputation is inextricably bound up with this one people. The psalmist emphasizes that he cries for help and mercy because he is *God's* slave (Ps 142:2: καὶ εἰσέλθῃς εἰς κρίσιν μετὰ τοῦ δούλου σου) and can therefore appeal to *God's* righteousness, which is again paralleled to *God's* "truthfulness," the LXX's rendering of covenant faithfulness. In Ps 142:1LXX, ἐν τῇ ἀληθείᾳ σου (באמנתך) parallels ἐν τῇ δικαιοσύνῃ σου, which again anticipates its covenant corollary, God's חסד/ἔλεος, in 142:8. In short, in the words of Ps 142:10, the sinner confidently calls upon God to teach him to do God's will "because you are my God" (ὁ θεός μου). For the parallel within Ps 142:11 itself makes clear that God's righteousness is explicitly defined as God's concern for his own "name" as "Lord," so that maintaining his reputation and character by answering the psalmist's cry is in essential accord with God's truthfulness. This divine righteousness, rather than precluding the sinner's plea for mercy, can therefore be the very basis for the sinner's appeal.

Psalm 143/142LXX is part of a larger canonical motif in which God's righteousness is expressed in his steadfast commitment to remain faithful or "true" to his covenant obligations (= promises). These obligations entail helping those who humbly rely on God alone as their king, here expressed in the prayer of Ps 142:1LXX.[10] God's own reputation is consequently at stake when his people take these promises seriously and look to him for help (Ps 142:9LXX); not to help those who depend on him would call his own righteousness into question. Preventing this from happening is therefore an essential aspect of God's "obligated righteousness" as Israel's king.[11] Conversely, God is not committed to help those who do not trust in him. Seen in this covenant light, the unconditional acts of the divine king (the covenant prologue) are to lead inextricably to a response of faith on the part of his people (the covenant stipulations). This corresponds to Paul's own purpose as an apostle of Jesus Christ to bring about the "obedience of faith among all the Gentiles on behalf of [God's] name" (Rom 1:5).[12]

---

10. I.e., what it means for YHWH to "do righteousness" (cf. Jer. 9:23) is that "Yahweh is a God who acts true to himself and preserves proper order in the world" (Scullion, "Righteousness," 728). Cf. e.g., Gen 18:19; 38:26; Exod 23:7; Lev 19:36; Deut 16:18; 33:11; 2 Sam 8:15; 1 Kgs 8:23; Pss 23:3; 37:6; 72:1-2; 106:2-3; 119:7, 62, 75, 138; 143:2; Prov 17:5; Isa 1:26-27; 5:16; 9:6-7; 28:17; 33:5; 43:9, 26; 48:1; 56:1; 58:2; Ezek 3:16-21; 18:5, 19, 22, 27; 33:14, 16; 45:10, etc. God's righteousness encompasses us individually, as well as the cosmos (cf. Pss 33:4-6; 89:11-17). For the single OT use of the exact expression, "the righteousness of God" (צדקת יהוה/δικαιοσύνη κύριος), see Deut 33:21.

11. For the glory of God, i.e., acting "for the sake of his name," as the basis and goal of God's action to save and to judge as the expression of his righteousness, see e.g., Exod 7:3-5; 9:14-16; 14:4; 1 Sam 12:22; 2 Sam 7:23; Pss 25:11; 79:9; 106:8; Isa 43:6-7, 21, 25; 44:23; 46:13; 48:9-11; 49:3; Jer 13:11; 14:7, 9, 20-21; 33:8-9; Ezek 20:9, 14, 22, 44; 36:20-32. I owe the insight that God's righteousness consists in his unswerving commitment to maintain his "glory" or reputation as the sovereign, free Lord to Piper, *The Justification of God*, 81-101.

12. In unpacking the meaning of faith the reference to παντὶ τῷ πιστεύοντι in Rom 1:16 should not be read apart from the "obedience of faith" (ὑπακοὴ πίστεως) in Rom 1:5. Campbell's stress on the organic unity of being-activity is again helpful here. As another example of this differentiated, organic unity, the genitive πίστεως in Rom 1:5 is best construed not as an epexegetical genitive, in which obedience is redefined as faith (as in much Lutheran theology), or even as a genitive of source, in which faith leads to obedience as a subsequent step or stage in the Christian life that entails a distinct response over against faith (as in much Reformed theology, with its "third use of the Law"). Rather, the meaning of Rom 1:5 correlates with the use of the middle voice in Gal 5:3, where faith's expression in love is the fulfillment of the law (Gal 5:14; see below). In the same way, in Rom 1:5 faith *itself* is expressed in obedience. Thus, since in the genitive construction of Rom 1:5 *obedience* is the lead noun incorporating faith as its descriptor, when Paul restates his purpose as an apostle in Rom 15:16-18 he can do so in terms of bringing about obedience among the Gentiles without mentioning faith at all.

Thus, contra Campbell, though the covenant is established *unconditionally* as an act of God's sovereign and free grace, it is also *conditional*, calling for faith's obedience as its stipulation, albeit a stipulation that is engendered, motivated, and *sustained* within the covenant relationship by God's own presence and power as king.[13] There are therefore *two* reasons for the psalmist's prayer in Ps 142. The ground clause in Ps 142:10 that the Lord is the psalmist's God (ὅτι σὺ εἶ ὁ θεός μου), so that the psalmist is God's servant (142:2), is matched by the ground clause in 142:8 that the psalmist hopes/trusts in God (ὅτι ἐπὶ σοὶ ἤλπισα; cf. כי־בך בטחתי). In other words, in the second "anthropological" instance, the psalmist cries out to God for help and mercy (!) because the psalmist has taken refuge in God alone, having stretched out his hands to the Lord as one whose soul is like a waterless land (Ps 142:6, 9).

So regarding Paul's theology proper, I would reverse Campbell's emphasis that "the discourse of kingship is primary, dictating the shape of any covenant in play" (207n12). As an apostle of the Messiah, Paul conceives of himself as a servant of the new covenant (2 Cor 3:5-6); accordingly, he develops his argument from Scripture in 2 Cor 3 in explicitly new covenant/old covenant terms (cf. 2 Cor 3:14). Second Corinthians 3 thus functions as a hinge between Galatians and Romans, picking up Paul's "allegory" in Gal 4:21-31, which is based on the same two covenant structure, and

---

13. See *Deliverance*, 862-64, 890, where Campbell convincingly links Gal 5:5 with Gal 3:11 and reads Gal 3:12 as a reference to eschatological life, but then limits the reference of πίστις in 3:12 solely to Christ's death and resurrection, though he takes Gal 5:5 to refer to the faith of Christians: in Gal 5:5, the Galatians are not being called "to have faith and hope in terms of their own pious resources; rather ... to live in the unshakeable and irresistible faith and hope *that Christ has already established for them*—The Galatians' faith is resourced from elsewhere, and its end, in the glories of life at the eschaton, is already certain, *as long as they do not forcefully abandon this location*" (891, second emphasis mine, pointing to Campbell's own version of the "conditional" soteriology he critiques). Compare esp. *Deliverance*, 101-4, 108, 116, 163-64, 179, 617, 705, 975n13 and 712-13, 817-21 on faith as a "marker of salvation," rather than "a solitary condition" in "fulfillment of a contractual condition," with Campbell's portrayals of Paul's soteriology, which "continually creates room for the human rejection of God's constitutive initiative" (161) based on human freedom (162, cf. 908). Rather than this call to perseverance leading to anxiety, however, believers can await God's deliverance in hope, "completely assured of that event as the Spirit involves them in *Christ's* fidelity" (892, emphasis his). Paul's gospel therefore "provides real eschatological security, in Christ and the Spirit—so 5:5—and real ethical efficacy, from the same sources—so 5:6" (892). Hence, as with the more traditional view, Campbell posits that believers can have assurance, since their faith and its ethical expression are God's apocalyptic work by the Spirit (cf. 892). Indeed, for Paul, the faith of the Christian is just as much a divine, apocalyptic act as the Christ-event and power of the Spirit that bring it about.

anticipating Paul's subsequent use of Scripture in the key fulfillment passages of Rom 1:4, 9–11, 16–17; 3:19–26; 4:1–25; chs. 9–11; and 15:4–13.

From this same covenant perspective, Paul's passing on of the seminal tradition concerning the gospel as the fulfillment of Scripture in 1 Cor 15:1–5 must be held together with his previous reference in 1 Cor 11:23–26 to the tradition of the new covenant embodied in the Lord's Supper. Strikingly, this earliest tradition concerning the gospel includes a strong conditionality at its heart (1 Cor 15:1[14]). So too, the words Paul "received from the Lord" (1 Cor 11:23) support why it is that the Corinthian disregard for one another (i.e., their lack of love as the greatest of the spiritual gifts) breaks the (new) covenant stipulations to such a degree that their "celebration" can no longer even be considered the Lord's Supper (1 Cor 11:20–21). Hence, having profaned the body of the Lord (= breaking the covenant stipulations), some Corinthians are being judged with death (1 Cor 11:27–30).

The role these texts play in Paul's theology should not be minimized: the conditionality of the gospel must be maintained, but we must make equally sure that we distinguish between a pre-election/redemption conditionality, which is rejected by Paul (and all of Scripture), and a post-election/redemption conditionality that is at the heart of the covenant structure. The covenant structure moves from the unconditional covenant prologue to the conditions of the covenant stipulations to the resultant covenant blessings and curses, a structure that is central to all of Scripture.[15]

THE APOCALYPTIC COVENANT

The unconditionality of God's gracious acts as king and the conditionality of his people's response of faith are not in conflict within a covenant relationship; the former *both* creates *and* sustains (not merely calls for!) the latter.[16]

---

14. 1 Cor 15:1–2: "Now I would remind you, brethren, in what terms I preached to you the gospel, which you received, in which you stand, by which you are saved, if you hold it fast—unless you believed in vain (εἰ κατέχετε ἐκτὸς εἰ μὴ εἰκῇ ἐπιστεύσατε)" (RSV).

15. I have tried to map out the nature of this covenant structure throughout the canon in my "Covenant Relationship," 20–65. For this same pattern in the Petrine tradition, see my "(Un)Conditionality of Salvation," 240–62.

16. It is unclear in what way, for Campbell, faith functions "more as a *marker* of salvation than a solitary *condition*; it is a marker of participation in the faithful and resurrected Christ, which thereby implicitly *guarantees* for the believer a future participation in the resurrection that Christ has already achieved" (*Deliverance*, 817, emphasis his). The functional difference between a "marker" and a "condition" is not clear. Thus, for example, for Campbell "faith" is brought about by God, his word, and the Spirit, and mediated by his messengers, but not caused by them (819), so that faith "stems from

The covenant relationship between God and his people is not legalistic at its inception, nor is it a synergistic contract in its continuation. Every aspect of the covenant is apocalyptic, since the covenant relationship is wholly dependent on God invading and continuing to invade the believers' lives to deliver them (Phil 1:6). As Campbell himself has insightfully pointed out in *Deliverance*, this emphasis counters so much of the "new perspective," which has simply shifted legalism from "getting in" to "staying in," thereby creating a synergism between God and humanity.[17] All legalism and synergism in relationship to God is to be rejected, including any "optimistic nomistic Pelagianism" by Pauline opponents who argued that transgressions could be overcome by disciplined pursuits of the mind (205).

In order to avoid slipping back into any kind of synergism in describing Paul's apostolic goal of creating covenant keepers, the determinative, apocalyptic (!) role of the Spirit must be kept in view. Campbell too emphasizes this creative, elective, liberating role of the Spirit as that which creates the new life of faith.[18] It is therefore surprising that at the same time

---

participation in the faithful (Christ)" and is evidence and "*a marker of divine involvement, not the fulfillment of a contractual condition*" (820, emphasis his). Such contrasts work only if, by a "condition," one always means a "contractual" condition rather than a covenant stipulation.

17. As Campbell points out, *Deliverance*, 103, Sanders' view simply shifts "legalism" to keeping the covenant, rather than to entering into the covenant. So there is not a great deal that separates covenantal nomism from legalism "in strictly theoretical terms." For Sanders, the giving of covenant in the *past* only establishes the "possibility of salvation," i.e., establishing the covenant is "a moment of divine, if contractually limited generosity" (103). With covenantal nomism legalism still exists in the *present and future*, in which salvation is dependent on fulfilling the conditions and evaluating individual performance of them in the present and future. "In short, it seems that the essential theoretical differences between covenantal nomism and legalism have effectively collapsed," since both are contractual (conditional) (104).

18. See *Deliverance*, 64, where it is stressed that the Spirit inaugurates humanity's rescue from Sin and Death and accompanies it along its agonizing way to the final consummation of redemption (64; Rom 8:23–27). Moreover, salvation is "*fundamentally transformational*," from termination to reconstitution (Rom 6:1–11; 7:1–4; 64, emphasis mine). It is the Spirit who effects this transformation with reference to Christ. "In Christ" or its close equivalent thus summarizes this process of transformation (6:4, 8, 11, 23; 8:1, 9–11, 39; opposite sense perhaps in 7:5; 8:8, 9; 64), which entails an important ethical dimension (6:19, 22–23; 65). "*That is, a transformation of the ethical capacity of humanity seems intrinsic to the entire salvific process; it is part of the event of grace* (6:15, 23)" (65, emphasis mine). Hence, soteriology is a "holistic process that extends far beyond mere corroboration" (66). Indeed, "the saving transformation of the human being through participation in Christ in the Spirit *is* simultaneously an ethical transformation. Ethics merely denotes the behavioral aspect of this overarching process" (83, emphasis his). "The unconditional, revelatory, transformational, and liberational aspects of this event mean that it is appropriately described as 'apocalyptic'" (66). "An 'apocalyptic' approach to Paul emphasizes the revelatory and hence unconditional

Campbell questions what he calls Calvinism's "unaccountable privileging of faith" on the grounds that it attributes salvation directly to God, so that "no saving criterion is now necessary at all. God simply saves individuals at the requisite point."[19] Surely for Calvinism, as for Campbell, faith is privileged and essential since it is the essential, salvific work of the Spirit; neither can exist without the other. How these two points fit together in Campbell's view remains unclear.

Here the tandem emphasis of 1 Cor 6:11 on both Jesus and the Spirit is significant: "But you were washed, you were sanctified, you were justified in the name of the Lord Jesus Christ (cf. Rom 3:24-26 in anticipation of Rom 5:9) and in the Spirit of our God (cf. Rom 8:1-4?)."[20] The presence of the Spirit is not just a divine, apocalyptic invasion of this world that rescues those baptized into Christ *from* sin negatively (Rom 6:1-14); positively, the Spirit is also the causative, new-creation source of Torah keeping as fulfilled in love (Rom 2:29; 7:6; 8:3-6, 11-14; 14:17). There is "no (judgment of the) law" against the "fruit of the Spirit" precisely because the latter keeps the law (cf. Gal 5:22-23 with Gal 5:14, 16, 18). This keeping of the law by the Spirit is part and parcel of God's apocalyptic deliverance from the power of this present, evil age (Gal 1:4). God's grace through Christ includes the gift of being delivered both from the penalty of sin—that is, from its curse (Gal 3:13)—and from the power of sin—that is, from its works of the flesh (Gal 5:19-21; Rom 8:13). The Spirit makes alive (2 Cor 3:6; Rom 7:6; Gal 5:25) and brings life and peace (Rom 8:6) because it submits to God's law and hence pleases God, which the flesh cannot do (Rom 8:7-9).

Within this paradigm for reading Paul, there is no need to construe δικαιόω in Rom 2:13 differently than in Rom 6:7, since in both cases it is an indicative-performative speech-act (cf. 209-10). As such, it both evaluates *and* effects that the life of the righteous is justified and hence freed from

---

nature of the soteriology" (903). For Campbell, therefore, it is important to see in Paul's argument that "the fidelity of Christ" mirrors "the fidelity of the Christian," since "Christians are faithful because they are being molded by the Spirit into the likeness of the faithful Christ" (527).

19. *Deliverance*, 59 (emphasis removed). As he queries, why in the Calvinist version of justification theory is faith necessary to be saved, when it is part of the Christians' overall transformation as those who are saved? "Since there is no condition for salvation, what is faith doing in the argument?" (59). Indeed, "if . . . the Calvinist variant's construal of justification cannot give a plausible account of the role of faith in Paul's argument, then its prospects are hopeless" (59).

20. For an insightful treatment of the need to incorporate within the doctrine of justification, with its focus on forgiveness based on the cross of Christ, the transformative, eschatological, and cosmic role of the Spirit in redemption as the inauguration of God's final righteousness and justice (thus replacing the need for an abstract notion of the imputation of Christ's merit), see Macchia, "Justification," 202-17.

the claims and consequences of sin both personally and forensically. For as Rom 2:25-29 makes clear in anticipation of Rom 8:4, the righteous are not condemned precisely because, by Christ and through the power of the Spirit of Christ, they keep the just requirements of the law. Paul emphasizes that it is not merely the possession of the law or the attempt to keep it in one's own strength that counts, but what matters is *actually* keeping the law by the power of the Spirit (cf. the reference to keeping τὰ δικαιώματα τοῦ νόμου in Rom 2:25 with keeping τὸ δικαίωμα in Rom 8:4). In *Deliverance*, Campbell seems to agree with this reading of Rom 2:25-29 as summarized in the letter/Spirit contrast of 2:29,[21] though in the end he opts for a participationist reading that is "law free."[22] But in Rom 2:26 the uncircumcision of the Gentile who keeps the law is reckoned as circumcision (εἰς περιτομὴν λογισθήσεται), just as in Rom 4:5, 9 his faith is reckoned as righteousness (λογίζεται ἡ πίστις αὐτοῦ εἰς δικαιοσύνην), while in Rom 6:16 it is obedience that leads to (is reckoned as?) righteousness (ὑπακοῆς εἰς δικαιοσύνην). The conceptual-theological link between keeping the law, faith, and obedience in Rom 2; 4; and 6 seems clear. In the same way, the letter/Spirit contrast from Rom 2:27-29 is repeated in Rom 7:5-6. Paul's soteriology thus appears

---

21. As he puts it, *Deliverance*, 569-70,

> Circumcision remains largely what it is within the Jewish propaganda literature—a symbol. And, as with all symbols, without the underlying reality—which must necessarily be grounded in divine action for Paul—it is empty. Consequently, Paul's cryptic criticism here is fundamentally realistic. The heart, as a metaphor for humanity's ethical condition, cannot be "circumcised" by any *literal* surgery ... or by literalism *per se*. ... To change human nature and its ethical workings requires divine involvement through the Spirit of creation. ... Paul holds that only participation in Christ's death and resurrection, through the divine Spirit, can change the sinful ontology of humanity—for both Jew and pagan. ... Hence, the ethical inadequacy of the Teacher's gospel is for Paul grounded in its ontological incapacity, which is rooted in turn in an inadequate evaluation of the work of Christ and the Spirit in the Christian life.

22. "The resurrected ethical condition in Christ, undergirded by the Spirit (and symbolized in baptism) is law free in the sense of not taking its primary ethical orientation from God's written commands in Scripture (a posture that Paul accuses ... of being deceptive and death dealing)" (607). So Paul lays out "a distinctive ethical system informed by participation in Christ through the Spirit; ... the inauguration of the resurrection of the Christian into a distinctively law-free praxis" (607).

closest to that of the radical, monergistic nomism seen in many of the Qumran documents.[23]

ANOTHER PARADIGM

Campbell declares that "we know well by now that Paul is utterly opposed to any account of salvation—that is, to any gospel—couched in these terms"—that is, in large measure in the terms I have just suggested! Such a gospel, in Campbell's view, "is simply wrong all the way across and all the way down" (210). I am not convinced, however, since it is Paul's fear of Christ's retributive judgment (2 Cor 5:10) that drives him to beg the Corinthians to be reconciled to God based on the cross of Christ (2 Cor 5:11, 18–20). Second Corinthians 5:10–20 corroborates the equally Pauline Rom 2:5–16 (cf. Rom 14:10–12), which is also based on Paul's awareness of the day of the Lord, "when God judges the hidden things of people according to [his] gospel through Christ Jesus" (Rom 2:16). For the same cross that brings forgiveness also creates the new, eschatological life of the new creation that lives for Christ in anticipation of that day of judgment (2 Cor 5:15, 17, 21; 6:1–2).

Hence, for Paul, rather than being a Jew or Gentile in accordance with the identities of the old covenant of the old age, what matters in the new age of the new covenant is the new creation brought about by Christ (2 Cor 5:17). Paul's programmatic statement in 2 Cor 5:17 summarizes the previous themes associated with the new creation, in particular, the parallels between Gal 5:14; 6:15; and 1 Cor 7:19:

---

23. Campbell, *Deliverance*, 108, sees Qumran's soteriology as unconditional due to its emphasis on election and its attributing all actions to the "Spirit of Light" unconditionally. There are thus four types of soteriologies for Campbell: (1) Justification legalism, (2) Covenantal nomistic legalism, (3) Eschatological-Participationism, (4) and Qumran, which is "overwhelmingly nomistic" (116), but according to Alexander is "an unconditional soteriology" that is "qualitatively different from either legalism or covenant nomism" (118). Cf. 1023n22, where in response to the "perfectionist axiom" of Justification theory, Campbell sees that Qumran plays a key role in understanding the demands of the law in that in Qumran the Jewish language of perfection "is invariably counterbalanced by compensatory mechanisms—means of atonement and restoration, and also direct ethical assistance toward perfection. At Qumran, the covenanters—at least in some texts—were elected to salvation, and assisted in perfect law observance by the Spirit of Light, thereby overcoming the evil inclination." Campbell points out that the absence of these "mechanisms" is what creates difficulties for Justification theory (1023n22).

Gal 5:6a	οὔτε περιτομή τι ἰσχύει
	οὔτε ἀκροβυστία
Gal 6:15a	οὔτε περιτομή τί ἐστιν
	οὔτε ἀκροβυστία
1 Cor 7:19a	ἡ περιτομὴ οὐδέν ἐστιν
	καὶ ἡ ἀκροβυστία οὐδέν ἐστιν
Gal 5:6b	ἀλλὰ πίστις δι' ἀγάπης ἐνεργουμένη
Gal 6:15b	ἀλλὰ καινὴ κτίσις
1 Cor 7:19b	ἀλλὰ τήρησις ἐντολῶν θεοῦ[24]

As these parallels demonstrate, Paul's statement concerning the "new creation" in Gal 6:15 is sandwiched between the mutually interpretive parallels of Gal 5:6, on the one hand, and 1 Cor 7:19, on the other. For Paul, what now counts in the new, eschatological era is no longer one's identity under the old covenant as circumcised and uncircumcised. What now "exists" (cf. 1 Cor 7:19a) is the "new creation," which is equated with "faith working out with regard to itself through love" (Gal 5:6),[25] which in turn can be framed in terms of "keeping the commandments of God" (1 Cor 7:19).[26] Here too

---

24. The interpretive parallel between these contrasts was first set forth simply in my *God of Promise*, 196.

25. The force of ἐνεργέω in the middle is difficult to render in English, since it indicates that the faith which works is also impacted by its activity, being "directly and personally involved in the process," so Taylor, "Deponency," 174. Betz, *Galatians*, 263n97, suggests for its translation, "become effective," "come to expression," pointing to the "fruit of the Spirit" in 5:22–23 as its referent. Campbell, *Deliverance*, 887, renders it as faith being "active in relation to itself—putting itself into effect ... by means of 'love.'" On the necessary embodiment of dispositions such as "faith" in one's way of life, individually and communally, see now Thiselton, *Hermeneutics of Doctrine*, 19–61, and its application to Pauline "justification by faith," 347–54. For the working out of other Christian dispositions, see 2 Cor 1:6 (comfort in endurance); 1 Thess 2:13 (the word of God in believers); Col 1:29 (Christ's ἐνέργεια in Paul's life); Eph 3:20 (God's power in believers); Rom 7:5 for its counterpoint in terms of the "passions of sins" (τὰ παθήματα τῶν ἁμαρτιῶν) working out (ἐνηργεῖτο) in one's life in the "flesh" (σάρξ); and 2 Cor 4:12 for both death and life working out (ἐνεργεῖται) in one's life. As Betz, *Galatians*, 264, thus rightly concludes, it is impossible for Paul to separate faith and love into "theory" and "practice."

26. For the conviction that "a comparison of the second members in the three passages is instructive," see already Burton, *Galatians*, 356. Burton, 356, sees πίστις and ἀγάπη in Gal 5:6 as "purely ethical terms, descriptive of the fundamental moral attitude of the Christian," while "keeping the commandments" in 1 Cor 7:19 is "a more external characterization of the Christian life and more formal." Over against both, "new creation" in Gal 6:15 is "less definite as to the moral character of the new life than either of the other expressions," though it "directs attention to the radical change involved rather than to the external expression or the moral quality of the life thus produced."

we see God's apocalyptic work of establishing the new creation decoded in terms of the realities of the new covenant—God's unconditional grace creating the keeping of the covenant conditions. In *Deliverance*, Campbell himself makes this point in regard to the conditionality expressed in Gal 5:5, which sets up these passages.[27]

THE WAY FORWARD

Of course, in offering this response I am simply matching one paradigmatic reading of Paul against another. In the end, then, Campbell's work can be evaluated only by reading both the whole and its parts from a counterdirection to see which one fits better overall. One of the great values of Campbell's work is that it forces one to do just that, instead of simply taking old answers for granted.

I have learned a great deal from Campbell's encyclopedic, often brilliant and insightful work. I am not yet convinced, however, by his radical solution to the problem of how to map out the move in Paul's theology from Rom 1–4 to 5–8. But I am convinced that I should not read Paul "forward" theologically. Campbell is right that justification by faith for Paul was not conceived to be the result of turning, out of despair, from one's independent, failed attempt to live a moral life, usually based on some kind of natural theology, to God's revelatory, "law-free," salvific gospel. I also agree with Campbell's critique of the means of salvation within the justification paradigm, in which its inherent legalism can only be solved by an imputed righteousness.

My own reading sits between the traditional view and Campbell's rereading. I propose that the way to combat importing "Western contractualism" into our reading of Paul, while at the same time preserving the coherence of Paul's letters, is not to replace a contractual view of the divine-human relationship with an exclusively apocalyptic, participatory eschatology. Rather, we should recover the biblical category of an apocalyptically understood, thoroughly monergistic, yet conditional covenant relationship between God and his people, and through this covenant relationship, between God and his world (cf. Rom 8:18–25 with Ps 97:7–8)

The deposit of these contrasts in 2 Cor 5:17 demonstrates, however, that such contrasts are only apparent.

27. See above, note 31.

DOUGLAS CAMPBELL'S RESPONSE TO SCOTT HAFEMANN

There is much to affirm and even applaud in Scott's learned essay from which I learned a great deal. But it is important to recognize that it is, in the end of the day, a salvation-historical stealth attack! As such, it inaugurates a fascinating conversation that I will only be able to make some regrettably brief remarks in response to here. (The position he represents so ably here ultimately requires a detailed consideration, which I hope to supply in due course.)

To redescribe the situation in broad brush strokes that are hopefully not without some accuracy: in *Deliverance* I identify and try to subvert a rather individualistic interpretative discourse in relation to Paul that I view as rooted exegetically in Romans 1–4—the Justification discourse. Scott, however, really represents another major Pauline interpretative discourse, namely, a salvation-historical approach. Hence, he is clearly in sympathy with a certain amount that I am suggesting, but then is not so sure about other aspects of the participatory and apocalyptic discourse that I go on to affirm. However, *Deliverance* does not position itself especially clearly with respect to Scott's concerns and those who share them, in part, because any engagement between participatory and salvation-historical accounts of Paul must do detailed work on Romans 9–11, whereas an engagement with the Justification paradigm only needs to address parts of 9:30—10:17 (and so on). In short, the detailed conversation between apocalyptic and salvation-historical advocates in relation to Paul has yet to happen (at least as far as I am concerned). A few gestures toward the shape of that future conversation will have to suffice here.

I appreciate Scott's suggestions that covenantal resonances are in play in Ps 98—that is, more than I allowed—and hence arguably in the allusion by Rom 1:17 to this text. However, I wonder if the scriptural echo provides a sufficiently firm and overt textual basis from which to insert what amounts to a grand OT narrative of covenantalism into Paul's subsequent arguments in Romans. My reading suggests that the echoed psalm of kingship provides a semantic possibility for the phrase δικαιοσύνη Θεοῦ that then informs Paul's argument quite directly, albeit in a limited fashion; in this psalm at this moment God is acting like a king in an executive action of deliverance. Hence I suggest interpreting the phrase in these terms; this is what it *means* as illuminated semantically by this intertext. And a Christological construal of the associated πίστις Ἰησοῦ Χριστοῦ genitives and associated phrases (see 1:17b; 3:22, 25, 26)—that is, in terms of the faithfulness of Christ—then invites Paul's auditors to understand it further in explicitly Christological terms.[28] The right activity of God here is in fact the deliverance of God that has been definitively revealed in the life, death, and resurrection of Christ. This is its concrete reference point. So the pressure of interpretation actually runs backward in 1:17 and any associated texts (i.e., from Paul's point of view) *from* the Christ event *to* his interpretation of a scriptural text.

If these points are clear then I need to ask to what extent Scott is actually overtly justified in textual terms to go beyond them to his rather more panoramic assertions. His compelling narrative is arguably a fundamentally historicizing and canonical exercise that is somewhat inappropriate for Paul himself. (It is, of course, deeply congenial to modern scholars concerned to interpret the canon constructively and appropriately!) And I fear that its persistent advocacy will generate a number of problems in due course, although now is not the time to explore those in detail.[29] But if I am resisting some of Scott's assertions here I would suggest that at other points what is required is only clarification.

Scott highlights several instances in my interpretations of what he calls conditionality, thereby really suggesting that conditionality cannot be repudiated *in toto* (that is, outside a theological schema committed to what we might call causal or "hard" predestination, which both Scott and I do not endorse). Even I apparently lapse into conditionality periodically, he implies, while repudiating the harsh form found in Justification theory. And a covenantal account of the OT consequently needs to retain a degree of conditionality as well, defining this carefully. Correlative to this is a particular notion of judgment, which opens up a more accommodating position in turn in relation to some of the texts in Romans 1–3, that I have more difficulty with. And a clarification here should prove helpful, although I suspect that my views have developed on this issue since *Deliverance* was written, the manuscript being completed at the end of 2007. So Scott should not be chided for missing this material, which was probably not present in *Deliverance* to the degree that it now probably would be.

Scott is really assuming with this line of criticism that any human responsiveness or agency, which are operative in most narratives of human ethics and accountability, must entail ultimately a contractual or

---

28. See my essay "The Faithfulness of Jesus Christ."

29. I worry (among other things) that it will still become involved in a foundationalist and negative construction of the Other, leading to problems in relation to mission and the construction of Judaism. I worry that it will override the implicit operation of Nicene categories within Paul's thinking. And I worry that its broad historical claims are ultimately fragile, that is, it presupposes a coherent and successful account of the OT data when many OT analysts would either offer equally powerful but different accounts or would dispute this very possibility.

conditional situation. So when he detects affirmations of Christian agency or responsiveness in my account of Paul he goes on to assume conditional and contractual entailments. However, this is to commit what one might call the great Liberal sin, namely, the assumption that human freedom is best articulated in terms of human choice and hence can only be articulated ultimately in arrangements that are conditional and contractual. To preserve any notion of human freedom, human will must be affirmed and human choice expected. This is not a Christological account of agency.

As Barth (among others), leaning on the work of Maximus the Confessor, emphasizes tirelessly,[30] human agency is best understood in terms of perfect obedience and *correspondence* to divine promptings and leadings—musical analogies often being very helpful for grasping this situation, whereas spatial conceptualizations, beloved of modernity, tend to distort it.[31] Perfect freedom is found in perfect obedience, as voices in songs sung freely correspond and directly harmonize with the tune, the conductor, and the rest of the choir. Conversely, to will or to choose to turn away from this relationship of correspondence is to struggle against the appropriate order of things—to cut against the grain—and to plunge into self-destructive sin (in the terms of the foregoing analogy, to disrupt and destroy the choral performance). Consequently *will* and *choice* are actually domestications of human *sin*! And this will all be judged by God, and implacably (although in a certain sort of way). Humanity will also be held constantly accountable.

These realizations generate in turn a particular account of the covenant. This arrangement describes how the principal component within the relationship between God and humanity, presaged in the relationship between God and Israel, is unconditional election and ongoing commitment by God to the group covenanted to. Moreover, everything is provided by the covenanting God. As a covenant with humanity/Israel, however, a response of perfect obedience to the relational expectations of the covenant is necessary. Of course, that response has generally been anything except perfectly obedient, entailing ongoing rescue operations by the covenantal God, and ongoing education into the destructiveness and stupidity of sin. But the covenant expects human responsiveness, although conceived of strictly in terms of correlative obedience.

The important implications in this brief explication for the interpretative stances of both Scott and I are that both his covenantal and my participatory emphases can wholeheartedly together affirm human freedom and responsiveness, and human accountability in turn, while resisting any

---

30. See esp. *Church Dogmatics* III/1, III/2, and IV/2.
31. See here now helpfully Begbie, "Room of One's Own?"

further explanation of these dynamics in terms of will and choice, these being the further articulations that necessarily unleash a destructive conditionality and contractualism. And one further positive result flowing from this is the ability to affirm that God's covenant is thick with the appropriate ethical expectations but not conditional upon them; it is unconditional, eternal and *unbreakable*, as any commitment by a fundamentally loving God should be. But these emphases in no way reduce or elide divine judgment and human accountability, or even freedom; rather, these secondary dynamics are explicable within this basic framework (i.e., in a way that has theological integrity and does not lapse ultimately into infralapsarianism or other acute theological problems). Indeed, all these dynamics are *strengthened* by them. (No accountability is more powerful or acute than covenantally generated accountability.)

In short then, I suggest that an appropriate understanding of agency in terms of correspondence—ultimately of course in Christological terms—speaks to Scott's identification of frequent emphases in my work on the human responsiveness operative through Christ; these do not entail contractualism in any shape or form. And it also assists *his* account of the covenant, as that is articulated by so much of the OT—although, I would suggest again, as that is definitively revealed, articulated, and fulfilled, by Christ. Indeed, to be truly free and responsive to God is necessarily to resist any articulation of these notions by conditionality or contractualism, the latter being the conspicuous conceits of modernity and, even worse, ultimately corrupting of true and authentic relationships. And I am, of course, grateful to Scott for prompting me to deepen these claims implicit in my earlier work here, and also for his corrections in relation to some of Paul's invocations of covenantal material.

3

Paul's "History-of-Redemption" Use of the Old Testament in 2 Corinthians[1]

Second Corinthians reveals the amazing breadth of Paul's knowledge of the Scriptures. No fewer than fifteen explicit Old Testament quotations and forty-six allusions appear in 2 Corinthians.[2] The tripartite canon of Law, Prophets, and Writings is almost equally represented, with the predominant cluster of texts coming from Exodus and Deuteronomy; Isaiah, Jeremiah, and Ezekiel; and Psalms and Proverbs. When the subject matter of these passages is taken into account, it is striking that they cluster around the first exodus and its covenant, the prophetic promise of a "second exodus" redemption and new covenant or new creation, and the suffering of the righteous. This distribution corresponds to the fact that 2 Corinthians centers on the nature of Paul's ministry as an apostle of the new covenant (3:4–6) whose life "in Christ" is characterized by his own suffering (1:5–10; 2:14; 4:10–11; 6:3–10; 11:23–33; 12:7–10). In what follows, we will focus on

---

1. From Scott J. Hafemann, "Paul's Use of the Old Testament in 2 Corinthians." *Int* 52/3 (1998) 246–57.

2. According to the Nestle-Aland text (27th ed.). Of course, the NA tradition is often questioned, both in what it includes (e.g., Prov 7:3 in 3:3) and in what it excludes (e.g., Jer 31:31–34 in 3:6, Jer 1:10 in 10:8). It is used here merely to give an indication of the scope of Paul's reflection on the Scriptures. On the quotations and allusions in chs. 1–9 and their relationship to Paul's christological statements, see Hafemann, "Paul's Argument," 277–303. For chs. 10–13, see 10:4 (Prov 21:22), 8 (Jer 24:6), 17 (Jer 9:22–23); 11:3 (Gen 3:13), 20 (Ps 53:5), 24 (Deut 25:3); 12:7 (Num 33:55, Ezek 28:34); 13:1 (Deut 19:15).

Paul's direct quotations, having first established the biblical framework of his thought.

THE BIBLICAL FRAMEWORK OF PAUL'S THOUGHT (2:14—3:18)

Beginning in 2:14, Paul initiates the most sustained defense of his apostolic ministry found anywhere in his letters (2:14—7:16 and 10:1—13:10).[3] Within this former section it has long been recognized that 2:14—3:18 is the theological heart of the epistle, providing the framework for understanding the rest of Paul's discussion in chapters 4-9, and perhaps also chapters 10-13. The significance of 2:14—3:18 thus reflects the central role Scripture played in Paul's self-understanding, since Paul develops his theological concepts in 3:1-18 by offering the most extended interpretation of an Old Testament text found anywhere in his epistles.

Paul begins his apology by presenting an argument for the legitimacy of his ministry based on his suffering as the vehicle through which the presence and power of the Spirit are mediated to God's people (2:14—3:3). This twofold argument from the role of suffering and the Spirit in Paul's ministry is grounded in Paul's conviction that the prophetic promises of the new covenant are being fulfilled through his own life and service under Christ. Through Paul's ministry God pours out the Spirit not merely on a remnant of the people, as under the Sinai covenant, but (in fulfillment of Ezek 11:19; 36:26 [2 Cor 3:3]; and Jer 31:31-34 [2 Cor 3:6b]) on the entire community of the new covenant as seen in the transformed hearts of the people of God. In order to support such a bold assertion, Paul returns to the narratives of the call of Moses (Exod 4:10; 2 Cor 2:16b; 3:4-6a)[4] and the veil of Moses (Exod 34:29-35; 2 Cor 3:7-18).

Against this scriptural background, Paul argues that, as an apostle of the new covenant, he has been called like Moses (2:16b; 3:4-6a), but with a very different ministry (3:6b-18). Moses was called to mediate God's will to

---

3. This section and the general perspective of this article are largely dependent on my earlier works, *Suffering and the Spirit* and *Paul, Moses, and the History of Israel*.

4. The language of "sufficiency" (Greek: ἱκανός, ἱκανόω) used in 2:16 and 3:4-6a alludes to the call of Moses in Exod 4:10, where in the Septuagint Moses responds to his call to deliver Israel from Egypt by declaring that he is not "sufficient" (ἱκανός) for his calling. In the context of Exod 4, Moses is then made sufficient by God himself. Like Moses and the prophets, who are also portrayed in Scripture as being called "like Moses" (cf. Deut 18:18), Paul too sees his sufficiency as coming from God in spite of his own insufficiency (cf. 3:4-6). Hence, the implied answer to 2:16b is "I am (!), by God's grace," which is then supported by verse 17.

a people whose hearts remained hardened, so that, without the Spirit, the law remained merely a "letter" that "kills" as part of a "ministry of death" and "condemnation" (3:6-7, 9). Indeed, Israel could not encounter the glory of God mediated by Moses without being destroyed. As a result, Moses had to veil himself in order to keep the glory on his face from consuming Israel.[5] The veil of Moses is therefore first an act of God's judgment, because it separated God's presence from the people; second, it is a manifestation of God's continuing covenant commitment, because it allowed God's glory to continue in the midst of the people without destroying them (cf. Exod 33:14-16). This is Paul's point in 3:7.[6] In stark contrast, under the "new covenant" Paul has been called to mediate God's will to a people whose hearts have been "given life" by the Spirit as part of a "ministry of the Spirit" and "righteousness" (3:3, 6, 8-9). The evidence of the dawning of the new covenant in Christ and of Paul's corresponding legitimacy as an apostle is the radical change in the spiritual condition of the people that is now taking place by the Spirit through Paul's ministry (3:1-3). (Indeed, Paul is aware that without the Spirit the gospel too kills; cf. 2 Cor 2:15-16a; 1 Cor 6:9-10; Gal 5:21.)

Due to Israel's "stiff neck," the glory of God had to be continually rendered inoperative by the veil (καταργέω; 3:7). Verses 11 and 13 claim that the Sinai covenant's mediation of divine glory was itself "continually being rendered inoperative" (καταργέω; 3:11, 13; my translation). The veiling of Moses's face thus demonstrates that the Sinai covenant, from its very beginning, did not accomplish its original purpose of establishing God's immediate and abiding presence among a sanctified people (cf. Exod 19:5-9;

---

5. Cf. Exod 32:9; 33:3, 5; 34:9 as the backdrop to 34:29-35, where Moses veils himself because of Israel's fear that God's glory would bring judgment.

6. The verb καταργέω is usually translated in 3:7 and elsewhere in the passage as "fading away" (cf. 3:11, 13, 14), as if Paul were saying that Moses veiled himself to keep Israel from discovering that the glory was fading in order to keep them from the truth and to protect his own authority. When Moses returned to the tent of meeting, he removed the veil, thereby "recharging" the glory on his face. Read in this way, it is obvious why students of this text have concluded that Paul radically reinterpreted Exod 34:29-35 against its original context, since there is no indication in Exod 34:29-35 that the glory on Moses's face was "fading away," or that Moses veiled himself to hide something from Israel. Such a translation and conclusion regarding Paul's intention, however, are not warranted by the evidence. A study of καταργέω throughout the Pauline corpus presents a narrow semantic field for its meaning and a uniform context for its use. Its Pauline context is consistently eschatological and its meaning is best translated in accordance with its use elsewhere in the ancient world: "to render (something) inoperative, ineffective, powerless," or "to nullify (something) in terms of its effects or impact." In no case does the verb refer to the gradual "fading away" of some aspect of reality. The lexica and scholars who adopt this reading rely only on 2 Cor 3 itself for such a rendering.

20:20). In contrast, Paul describes the new covenant ministry as that which "remains," "lasts," or "persists" (3:11; NRSV: "the permanent"). Paul's return to this verb (μένω) recalls its earlier use to refer to the work that "remains" beyond the eschatological judgment (1 Cor 3:14), and to faith, hope, and love as the three things that "remain" in the future eschatological era (1 Cor 13:13). In this latter context, καταργέω forms the counterpart to μένω as a description of those things that are nullified, or do not "remain" eschatologically (cf. 1 Cor 13:8, 10, 11). Moreover, the quotation from Ps 111:9LXX (2 Cor 9:9) indicates that this "remaining" at the eschatological judgment of *Paul's* ministry and its consequences can be linked by Paul to the psalmist's declaration that the *Lord's* "righteousness remains forever." That which lasts eschatologically "remains" precisely because it corresponds to God's "righteousness" which "remains" (cf. Rom 9:11). For only what is based on God's own righteousness can stand the test of God's "righteous judgment" (e.g., Rom 2:5). In contrast to the Sinai covenant, the new covenant "remains" in force since it reveals the righteousness of God, which will last forever (cf. Jer 32:37–40). It is this "remaining" new covenant of the Spirit, based on the righteousness of God, that Paul is called to minister (2 Cor 3:4–11).

Hence, Paul has the confident expectation (cf. 3:12, "hope") that under the ministry of the new covenant the Spirit is being poured out to change the hearts of God's people. Moses "put a veil over his face to keep the people of Israel from gazing at the end [τέλος] of that which was being rendered ineffective or inoperative in terms of its consequences"—that is, the death-dealing judgment of the glory of God upon a "stiff-necked" people under the Sinai covenant (3:13b; my translation). But rather than having to "veil" his message, Paul preaches with boldness, knowing that under his ministry the Spirit is changing the hearts of God's people so that God's glory brings about their transformation, not condemnation and judgment. The new covenant thereby fulfills the original purpose of the covenant at Sinai. In 2 Cor 3:16–18 Paul consequently modifies Exod 34:34 to link Moses to those who now enter into God's presence "unveiled" because the Spirit has granted them freedom from their hardened hearts. The fact that Paul can picture the consequence of this "unveiled" encounter with the glory of God in terms of transformation into the "image of God" (cf. Gen 1:26–27) indicates that Paul views the dawning of the new covenant as the inauguration of the new creation as well. And the means by which this "second exodus" new creation has now taken place in Corinth is Paul's ministry of the Spirit, mediated through his own suffering as an embodiment of the gospel. On the other hand, the veil of Moses represents the hard-heartedness of Israel that has characterized the history of Israel under the Sinai covenant (2 Cor 3:14ab). Paul recognizes that this "veil" of hardness still resides over unbelieving

Israel in their reading of the old covenant, since only the Christ can remove the veil of a "hardened mind" (3:14c).

To support this point Paul appeals to a common scriptural pattern: Israel's current rejection of God's work is evidence that Israel remains in the same hardened state that has characterized the people as a whole from the beginning.[7] This interpretation of Israel's history is reflected in Paul's use of the phrase "[even] to this [very] day" (3:14-15), which recalls the parallel designation in Deut 29:3LXX. There Moses declares that, despite the people's deliverance, God "has not given [Israel] a heart to know, and eyes to see, and ears to hear until this day." Within its original context, God's prerogative not only explains Israel's past disobedience, but also grounds Moses's proclamation that, despite God's warnings, Israel will continue to break the covenant in the future and suffer the judgment of the exile as a result (cf. 29:18).

Jeremiah and Ezekiel had likewise declared that Israel's plight in their time was evidence that the people's rebellion had continued unabated from the days of the fathers "[even] to this [very] day."[8] Hence, in 3:14-15, as in 3:3-6, Paul again builds his argument on the testimony of the Law and the Prophets. Rather than calling into question Paul's ministry and message, Israel's rejection of the gospel is evidence of the same hardened condition that Moses encountered and predicted would continue into the exile, and that the prophets also endured throughout their own ministries.

Paul argues that the proof of Israel's continued hardening is a "veiled" (morally hardened) reading of the Sinai covenant, since the Scriptures point to the fact that the eschatological renewal by the Spirit would and has dawned in (the) Christ. Paul's introduction of the terminology "old covenant" is a declaration of his eschatology, not a deprecation of the law (3:14). Paul refers to the Sinai covenant as "old" only because he is convinced that Jesus, as the Christ, has inaugurated the "new covenant" of Ezek 36:26-27 and Jer 31:31-34 (3:3, 6).

---

7. The pattern of argument from Israel's current rebellion (and consequent judgment in the exile) to the people's being hardened from the beginning appears in Isa 63:7-19; 65:2-7; Jer 3:25; 7:18-26; 11:7-10; 15:1 (where not even Moses himself could prevent the ensuing judgment of God!); 16:11-13; 17:23; 19:15; 44:9-10; Ezek 2:3; 20:8-36; Amos 2:4; Zech 1:2-4; 7:11-14; Lam 5:7; Mal 3:7; Neh 9:16-31; Pss 78:5-8, 54-64; 106:6-39; and Paul's own mixed citation of Deut 29:3 and Isa 29:10 in Rom 11:8, where the latter text concerning Israel's hardening in Isaiah's day is explicated in terms of Israel's having been hardened during the days of Moses.

8. See Jer 3:25; 7:25; 11:7 (MT); 32:20-21 (MT); 44:10 (MT); and Ezek 2:3.

THE BIBLICAL BASIS FOR PAUL'S CONFIDENCE IN HIS MINISTRY (4:1–6)

Paul now draws the conclusion that flows from his apostolic role as a mediating agent of the Spirit in fulfillment of the prophetic promises of the new covenant (cf. 3:12): Paul does not lose heart. Instead, as a recipient of this mercy, Paul "recommends himself" by living openly and preaching the gospel without compromise (cf. 2:17; 4:1), knowing that a rejection of his message can only mean that the "god of this age" has blinded the minds of unbelievers to the glory of Christ as the image of God that is being revealed in the gospel (4:2–4). What is true for Israel is true for the Gentiles as well (3:14–15; 4:3–5). Rejection of Paul's gospel is a sign that one's heart has not been transformed by the Spirit.

Earlier Paul supported the legitimacy of his apostolic "suffering" for the sake of the Corinthians by pointing to his calling (2:16b; 3:4–6a). Paul now undergirds his role as an apostolic "slave" to the Corinthians by again pointing to his calling (4:6). In the earlier passages he had pictured his call in relation to the call of Moses. Now he uses terms taken from the creation of light in Gen 1:3, reiterated in Isa 9:1 (a prophecy of redemption in which a "light will shine" upon those dwelling in darkness), to picture the "new creation" to come. Inasmuch as the "god of this age" has blinded people to the glory of God in Christ, only the God of creation, the one who originally called forth light out of darkness, can overcome this blindness by making the divine light "shine in our hearts." Paul's conversion-call on the road to Damascus is a living example of this "new creation": As a result of having encountered God's glory in Christ (4:6), Paul now lives as a slave of the church he once persecuted. The same power that created Adam in God's image is now being unleashed in "re-creating" God's people in Christ. This is confirmed by Paul's use of the "image [or] likeness of God" from Gen 1:26 to describe both the goal of transformation (3:18) and the identity of Christ (4:4). To be transformed by the Spirit into the image of God's glory (3:18) is to be conformed to the "image of God" as manifest in Christ, the "second Adam" (4:4; cf. 1 Cor 15:42–49; Rom 5:12–21; 8:28–30). To "see" the glory of God in Christ with an "unveiled face" is to begin to come face to face with the presence of God as enjoyed by Adam before the fall (3:16–18; 4:4, 6). This divine act of new creation under the new covenant, which Paul himself experienced, is the basis of Paul's confidence. Thus, the antithetical parallels between 4:4 and 4:6 illustrate not only Paul's own redemption, but also Paul's ensuing ministry as the means by which the new creation of the new covenant is being inaugurated in the midst of this present evil age (cf. Gal 1:4):

The god	God
of this age	of creation ("Let light . . . ")
has blinded	made light shine
the minds of unbelievers	in our hearts
so that they cannot see	to give us
the light of the gospel	the light of the knowledge
of the glory of Christ	of the glory of God
who is the image of God.	in the face of Christ.

THE BIBLICAL PERSPECTIVE REGARDING PAUL'S SUFFERING (4:7-18)

In 2 Cor 4:1-6 Paul has expressed his confidence as a minister of the Spirit (cf. 3:8, 12-13), and he returns to this point at the end of the chapter, framing this unit of his letter with two declarations of encouragement (4:1, 16). Yet inasmuch as Paul's confidence is based on the reality of God's glory in and through his life, Paul must counter his opponents' influence by again reminding the Corinthians that this glory is not made manifest through a "health and wealth" gospel or lifestyle, but in the "clay jar" of his weakness and suffering (4:7; cf. 1:3-11; 12:7-10). The image of a "clay jar" (earthen vessel) was a common metaphor for human weakness in the ancient world, including the Qumran writings.[9] The reference in 4:9 to not being "forsaken" in his weakness is therefore significant; its background in the LXX indicates that this is a "divine passive" that speaks of being forsaken by God (cf. Gen 28:15; Deut 31:6, 8; 1 Chr 28:20; Pss 15:10; 36:25, 28; Sir 2:10).[10] Paul's reliance on this scriptural worldview reveals his understanding that his sufferings are not a matter of coincidence, but, like Jesus's own experience on the cross, are part of God's sovereign plan to reveal power by sustaining Paul in the midst of his afflictions (4:8-11).

It is not surprising, therefore, that in 4:13 Paul summarizes the force of vv. 7-12 in terms taken from the Scriptures. Rendered literally, the opening clause of v. 13 reads, "having the same spirit of faith according to what has

---

9. E.g., note the references to clay pots as weak and prone to break in Ps 30:13LXX; Isa 30:14LXX; and in 1QS 11:22; 1QH 9:23-24; 11:21-22; and 12:30. (The column/line numbering for 1QH here follows the new reconstruction found in Stegemann, et al., editors, DJD 40 [Oxford: Oxford University Press, 2009].)

10. I owe this insight to Savage, *Power through Weakness*, 169.

been written."¹¹ Hence, Paul begins his new paragraph by referring to what has just been said as "the same spirit of faith," best interpreted as "the Holy Spirit who produces faith," not the "essence" or "nature" of faith. Paul's point is that the profound character of his life as an apostle is not unique. Paul stands in the long line of the suffering righteous from the past, here expressed in imagery drawn from Ps 116:10 (115:1LXX).¹² The psalmist finds himself in a situation of "death," only to be rescued by the Lord in response to his desperate cry for help (116:1-9). The psalmist's response to God's rescue of him is to fulfill a "vow" of thanksgiving as his "sacrifice of praise." An essential aspect of this praise is the psalmist's conclusion from his experience of suffering and divine rescue that he is indeed God's servant (116:16). So too, Paul's own experience of God's rescuing him from death leads to this same response of praise (2 Cor 1:3, 11; 2:14; 4:8-9, 15) and to the same conviction of his status as God's servant (3:1-6; 4:1-7). Far from being merely a pious outburst or scriptural coloring, Ps 116 provides an interpretive lens through which Paul sees the significance of his experience in (the) Christ, the Suffering Righteous One. The God who raised the Lord Jesus will also raise Paul with Jesus, together with all those who will stand resurrected in God's presence (4:14). For as Paul knew from Ps 116:9 (114:9LXX), now confirmed by Jesus's empty grave, the experience of having been preserved by God in the past leads one to declare defiantly for the future, "I shall walk before the Lord in the land of the living!"

In 4:16-18, Paul returns to where he began in verse 1. There the contrast was between losing heart and ministering with integrity in spite of his suffering. Here the corresponding contrast is between losing heart and the daily renewal of Paul's "inner man" ("inner nature") in spite of the "wasting away" of his "outer man" ("outer nature"). In light of these parallels, "outer" and "inner" probably refer to the moral transformation of Paul as a believer (his "inner man") in the midst of the suffering and sin of this present evil age (his "outer man"), not to a dualistic "body/soul" dichotomy.¹³ The "inner

---

11. For this same summary formula, cf. 3:4, 12; 4:1, 7.

12. That Paul pictures his proclamation and suffering in 4:13 in terms of the biblical tradition of the suffering of the righteous is confirmed by his use of related OT passages concerning the suffering of the righteous in 1 Cor 1:19, 31; 2:9; and 3:19-20. For the OT backdrop to Paul's understanding of his suffering, see Kleinknecht, *Gerechtfertigte*, 242-84. Kleinknecht points to the OT tradition of the suffering of the righteous, interpreted christologically, as the backdrop to Paul's thought in 2 Cor 1:3-11 (cf. Pss 71:20-21; 94:19; 23:4-5; 69:33-34; Isa 66:11; Jer 16:7); 4:7-18 (cf. Isa 30:13; Jer 19:11; Ps 2:9; esp. Pss 31:13; 37:28; *4 Ezra* 4:11; 7:88-89; *T. Jos.* 1.3ff; 2.3ff.; in addition to Ps 115:6-7); 6:1-10 (cf. *1 En.* 66:6; Pss 139; 118; Isa 49:8a; in addition to Ps 118:17-18); and 8:9 (cf. Isa 53:5).

13. For the "inner/outer" distinction as moral categories parallel to "old man/new

man" and "outer man" both refer to Paul in his entirety as one who lives eschatologically in this overlapping of the ages. "In (the) Christ" Paul belongs to the age to come ("inwardly") at the same time that he continues to live in the midst of this evil age ("outwardly").

This eschatological interpretation of the "inner man/outer man" contrast is confirmed by the common Jewish conception that in the age to come Adam's lost glory will be restored to the righteous who suffer.[14] Against this backdrop, the allusion to Gen 1:26–28 in 4:4, 6 is again picked up in v. 16, now associated with Ps 8:5–6. The "outer man" refers to the believer's existence under the decaying mortality inherited from Adam, while the "inner man" is the believer's existence in the new age already inaugurated by Christ as the "last Adam."[15] As we have seen, this transformation into the image of God takes place through encountering God's glory in Christ. Therefore, Paul does not lose heart, since as a member of the new covenant he is already participating proleptically in the new creation in anticipation of the "eternal weight of glory beyond all measure" (4:17).

THE APPLICATION OF THE SCRIPTURES TO THE CORINTHIANS

In view of the scriptural foundation developed in 2:14—4:18, Paul's argument throughout 2 Corinthians is best understood within a history-of-redemption perspective focused on the restoration of God's people in Christ under the new covenant. This means that reconciliation with God through Christ (5:18–21) is the beginning of the eschatological redemption of the world, the "new creation" (5:17; cf. Isa 43:18–19; 65:16b–23; 66:22–23). Indeed, in Isa 43:1–21 and 65:17–25 Israel's restoration from exile is described with new creation language as part of the extensive development throughout Isa 40–66 of the theme of Israel's restoration as a "second exodus." As G. K. Beale has argued, "'reconciliation' in Christ is Paul's way of explaining that Isaiah's promises of 'restoration' from the alienation of exile have begun to be fulfilled by the atonement and forgiveness of sins in Christ."[16]

Paul is convinced that this new creation, which is embodied in the community of the Spirit, takes place in response to the gospel proclaimed

---

man," cf. Rom 6:5–6; Col 3:5–14; Eph 3:16; 4:20–24.

14. Pate, *Adam Christology*, 61, 106, 126.

15. Ibid., 110, 112.

16. Beale, "Reconciliation," 556. Beale argues that this second exodus/restoration/new creation perspective is the basis of Paul's argument throughout chs. 5–7. For confirmation of this perspective, see Webb, *Returning Home*.

in Paul's own ministry (5:18b, 19b). At the center of the new creation as a "second exodus" redemption of the world is the manifestation of the glory of God in the midst of the people, now composed of those Jews and Gentiles who encounter God's glory in Christ. This is why Paul can identify his own proclamation of the gospel to the Corinthians, centered on its offer of reconciliation with God (cf. 5:20–21), with the role of Isaiah toward Israel (Isa 49:8), thereby making 6:1-2 one of Paul's greatest assertions of his apostolic authority and strategic role within the history of redemption. In fulfillment of Isaiah's expectation, the people of the new covenant are now experiencing in response to Paul's gospel the very "day of salvation" promised in Isaiah 49:8, and as such are themselves becoming part of the means by which this salvation is being brought about in the world.

As a consequence, Paul is concerned that those Corinthians who are still siding with his opponents, with their "other Jesus," "different Spirit," and "different gospel" (11:4), may have accepted God's grace "in vain" (6:1). For Paul's repetition of the solemn expression "[behold] now" in 6:2, by recalling 5:16-17, emphasizes his conclusion that the day of eschatological salvation promised to Isaiah has indeed arrived.[17] In other words, to go back on Paul's message at the dawning of the new creation is to be led away from the truth in the same way that Eve was deceived in the garden at the first creation (11:3; cf. 4:4). If Paul's gospel stands at the inauguration of the eschatological new creation, then to doubt its truth can be pictured in terms of the fall after the first creation! Conversely, as a new creation in Christ, the Corinthians must testify by their obedience and separation from evil that the consequences of the fall for all humanity (Gen 3) and for Israel (Exod 32–34) are being reversed in their lives (cf. 1 Cor 5:1—6:20). The transformation brought about by the Spirit is the evidence that one is, indeed, a new creation in Christ (3:18).

Within this paradigm it becomes clear that 6:14—7:1 is not a later insertion into Paul's argument, but a fitting application of Paul's covenantal perspective. The call to separate oneself from unbelievers in obedience and cultic purity (6:14–15; 7:1), like the calls to reaffirm allegiance to Paul and his ministry that frame them (6:11–13; 7:2–4), are grounded in the covenant formulas and their implications quoted in 6:16-18 (e.g., Isa 52:11, used in 6:17; in its original context those being redeemed in exile are called

---

17. So, e.g., Furnish, *II Corinthians*, 312–15, who points out that the expression "Behold!" (ἰδού) occurs frequently in the LXX and apocalyptic traditions to introduce solemn pronouncements, especially in visions and eschatological announcements concerning the "End." Furnish also observes that "now" (νῦν) points back to 5:16, which recalls Isa 48:6 ("the new things from now on"), and is used by Paul in 6:2 and in Rom 3:21; 5:9, 11; 8:1; 11:30; 13:11; Gal 2:20; and 4:9 to refer to the time of faith and salvation.

to separate themselves from everything unclean). As James M. Scott has demonstrated, Paul's use of these texts reflects the tradition of interpretation in which, on the basis of 2 Sam 7:14, 24, the regathered people of God come to be seen as the adopted sons and daughters of God (Ezek 20:34; Isa 43:6).[18]

But if 6:14—7:1 expresses in a negative vein the new covenant status and obligations of God's restored people, then their renewed willingness to participate in the collection for Jerusalem will be an undeniable positive expression of this same status. As Paul has admonished the Corinthians to separate from the wicked, he now extends a covenant call to identify with God's people through the sharing of financial resources with the needy believers in Jerusalem. Paul urges the people to share willingly and sincerely with the saints in Jerusalem as an expression of the grace they have experienced in Christ by quoting Exod 16:18LXX (2 Cor 8:15). God's promise to provide for the people during the exodus, as embodied in the manna and quail, has been reconfirmed in (the) Christ (cf. 8:9 with 1:20) and is now readily applied to the Corinthians as God's people of the "second exodus." The wilderness generation were to express continuing trust in God's provision by limiting their portion to "an omer apiece" (Exod 16:16), regardless of how much they gathered, sharing the rest with those who did not have their allotted amount. So too, the Corinthians are to share freely from their abundance, even as others will be called upon to share with them if the need arises (8:13–14). Such "cheerful giving" within the body of Christ demonstrates that "every grace" has been poured out abundantly in one's life (9:7–8a). The "sufficiency in everything, always" that comes from experiencing God's grace in Christ frees one to meet the needs of others "in every good work," being confident that God in Christ is able to meet one's own needs (9:8).

The principle that the sufficiency of God's grace for one's own needs is demonstrated in the willingness to meet the needs of others is not original with Paul, but an extension of wisdom teaching from Proverbs and Psalms. God blesses the one who generously shares food with the poor, rather than ruling over and enslaving them (cf. Prov 22:8LXX). The person is righteous who graciously gives to the poor out of a fear of God and delight in God's commandments (cf. Ps 111:9LXX). When Paul applies these texts to the Corinthians the promise of eschatological salvation is again in view, this time drawn from Isa 55:10 (2 Cor 9:7–10). Here too, Paul's understanding is informed by his conviction that in (the) Christ God has inaugurated the new age of the new "everlasting covenant" (cf. Isa 55:10 within the context of 55:1–5). Moreover, in Isaiah 55:10-11 the "seed" and "bread" brought

---

18. See Scott, "Use of Scripture," 73–99.

about by the rain and the snow are likened to that which is produced by God's word, which is sent out and will not return without accomplishing its designated task. So just as the righteous one in the psalm gives to the poor out of a delight in God's commandments (Ps 111:9LXX), the Corinthians' willingness to contribute to the needs of the saints expresses their righteousness in "obedience to [their] confession of the [sufficiency of the] gospel of Christ" (9:10, 13).[19] God meets the needs of the Corinthians abundantly so that they may meet the needs of others, thereby glorifying God, who makes their generosity possible (cf. 9:8, 12–15). The transforming impact of the "surpassing glory" (3:10)[20] of God's "surpassing grace" (9:14) under the new covenant is seen in the Corinthians' giving to others (9:6–15; cf. 4:7, 15). This "surpassing grace" toward the Corinthians is described in terms of the Corinthians' own ministry (cf. 3:3–9), which not only meets the needs of the saints, but also becomes the vehicle through which "many thanksgivings are abounding to God" (9:12; cf. 3:9). "Through the testing of this ministry" God is glorified (9:13). The ministry (διακονία) of the gospel "abounds" in its manifestation of the "glory of God" (cf. 3:9).

In the end, both the foundation and goal of Paul's apologetic, derived as it is from the biblical framework of the history of redemption, is consequently his radically theocentric perspective. The ground and purpose of his apostolic ministry—this is God's purpose throughout history—is the glory of God manifested and praised (3:7–18; 9:12–15). So Paul ends this section where he began, with thanksgiving to God (cf. 2:14a with 9:15). In so doing he follows the biblical injunction that the only genuine boast is "boasting in the Lord" (10:17; cf. 1 Cor 1:31; Jer 9:22–23MT/LXX). What ultimately matters to Paul is not the approval of the Corinthians (cf. 2:17; 12:19), but the commendation of God.

Paul's quotation of Jer 9:22–23 in 10:17 is intended to be the positive counterpart to the negative point Paul makes in 10:14–16. False boasting trumpets one's own accomplishments or the labors of others, while legitimate boasting "in the Lord" celebrates what the grace of God has accomplished in and through one's life—whether in establishing Paul's mission territory (10:13–16), or granting wisdom, righteousness, sanctification, and redemption in Christ (cf. Paul's other use of Jer 9:22–23 in 1 Cor 1:31). This

---

19. We take the subject of the quotation from Ps 111:9 in 9:9 to be the righteous man, as in its original context, and not God, as is common among commentators. In my view, Ps 111:9 picks up the subject of the purpose clause of 9:8b ("in order that you might abound in every good work"), rather than jumping back to the prior clause in 9:8a.

20. "Surpassing" in its impact (since it is not veiled), not "greater" in kind (cf. NRSV).

is the point of Jer 9:22–23, where the wise, strong, and rich are called to boast not in their own distinctive qualities, but in God, who is known on earth in mercy, judgment, and righteousness, since these are the things in which God delights. In turn, those who have experienced divine mercy and righteousness and are conscious of divine judgment manifest this knowledge in their own exercise of justice and righteousness (Jer 9:24–25; 2 Cor 5:10). This "boasting in the Lord" through one's own attitude and actions becomes the "boast" that marks one as legitimate before God and others.[21] "Boasting in the Lord" is the human counterpart to being "commended by the Lord" (10:17–18). Against the backdrop of Jeremiah, Paul's boasting about his authority is, in reality, a "boast in the Lord," who established Paul's apostleship in Corinth by pouring out the Spirit through Paul's ministry (10:13; cf. 3:3–10).

Finally, if Paul is an agent of God's eschatological redemption, he must also be an agent of God's eschatological judgment (2:15–16a; 4:4; 6:1–2). Accordingly, Paul's closing words to the Corinthians are words of warning in anticipation of his third visit. In the past, Paul postponed his return in order to give the Corinthians time to repent (1:23—2:4). But in his next visit, Paul will be forced to carry out his apostolic calling. With this in mind, Paul's final scriptural word to the Corinthians draws from the legal mandate in Deut 19:15 in preparation for his arrival (13:1). Paul calls those Corinthians who are still in rebellion against him to test themselves to see if they are truly "in the faith" (13:5). He prays that they will "pass the test" by reaffirming their support for his ministry and gospel (13:5–9). For in fulfillment of Jeremiah's promise that God will one day "build" a new covenant people, Paul's ministry under the new covenant—in contrast to Jeremiah's under the judgment of the Sinai covenant—is predominantly for "building up and not for tearing down" (13:10; cf. 10:8; Jer 1:10; 24:6; 31:4, 28; 33:7).

But if judge he must, then Paul will do so in accordance with the scriptural criterion. In acting "for the truth" in this way, Paul will simply be exercising the implications of the gospel itself (13:8). As we have seen, the framework of Paul's thinking throughout 2 Corinthians is that the new covenant brought about by the "second exodus" redemption in Christ is the inauguration of the eschatological new creation. This is a proleptic fulfillment of the postexilic restoration of Israel promised in the Prophets, in which God will dwell in the midst of the people. Hence, only those who are experiencing the transforming power of the glory of God in the face

---

21. For this point and my understanding of the role of Jer 9:22–23 in Paul's argument, see Hafemann, "Self-Commendation," 80–84, with its reliance on the work of J. Schreiner on Jeremiah.

of Christ can be considered members of the new covenant community. In preaching the gospel, therefore, Paul must also test the Corinthians' faith.

CONCLUSION

Paul's use of the Scriptures in 2 Corinthians underscores his conviction that (the) Christ has inaugurated the new covenant of the new creation. As a believer in Christ and apostle to the Gentiles for Israel's sake, it was this perspective that shaped Paul's self-understanding, served as an apologetic for his ministry, and supported his admonitions to the Corinthians. Thus, to encounter Paul is to encounter one whose life and labors were an extension of the scriptural worldview from which he understood his universe (cf. 1 Cor 10:6, 11; 15:3–4; Rom 1:2; 15:4).

Paul's use of the Scriptures in 2 Corinthians also reveals his confidence that the gospel he preached would bring about a transformation in the lives of God's people in accordance with the power of the Spirit being poured out under the new covenant. This transforming experience of encountering the glory of God in the face of Christ (3:18) is for Paul the beginning of the eschatological fulfillment of the restoration of Israel promised in the Law and the Prophets. As a result of the "second exodus," God is dwelling in the midst of the people! Hence, the Corinthians themselves, as the temple of the Holy Spirit (1 Cor 6:19; 2 Cor 6:16), are evidence that the promises of the prophets are being realized in and through Paul's ministry. This transformation of God's people supports Paul's legitimacy, so that he needs no "letter of recommendation" in Corinth beyond the Corinthians themselves (2 Cor 3:1–3). For in the end, the Scriptures lead Paul to conclude that the Corinthians, as "new creatures in Christ" (2 Cor 5:17), are testifying by their very lives that the effects of the fall are now being reversed through Paul's apostolic ministry.

4

The Comfort and Power of the Gospel
The Argument of 2 Corinthians 1–3[1]

For Paul, person and proclamation were wed together into an indissoluble whole. What Paul preached and how he lived combined to reveal publicly the same "glory of God in the face of Christ" which had so radically transformed his own life on the road to Damascus (2 Cor 4:6; cf. Gal 3:1). In his first canonical letter to the Corinthians Paul thus reminded the church of how his manner among them "in weakness and in fear and in much trembling" served to underscore that the persuasiveness of his message was based not on the latest wisdom of this world or rhetorical flash, but on "a demonstration of the Spirit and power" (1 Cor 2:3–4). For Paul had been sent to proclaim "Christ crucified" (1 Cor 1:23) and to live a correspondingly "cruciform apostolic" existence (1 Cor 2:1–4; 4:8–13)[2] "in order that [their] faith might not be in the wisdom of men, but in the power of God" (1 Cor 2:5). To those being saved, the suffering of the Christ *and* the suffering of his apostle were not a stumbling block or foolishness, but the vehicle through which the very power and wisdom of God were being displayed in the world (cf. 1 Cor 1:23–24 compared to 2:4–5).

---

1. From Scott J. Hafemann, "The Comfort and Power of the Gospel: The Argument of 2 Corinthians 1–3." *RevExp* 86 (1989) 325–44.

2. This is J. Christiaan Beker's apt phrase for Paul's apostolic lifestyle. See his discussion of this theme in his *Paul the Apostle*, 299–302. For the recent development of this theme, see now the works of Michael J. Gorman, *Cruciformity*; *Apostle of the Crucified Lord*; and *Inhabiting the Cruciform God*. For a detailed development of the theme of Paul's suffering in 1 and 2 Corinthians, see my work *Suffering and the Spirit*, 58–83, 126–76, upon which much of the following is based.

PAUL AND THE POLEMICAL SITUATION BEHIND 2 CORINTHIANS (1:1–2)

Between the writing of the letters we now call "First" and "Second" Corinthians, the situation in Corinth had changed drastically. When Paul wrote 1 Corinthians, the validity of his apostleship was not yet under attack within the Corinthian church, though its significance was being minimized in view of the many other "guides" which were now drawing the allegiance of various groups within the church (1 Cor 1:10–12). In 1 Corinthians Paul could therefore point to his suffering as the foundation for his legitimacy as an apostle and use both as the assumed basis of his authoritative admonitions to the Corinthians (cf. 1 Cor 4:14–17; 7:12, 25; 9:15–23). For at the time of the writing of 1 Corinthians, the problem was largely *within* the church, not between the church and her apostle.[3]

By the time 2 Cor 1–3 was penned, however, Paul's legitimacy as an apostle was *itself* being called into question *because* of his suffering. Under the influence of the "false apostles" who had now infiltrated the Corinthian church (cf. 2 Cor 10:4, 13–15), Paul's apostolic lifestyle of suffering was now being interpreted by some *within* the church as a sure sign that Paul's claim to be a true apostle of Jesus Christ was unsubstantiated. How could Paul claim to be a Spirit-filled apostle when his own life was so filled with suffering, anxiety, and mishap? Surely God's redemption in Christ was meant to free us from such effects of this evil age! The Christ suffered so that we would not! No one can claim to be an apostle of Jesus Christ who cannot "name and claim" God's promises in Christ!

Against such a backdrop Paul's nearly "standard" salutation in verses 1–2 takes on a poignant sense of importance. Paul is an apostle and he owes his apostolic calling to the "will of *God*" (v. 1). Paul did not owe his apostleship to some decision of his "to enter the ministry," but to the sovereign, predestined call of God in his life (cf. Gal 1:15). Paul can thus refer to his call to be an apostle as the "grace of God" (1 Cor 15:9–10; Rom 12:3; 15:15–16; Eph 3:1–6) since, as Gal 1:15–16 makes clear, Paul's "vocation and conversion were identical."[4] In 2 Corinthians, Paul likewise grounds his message

---

3. For a development of this view, see my *Suffering and the Spirit*, 41–83. For the more common view that already in 1 Corinthians Paul had to defend his standing as an apostle, see Fee, *First Corinthians*, 4–11, 28–29, 41, 48, 156ff., 392ff. etc., and Plank, *Irony*, 12–24.

4. Nock, *St. Paul*, 69. Though Stendahl is right in his essay, "Call," 7–23, that Paul was not converted to another religion on the Damascus Road, Paul's reorientation theologically and ethically was so drastic that some sort of "conversion" or transformation language is appropriate. I have therefore used the phrase "conversion-call" to bring these two concepts together.

of the Lordship of Christ and his own status as the slave of those to whom Christ calls him in his "conversion-call" on the road to Damascus (cf. 4:5-6).[5] Paul's call to Christ, his call to be an apostle to the Gentiles as a slave of the Christ, and his call to be the slave of those to whom God sent him were all one in purpose and all divine in origin.[6] Paul's opening introduction implicitly strikes at the very heart of the controversy now raging in Corinth and opens the way for the defense of Paul's legitimacy that will occupy so much of this letter. Either Paul is the true apostle, called by God, or his opponents are; but not both. There can be no compromise between Paul's claims and those of whom in 2 Cor 11:13-15 he calls "pseudo-apostles," "deceitful workmen," and "servants of Satan."

In the same way, Paul's designation of the Corinthians as the "church of God" and "saints," as well as his blessing of "grace and peace," also carry forceful connotations in this polemical context. On the one hand, Paul is reminding the Corinthians that, as "holy ones" (ἅγιοι), they are the people of God called to be separate *from* the world and separated *unto* God.[7] The reality of the Corinthians' faith is to be demonstrated in the reality of their obedience to the will of God. Those who encounter the glory of God are transformed by it (2 Cor 3:18). The "benefit of the doubt" that Paul extends to *all* the Corinthians at this point thus anticipates the appeals to come throughout 2 Corinthians. If the Corinthians are, in truth, the holy people of God, their genuine calling will manifest itself in obedience to the Pauline gospel. If not, the warnings of judgment found in 2 Cor 13:1-10 will become a reality. Hence, it is allegiance to Paul himself that will become the ultimate test of the genuine nature of the Corinthians' faith (cf. 2 Cor 5:20 with 6:1-13)!

From start to finish, then, Paul's salutation focuses his reader's attention on his own apostolic calling and legitimacy. If the "church of God in Corinth" were to reject Paul as an "apostle of Christ Jesus through the will of God," this would therefore not only be the ultimate irony, but also the ultimate tragedy. For, in reality, it is not *Paul's* apostleship that is on the line in 2 Corinthians, but the faith of those *Corinthians* who continue to reject Paul's proclamation of the gospel and apostolic life of suffering!

---

5. So too Stendahl, *Paul*, 45, and Kim, *Origin*, 5-11, 137-268.

6. See the work of Satake, "Apostolat," 96-97, in which he shows the parallel between Paul's use of καλέω ("to call") to refer to becoming a Christian in Rom 8:30; 1 Cor 1:9; 7:15; 1 Thess 2:12, etc. and his use of it to refer to his apostolic calling in Gal 1:15-16.

7. See the Old Testament roots of ἅγιος in the LXX of Exod 19:5-6; Lev 11:44; Num 23:9; Deut 7:6; 14:2; Ps 147:20, etc. See Martin, *2 Corinthians*, 3-4.

THE COMFORT OF THE GOSPEL
AND THE SUFFERING OF PAUL (1:3-11)

Paul begins the first major section of his letter by praising God with the בְּרָכָה (blessing)-formula typical of Jewish worship.[8] As Peter O'Brien has demonstrated, such introductory thanksgivings, far from being merely an unreflected outburst of Paul's piety, actually perform a threefold function in Paul's letters: epistolary, didactic, and paraenetic.[9] Paul's prayer of praise and its support in verses 3b-11 thus introduce the main themes of the letter, express Paul's key perspective on them, and contain an implicit appeal to his readers to join him in his outlook.

From Comfort to Comfort (vv. 3-7)

Even a cursory look at the vocabulary of this section makes it clear that the central themes of the letter are the "comfort" (παράκλησις/παρακαλέω) of God in relationship to "affliction" (θλῖψις) and "suffering" (πάθημα). The former occurs ten times in this short passage, the latter seven.[10] Indeed, the immediate ground for Paul's praise in verse 3a is that God is both the "Father of mercies" and the "God of all comfort" (3b). God's essential nature is one of granting to mankind his undeserved favor and, in this case, Paul is thinking explicitly of God's merciful work of comforting those in affliction.

The comfort in view in this passage is not the feeling of emotional relief or psychological support. Paul's further development of the theme of verses 3-7 in verses 8-11 demonstrates that in speaking of "comfort" Paul is referring to the common Old Testament theme of God's decisive intervention to

---

8. For the historical and linguistic background in Jewish tradition to 2 Cor 1:3, see the commentaries by Furnish, *II Corinthians*, 108, 116-17, and Martin, *2 Corinthians*, 7-8.

9. See his *Thanksgivings*, 233-40. For the other εὐλογητός-formulas in Paul, see Rom 1:25; 2 Cor 1:3ff.; Eph 1:3ff.; Rom 9:5; and 2 Cor 11:31.

10. This is even more striking in view of the fact that παράκλησις ("encouragement" or "comfort") and παρακαλέω (in the sense of "to comfort" rather than "to exhort") is a distinctively Pauline theme. The former occurs twenty-nine times in the New Testament, twenty of which are in the Pauline corpus, with eleven of these in 2 Cor (six in 1:3-7)! Of the seventeen times that παρακαλέω clearly means "to comfort" in the New Testament (Acts 18:27 contains a variant reading, and the sense is unclear in Acts 20:1f. and 1 Thess 4:18; 5:11), fourteen are in the Pauline corpus, with eight of these in 2 Corinthians (four in 1:3-7)! On the other hand, Furnish, *II Corinthians*, 110, points out that θλῖψις ("affliction") "is more often mentioned by Paul than by any other NT writer, and more often in 2 Corinthians than in any other letter (noun and verb, twenty-four times in the seven letters, twelve times in 2 Corinthians)."

rescue and relieve his people in times of distress and affliction. It is God's acts of deliverance, both past and future, that are the "comfort" of his people. God is the "God of all comfort" because he is the one who is "our refuge and strength, a very present help in trouble" (Ps 46:1).[11] As C. K. Barrett has put it, "It is clear that comfort means not that Paul is consoled *in* his afflictions, but that he is delivered *out of* them."[12]

Furthermore, although Paul uses the idea of comfort and encouragement elsewhere to refer to common Christian experience,[13] and even though Paul uses first person plural pronouns throughout this section, the continuation of Paul's argument in verses 4-6 makes it clear that here Paul is not thinking of humanity's plight in general, nor even of the suffering of Christians. Rather, Paul is referring specifically to his *own* suffering as an *apostle*.[14] But Paul is not looking for pity. The focus of attention is not on Paul's suffering, but on its results. Specifically, God has comforted Paul in the affliction he has experienced *so that* (εἰς τό + the infinitive δύνασθαι) Paul will be able to comfort others in their affliction (1:4). Moreover, Paul immediately makes it clear that the resource with which Paul will comfort others (i.e., the assurance of God's commitment to deliver his people) is the same comfort with which he himself has been comforted by God (i.e., his own experience of God's faithfulness). For this reason *God* is still to be praised as the "God of all comfort," even though the *apostle* does the actual

---

11. I owe this insight to the work of Hofius, "*Paraklesis*," 217-27. As Old Testament background Hofius points to Isa 12:1; 40:1; 49:13; 51:3, 9-14; 52:9; 57:18; Jer 31:13; 38:9; Pss 23/22LXX:4ff.; 71/70LXX:20ff.; 86/85LXX:1-2, 7, 12ff.; 94/93LXX:16ff.; 125:1, etc. See too Bar 4:30; Tg. Hos. 6:2.

12. Barrett, *Second Corinthians*, 60.

13. Cf. Rom 12:8; 15:4; 1 Cor 14:3; 31; 2 Cor 2:7; 7:6-7; Phil 2:1; Col 2:2; 4:8; 1 Thess 4:18; 2 Thess 2:16-17.

14. For an analysis of Paul's use of first person plural pronouns to refer to himself in 2 Cor 1-3, see my *Suffering and the Spirit*, 12-17; and in general, Cranfield, "Changes," 280-89. The best explanation for this usage is Wendland's suggestion that in using the literary plural Paul is reflecting his consciousness that he is speaking *as an apostle*; cf. his *Briefe*, 175. We are tipped off to this already in verse 3 with Paul's use of "blessed be the God ..." (εὐλογητὸς ὁ θεός), since this blessing formula is consistently used by Paul for experiences in which he participated. In contrast, Paul uses the "I give thanks to God" (εὐχαριστέω) formula to refer to the work of God in the lives of others. See O'Brien, *Thanksgivings*, 239. For the εὐχαριστέω-formulas in Paul, see Rom 1:8; 1 Cor 1:4; Phil 1:3ff.; Col 1:3-4, 12; 1 Thess 1:2-5; 2:13; 2 Thess 1:3; 2:13ff. Though O'Brien's distinction holds true in general, Rom 1:25 and 2 Cor 11:31 do not seem to fit the pattern. And in verse 4a Paul's focus on his own suffering is made explicit by his use of the grammatical construction πᾶς followed by a noun with the article (ἐπὶ πάσῃ τῇ θλίψει ἡμῶν; i.e., "in every affliction of ours"). For such constructions, "the reference is not indefinite and open-ended but is to something actually encountered," so Furnish, *II Corinthians*, 110. See too 2 Cor 7:4; 1 Thess 3:7.

comforting of others, since Paul's ability to encourage others is a direct result of God's prior work in his own life.

The main point of verses 4–5, therefore, is Paul's statement in 4b that, by means of the comfort he has received, he is able to console those who are in every kind of affliction. Verse 5 then supports (cf. the ὅτι of 5a) the fact that God has indeed comforted Paul. It does so by drawing a comparison between the sufferings of Paul and the comfort he has received through Christ. Paul's point is simple. The greatness of his sufferings has never outweighed the greatness of the encouragement he has received. No matter how severe the suffering, whether it be outward circumstances or inward mental and spiritual distress,[15] the comfort (= deliverance) Paul received from God through Christ has been equal to the challenge.

In verses 6–7 Paul continues to draw out the consequences of 4b by applying the principle of "from comfort to comfort" to the Corinthians. As the two sets of conditions in verse 6 indicate, whether Paul is afflicted or comforted, in either case, the result is still the same: *their* comfort (6a–d). Notice that this movement "from comfort to comfort" is not reciprocal. Paul does not say that when they are afflicted, he comforts them, and when he is afflicted, they comfort him. Verse 6 is not a description of a fellowship of suffering. Paul is the one suffering *and* being comforted, while the Corinthians are the ones who, *in both cases*, are being comforted. Although Paul will develop this point in greater detail later in the letter (cf. 1:8–11; 2:14–17; 4:7–15, esp. vv. 12, 15), the reason for this one-sided relationship of comfort is already hinted at in Paul's identification of *his* affliction (v. 4) with the sufferings of *Christ* (v. 5). Just as Christ suffered on the cross and was "comforted" at the resurrection on behalf of the church, so too Paul suffers and is comforted for the encouragement of his people.

The ultimate result of this comfort in the lives of the Corinthians is spelled out in verses 6e and 7. Paul's experience of affliction and comfort leads to a comfort among the Corinthians that works itself out in an "endurance" (ὑπομονή) of the same kinds of suffering that Paul is presently experiencing (v. 6e). In other words, the evidence that one is indeed being comforted through Paul's afflictions and comfort is the ability to endure the same sufferings as Paul endures. For to Paul "endurance" is not some sort of self-generated, stoic "power of positive thinking," but is rather "the obedient faith of those who can rejoice, precisely in the midst of adversity, in

---

15. For θλῖψις ("affliction") as outward circumstances, see Rom 2:9; 5:3; 8:35; 12:12; 1 Cor 7:28; 2 Cor 4:17; 6:4; Eph 3:13; Phil 4:14; Col 1:24; as an affliction of mental and spiritual states of mind, see 2 Cor 2:4; 7:4–5; Phil 1:17; 2 Cor 11:28 (!). For πάθημα as suffering and misfortune, see Rom 8:18; Phil 3:10; Col 1:24.

the confidence that God's love will not only perdure but will indeed prevail (Rom 5:1–5)."[16]

The endurance of faith in the midst of adversity that Paul highlights in verse 6e is thus a direct reflection of one's trust in God's ability to sustain and rescue his people in affliction. Paul's confidence in God's capability to do just that (cf. 1 Cor 10:13!) has been the underlying presupposition of this passage. Paul's hope for the Corinthians is therefore certain *because* (taking the participle εἰδότες in 7b to be causal) he knows that just as the Corinthians share in Paul's experience of suffering, they will also share in his comfort. Not to do so could only mean that God was not at work in their lives. For where God is at work, there is comfort in the midst of affliction, since God is, by his very nature, the "God of all comfort" (v. 3). But how do Paul's experiences of suffering and comfort actually produce this corresponding comfort among the Corinthians (vv. 6–7) so that he feels justified in equating his own suffering with the sufferings of Christ (v. 4–5)? And if Paul is right in verses 3–7, then what are the implications for the current conflict between Paul and his church? The purpose of verses 8–11 is to answer these questions.

The Apostolic Sentence of Death (vv. 8–11)

Whereas the opponents of Paul have convinced numbers of the Corinthians that Paul's suffering and weakness call his legitimacy as an apostle into question, Paul is now ready to show how his suffering, in reality, is at the very heart of what it means to be called as an apostle of Jesus Christ. Thus, far from being ashamed of his suffering, in verses 8–11 Paul calls his readers' attention to a recent example of it and its significance.

The nature and occasion of Paul's affliction in Asia are unknown and, in the end, unimportant. Paul's purpose here is not to give a news report. What is important is the severity of Paul's suffering as stressed in verse 8 and the theological principle that he draws from it in verses 9–10. Paul's suffering was so severe that he saw no way out but death (v. 8). But God's purpose in this affliction was not to kill Paul. Instead (cf. the ἀλλά in v. 9a), Paul received this "sentence" or "verdict of death" (τὸ ἀπόκριμα τοῦ θανάτου) in order that (ἵνα + subjunctive in 9b) Paul would not continue trusting in himself, but in the God who raises the dead (v. 9b).

Paul's theological move at this point is decisive.[17] As he has already done in 1 Cor 4:9; 15:30–32, Paul once again follows common Jewish

---

16. Furnish, *II Corinthians*, 111. See too Rom 15:5.

17. Indeed, Paul's purpose clause in 2 Cor 1:9b is so fundamental to Paul's thinking

tradition in interpreting his daily experiences of suffering as a "death." Now, however, Paul takes the additional step of interpreting his "death" in terms of the death of Christ, and his deliverance from this suffering as a type of Christ's resurrection. Like (the) Christ, Paul is called in his "death" (= his suffering) to trust the God who raises the dead. But Paul's call to trust in God in his affliction is not a blind leap into the dark, nor the last act of a desperate man. For Paul's present faith in the God who raises the dead (v. 9b) is grounded in the fact that God has demonstrated his faithfulness to sustain him in the past (v. 10a). Paul therefore has every reason to trust and hope in God to rescue him in the future (v. 10b).

Like the suffering righteous in the Old Testament and *the* suffering Righteous One, (the) Christ,[18] Paul is being led into situations of suffering in order that God may display his resurrection power of deliverance through him. Specifically, when we compare Paul's point in 2 Cor 1:9-10 with his prior discussion of his suffering in 1 Cor 4:8-13, it becomes clear that in both cases God is the one who is carefully orchestrating the circumstances of Paul's life (i.e., his "sentence to death" in 1 Cor 4:9 and 2 Cor 1:9) for the very purpose of revealing his wisdom and power through the apostle (cf. 2 Cor 2:14 as well; see below). But in 1 Cor 4:8-13 this revelation takes place through *Paul's* response of faith in the midst of his adversity, while in 2 Cor 1:9-10 it takes place through *God's* response of deliverance. That is to say, in 4:9 Paul's suffering is viewed in the context of the *cross* as its *corollary*, while in 2 Cor 1:8-11 Paul's suffering is being viewed in the context of the *resurrection* (v. 9b, 10b) as its *antithesis* (as also later in 2:14-17; 4:7-12; 6:1-10; and 11:23—12:10). In the former case, it was Paul's endurance that manifested God's power; now it is God's deliverance itself. Yet in both cases, Paul's suffering stands at the very center of his apostolic ministry as the revelatory vehicle through which the power and glory of God are being made known. It is not *in spite of*, but *in and through* Paul's suffering that his legitimacy as an apostle is established.[19]

In turn, rather than rejecting Paul for his weakness, the Corinthians ought to view Paul's suffering as a vivid display of the ability and willingness

---

that Nigel M. Watson takes this verse to be the clearest expression and summary of the center of Paul's theology that we have! See his "2 Corinthians 1:9b," 384-98, for the development of the main aspects of Paul's thought as reflected in this text.

18. Though it is beyond the scope of this essay, see the work of Kleinknecht, *Gerechtfertigte*, 208-304, for a discussion of the Old Testament theological backdrop to the catalogs of suffering in 1 Corinthians and 2 Corinthians. Of special significance for this passage is the situation of death and rescue portrayed in Ps 116/114-15LXX; but cf. the four quotes from the tradition of the suffering righteous in 1 Cor 1:19, 31; 2:9; 3:19-20.

19. I have developed these points in detail in my *Suffering and the Spirit*, 58-83.

of God to sustain and deliver his people from trial. Paul's life is an object lesson and extension of the same truth about God's faithfulness so clearly portrayed in Christ's cross and resurrection—namely, that God's power and grace are made known and perfected in and through suffering (cf. 2 Cor 12:9).

The epistolary and didactic purposes of Paul's opening thanksgiving have now been accomplished. Paul has introduced the comfort of God in the midst of afflictions as the central theme of the letter. Next, he has explained how his own suffering is the essential link in the mediation of the comfort of God to the Corinthians. Now, in verse 11, Paul concludes his thanksgiving by drawing out the implication of his understanding of the revelatory function of his suffering for the Corinthians. Verse 11 also contains an implicit exhortation in fulfillment of the paraenetic purpose of such introductory sections. In closing his thanksgiving, Paul invites the Corinthians to join him in *thanking* God for his suffering, the very thing that the opponents say disqualifies Paul as an apostle! Just as Paul praised God in verses 3–7 because of the Corinthians, in verses 8–11 he now encourages the Corinthians to praise God because of him. Verse 11 thus fulfills Paul's initial call to praise in verse 3. If, for their part, the Corinthians do not join Paul in praising God for his ministry, this refusal becomes an indictment of the Corinthians themselves (cf. 12:19–21).

THE BOAST OF PAUL AND THE PROMISES OF GOD (1:12—2:11)

In 2 Corinthians Paul is engaged in a dialogue on two fronts. As we have seen, Paul must deal with those Corinthians who have come to doubt his apostleship as a consequence of the intruders who have infiltrated the church. But what about those who have already repented of their disloyalty to Paul in response to his previous "painful letter" (cf. 2:5, 8–9; 7:7–16) and would now gladly join with Paul in thanking God for his ministry of suffering? While confronting the former, Paul must therefore also encourage those within the church who support him.

Nowhere is this more evident than in this next section of the letter. At this point Paul turns his attention to his recent relationship with Corinth in order to explain the theological rationale for his unexpected change in travel plans (1:12—2:4) and, by applying this same rationale, to give his supporters advice for dealing with the one who has caused so much pain (2:5–11). At the same time, Paul must keep one eye on his opponents, who have convinced some of the church that both situations are further evidence of his illegitimacy.

The Single Reason for the Many Plans (1:12—2:4)

Evidently, one of the accusations against Paul was that he was involved in an elaborate scam in an attempt to defraud the Corinthians (cf. 2 Cor 7:2; 8:20f.; 11:7f.; 12:13–18). As support for this accusation, Paul's opponents pointed to his apparently indecisive vacillation in travel plans in regard to his coming to Corinth. If Paul were a true apostle, filled with the Spirit, he should be able to rely on the guidance of God so that his commitments and plans would reflect the very surety of God himself. The true apostle's language is straight and pure, his "yes is yes" and his "no is no" (cf. 2:19). Paul's inability to carry through with his plans was thus seen to be yet another sign of his illegitimacy as an apostle and a reflection of Paul's duplicitous motives as one who decides "according to the flesh" (cf. 1:17).

Paul counters by reassuring the Corinthians that his exhortation for the Corinthians to praise God for Paul's life is not unfounded (note the γάρ in 12a). Paul *can* boast (i.e., his conscience does confirm) that his behavior has not been motivated by the "wisdom of sinful flesh" (σοφίᾳ σαρκικῇ), but derives, just as his call itself does, from the "grace of God" (v. 12b). Hence, Paul can assert that his actions have taken place as a result of the "uprightness and sincerity" that comes "from God" (taking τοῦ θεοῦ to be a genitive of source, v. 12a). Therefore—taking the γάρ of v. 13 to be inferential—Paul is not hesitant to write openly about his recent change of plans in 1:15—2:4, knowing that they too derived from the work of God's grace and the divine sincerity within him (vv. 13–15a).

Paul's main point in 1:15—2:4 is that his earlier decision not to come to Corinth on his way to Jerusalem from Macedonia (cf. 1 Cor 16:5–9), but to come directly to Corinth first (v. 15), as well as his later decision not to return to Corinth for a second visit (v. 23),[20] were not the vacillations of a man who makes decisions "according to the flesh" (v. 17), but the actions of one who is indeed "sealed by the Spirit" (v. 22). Paul supports this bold counterpunch by once again relating his experience to the revelation of God

---

20. As well as outlining the options for interpreting the identity of the offender in 2:5ff., Kruse, "Offender," 129–31, offers a good summary of the widely accepted reconstruction of the sequence of events between the writing of 1 Corinthians and 2 Corinthians.

in Christ. Just as God is faithful to his people in Christ, Paul has been faithful to the Corinthians in his travel plans (v. 18).

The key is to see that the definition of this "faithfulness" is (the) Christ himself (vv. 19–20a). Even though (the) Christ, in his earthly ministry, did not establish the kingdom of God in its fullness, he was nevertheless the full expression of the promises of God (vv. 19–20). For through Christ God's purpose to bring mercy before judgment became clear and was fulfilled. Hence, when Paul changed his travel plans twice in regard to the Corinthians, he was not breaking his apostolic word nor violating Christ's command to speak the truth with integrity.[21] For in each case Paul's change of plans was motivated by a desire to extend mercy to the Corinthians for their restoration (1:23—2:4)!

This was the one reason for Paul's many decisions. In order to remain *faithful* to the expression of God's glory (= power) in Christ (v. 20) and the work of the Spirit within him (v. 22), Paul *had* to change his plans in order to give the Corinthians the chance for the repentance that would spare them judgment. So it was in order to *affirm* the work of God in Christ (cf. v. 20b!) that Paul first decided to come to Corinth immediately when he heard of trouble in the church (v. 15), and then not to come back again after his "painful visit," but instead to write the "sorrowful letter" (2:1–5). Paul's changes in plans were an act of mercy on his part (1:23), as was his "sorrowful letter" (2:4), all of which were carried out in the hope of reestablishing the Corinthians' allegiance to him (cf. 2 Cor 7:8ff.). Thus, just as Paul's suffering was a platform for the revelation of God's glory in his power, so too Paul's actions become a conduit for the revelation of God's glory in his mercy.

From Mercy to Mercy (2:5–11)

The desire to extend mercy, which flows from the work and model of Christ, had guided Paul's relationship with the Corinthians. In the same way, this same principle is to guide the Corinthians' relationships with one another. So Paul once again turns his attention back to the Corinthians in order to admonish them to follow in his footsteps. Specifically, Paul now instructs the Corinthians to extend mercy to the repentant sinner (2:7). Whoever this person was, Paul's judgment is that the punishment had accomplished its divinely intended goal of producing the grief that leads to repentance

---

21. For an analysis of 2 Cor 1:17–18 against the backdrop of Matt 5:37 and Jas 5:12, which details how Jesus's prohibition against oaths could have become used by the Corinthians to accuse Paul of breaking his promises, see Wenham, "Echo," 271–79.

(cf. 2 Cor 7:9f.; 2:6). In response, the Corinthians must welcome him back into the community with forgiveness, comfort, and love, lest he be "overwhelmed by excessive sorrow" (2:7f.).

Paul's seriousness at this point is striking. His command to accept the offender takes on the status of a test of faith (2:9; cf. Matt 18:23–35). For to Paul, the indicatives of the gospel and the imperatives that flow from them cannot be separated, since they represent one integral reality. Paul therefore ends this section by reminding the Corinthians of the ultimate purpose for his admonitions: to prevent the Evil One from using this situation against the church (v. 11). For Satan's schemes all revolve around destroying the mutual acceptance and forgiveness that are to characterize God's people as the sign of God's redeeming work (cf. Rom 15:7). And no church had struggled with this more than the Corinthians. Indeed, most of the commands throughout 1 Corinthians center on some aspect of church unity (cf. 1 Cor 1:10; 3:1–3; 4:14, 16; 5:4a, 5a, 7a, 8b; 6:1, 4, 6–7; 6:18, 20; 8:9, 13; 10:14; 11:33–34; 12:14ff., etc.). So before turning his attention back to his own apostolic ministry in 2:12, Paul once again reminds his readers of the seriousness of the "test" that now confronts them. Nothing less than the validity of their own salvation is on the line (2:9). Those who have repented and experienced mercy from God have no choice but to extend mercy to those who have sinned against them but have now likewise repented. Not to do so would be to call one's own experience into question.

PAUL'S DEFENSE OF HIS APOSTOLIC MINISTRY: SUFFERING AND THE SPIRIT (2:12—3:3)

From the beginning of his letter Paul has weaved together his own experience as an apostle with his admonitions to the Corinthians, the former providing the theological support for the latter (cf. 1:3–10 with v. 11; 1:12—2:4 and 2:10 with 2:7–8). His proclamation and person have been one. What he practices and experiences he also preaches. But the focus of attention has been largely on Paul himself. In keeping with this focus, Paul now begins the most detailed defense of his apostolic ministry found in any of his letters, a defense that lasts through chapter 7, though the heart of Paul's apologetic is the twofold argument for his sufficiency and boldness as an apostle in 2:14—3:18.

Paul's apparently sudden switch back to his travel plans in 2:12-13 provides the transition back to Paul's ongoing defense of his apostolic ministry. As such, this small and seemingly insignificant mention of Paul's anxiety over Titus in Troas and its consequent result carries tremendous import for Paul's argument. Paul's refusal of the open door in Troas was not the mistake of someone overcome with worry, but yet another expression of the *suffering* that Paul undergoes for the sake of his churches (cf. 2:13 with 11:28!). It was Paul's concern for Titus and the *Corinthians* that led Paul onward to Macedonia (cf. 7:5–7). This is the significance of the emphasis in verse 13 that Paul said goodbye to those in Troas before he left town. Paul was not ashamed of his decision to leave the open door; he did it openly as yet another act of love and suffering on behalf of God's people. Rather than merely giving more information about Paul's itinerary, 2:12-13 call our attention back to the central theme of Paul's suffering as an apostle first introduced in 1:3-11.

From this point on, and throughout Paul's argument in chapter 3, Paul's thought becomes very complex.[22] It should be kept in mind, however, that the crux for interpreting this section revolves around two questions. First, we must understand the function and meaning of the metaphor of verse 14 within the context of the Corinthian correspondence as a whole. Second, we must establish the relationship between Paul's argument in 2:14-17 and 3:1-3 before these units are related to the comparison with the ministry of Moses set forth in 3:4-18.

Paul's Ministry of Suffering (2:14-17)

Ever since Calvin, commentators have balked at Paul's image in 2:14 of his being led in a triumphal procession. For as an essential aspect of this institution in the Roman world, those prisoners of war who were led in these victory parades were being led to their *death*.[23] In the face of such an image, students of Paul have tried to reinterpret the metaphor in a variety of ways, either to emphasize Paul's triumph, God's triumph, or both. But the emphasis of verse 14 is clearly on *Paul* as the one who is being led in the procession. And the use of the word θριαμβεύω elsewhere shows that it cannot be taken as causative ("causes [us] to triumph"). The only attested meaning of this word in Paul's day is, "to lead one (to death) in the triumphal procession." Yet how could Paul praise God in verse 14 for leading him to his *death* as a conquered slave in a triumphal procession?

---

22. For the exegetical substantiation for the following overview, see the detailed analysis of 2:14-17 in my work, *Suffering and the Spirit*.

23. For a detailed discussion of the triumphal procession, see Versnel, *Triumphus*. Of special interest for the New Testament period, and 2 Cor 2:14 in particular, are the accounts of the triumphal procession in Dionysius of Halicarnassus, *Ant. Rom.* II.3; VIII.67.9-10; IX.36.3; 71.4; Plutarch, *Rom.* 25.4; *Thes.* 4.2; *Aem.* 32.1—36.6; *Ant.* 84.2—86.3; Appian, *Mith.*, 12.116-17; and Josephus, *J.W.* 6.414-19, 433-34; 7.153-55.

In view of our earlier study of 1:3–11, and in the context of 2:12–13, the answer should now be clear. Paul's opening phrase in verse 14, "thanks be to God," is the same kind of thanksgiving formula as that found in 1:3 — namely, the introductory formula of blessing that calls attention to Paul's own experience. Thus, the formula in 2:14 performs the same epistolary, didactic, and paraenetic functions we saw in chapter 1. Like 1:3–11, 2:14–17 is also designed to be a thesis-like statement that sets the tone and themes of what follows, with a focus on an implied admonition to the Corinthians to accept Paul's point. It should not be surprising, then, especially in view of 2:12–13, that Paul's theme in 2:14 is once again his suffering. For Paul's experience of anxiety mentioned in 2:12–13 is yet another example of the "death" which Paul undergoes as an apostle of Christ (cf. 1 Cor 15:31; 2 Cor 11:28). The metaphor of the triumphal procession simply expresses, in yet another graphic analogy, the central role of Paul's suffering in his calling to be an apostle (cf. 2:14 with the "death" analogies in 1 Cor 4:9; 2 Cor 1:9; 4:11!). Rather than despair, Paul can consequently respond in thanksgiving when he reflects on his suffering in Troas.[24] Paul knows that it is precisely through his suffering that God is revealing "the knowledge of himself in every place" (2:14b).

Notice once again that Paul's praise in verse 14 is based on his implicit recognition that God is the one who is in sovereign control. God is the subject of θριαμβεύω in verse 14. *He* is the one who both leads Paul to his "death" (= suffering) and then uses it to reveal himself to the world. Paul thus supports his praise in verse 14 by pointing to the twofold effect that God's self-revelation through Paul's suffering brings about in the world (note the ὅτι in v. 15a). It is evident that God is indeed revealing himself through Paul's suffering *because* the "aroma of Christ," which Paul's life of suffering spreads, brings about the same twofold response that Paul described for the word of the cross in 1 Cor 1:18–25. Those who are being saved welcome Paul's suffering as the appropriate expression of his apostolic calling, while those who are perishing reject it as foolishness (2:15–16). The

---

24. There is thus no reason to posit a break in the letter between 2:13 and 14 so that 2:14ff. becomes part of an independent literary fragment, as so many commentators argue. The link between 2:13 and 14 is Paul's experience of suffering in 2:12–13 and his theological reflection on it in 2:14ff. presented in the metaphor of the triumphal procession. See too Murphy-O'Connor, "Paul and Macedonia," 99–103, who argues for the unity of the text at this point based on the "resonances of the term 'Macedonia' in 2:13" as found in passages such as 1 Thess 1:6–8 and Phil 2:14–16 (100–101). But whereas Murphy-O'Connor must rely on the somewhat subjective analysis of "the associative way in which Paul's mind worked" (102), my suggestion can take "Macedonia" in 2:13 quite literally, as well as keep the focus in this context on Paul himself, rather than introduce the foreign idea of the "apostolic impact of the churches of Macedonia" (102).

implied admonition to the Corinthians is therefore clear. How they respond to Paul's declaration in verse 14 concerning his suffering will indicate on what side of the life and death watershed they stand.

If what Paul says in verses 14–16b is true, then the rhetorical question in 16b takes on a startling force. Rather than taking it as a sign of humility, as many commentators do, Paul's question ("Who is sufficient for these things?") is actually intended to be answered, "*I am!*" Since Paul is the one through whom God is revealing himself, Paul is in fact the one whom God has called to be his agent or mediator of revelation. Verse 17 confirms this interpretation. The γάρ ("because") of verse 17 indicates that this verse is intended to support the implied positive assertion of 16b. If Paul had just denied his sufficiency for the task, there would be nothing to support with this comparison. In addition, Paul's acknowledged sufficiency is the unexpressed presupposition of 3:4-6, where Paul returns to outline the source of his sufficiency, not to deny it.

Moreover, once verse 17 is seen to be a reference to Paul's practice of preaching the gospel free of charge, rather than to his watering it down in some way,[25] it becomes clear that here too Paul is again pointing to his suffering as the distinguishing mark of his apostolic legitimacy and of his love for the Corinthians (cf. 1 Cor 9:12–18 and 2 Cor 11:7–15; 12:13–16). This is evident in that Paul's declaration in 2:17 reflects the fact that many of the sufferings listed in 1 Cor 4:11–13 and 2 Cor 11:26–27 are a direct result of Paul's decision to support himself with his trade.[26] The point of verse 17 is that Paul should be considered a legitimate apostle *in contrast* to the many who are selling the gospel precisely *because*, not in spite of the fact that, he preaches to the Corinthians without charge. Conversely, Paul's description of his opponents in 2:17 as those who "sell the gospel like retail merchants in the market place" (καπηλεύω) raises suspicion concerning their true motives in preaching. In contrast, Paul's suffering as a result of his decision to preach the gospel without charge is a clear testimony of his genuine love for and commitment to the Corinthians (cf. 2 Cor 11:11; 12:15). If anyone is trying to defraud them, it cannot be Paul.

In sum, verses 16–17 affirm that Paul *is* the sufficient one (though his sufficiency is not from himself, cf. 3:4-5) precisely because he is the one

---

25. The issue revolves around the translation of καπηλεύοντες τὸν λόγον τοῦ θεοῦ in 2:17a and its relationship to δολοῦντες τὸν λόγον τοῦ θεοῦ in 2 Cor 4:2. For examples of those who take καπηλεύω to mean "water down," see the commentaries of Meyer, Heinrici, Hodge, Plummer, Windisch, Barett, Tasker, and J. Hering; for another presentation of my view, see Furnish's commentary on 2:17; Martin argues that the verb expresses the meanings of both "sell for profit" as well as "adulterate" or "water down."

26. See Hock, *Social Context*, 28, 35–37, 60, 78n17, 84n94.

who has been called to suffer for (the) Christ on behalf of the churches. Rather than calling his apostleship into question, Paul's suffering is itself the very evidence of his legitimacy. For this reason Paul praises God when he thinks back to his experience in Troas because he knows that it is through his ministry of suffering that the word of the cross is not only proclaimed but embodied.

Paul's Ministry of the Spirit (3:1–3)

What is the evidence that Paul's assertions in 2:14–17 are true? To those in Corinth who considered suffering to be the direct antithesis of the power of God unleashed in the Spirit, Paul's declarations that his suffering was the divinely orchestrated vehicle of God's self-revelation would sound like special pleading. Certainly the false apostles could counter with their signs and demonstrations of the Spirit, not to mention with the fact that they were being paid for their ministry as a sign of its value and recognition. After all, it could be argued, the Spirit has come to *deliver* us from this evil age, not to enable us to *endure* it. And the Corinthians, due to their spiritual pride and over-realized eschatology, had been in no position simply to accept Paul's radical interpretation of his suffering in 1:3–11 and now again in 2:14–17.

Paul's response to this expected, and unfortunately "natural" reaction is to raise the issue himself in order to quell the counterattack before it begins. He does so with the kind of rhetorical questions familiar to us from the diatribes in the letter to the Romans (cf. Rom 3:9; 6:2, 15; 7:7, 13; 9:14; 11:1, 11). The purpose of these questions is to prevent one's audience from drawing a false conclusion from the argument presented. Thus, in 2 Cor 3:1 Paul introduces two questions, the latter intended to interpret the former, which together are intended to stop the Corinthians from drawing the false conclusion that Paul's argument in 2:14–17 is merely an unsubstantiated "self-commendation." If it were, then Paul would, in fact, have no evidence of his *own* to back up his claims, which in turn would mean that he would need letters of recommendation from *others* to support his ministry. Thus, when Paul denies his need for letters of recommendation, he is also denying the fact that he is commending himself. As the structure of the two rhetorical questions of 3:1 indicates, the issues of self-commendation and letters of recommendation are in reality one and the same: does Paul have evidence from his own ministry to substantiate the claims of 2:14–17 concerning his suffering?

The Corinthians themselves are the answer to this question. Paul is not merely commending himself and therefore does not need letters of recommendation to supplement his claims because the *Corinthians* are his letter of recommendation (3:2a). Specifically, it is clear to all that they are Christians, that is, a "letter of Christ" (3:3a), and that the Corinthians owe their very lives as Christians to Paul as their spiritual father (cf. 1 Cor 4:15; 9:1-2; 2 Cor 10:14; 11:2). Moreover, if their own experience is not evidence enough, then once again Paul's own life is a public testimony to his sufficiency as an apostle. When people look at Paul, they can see from his very way of life that the Corinthians are written on Paul's "heart" (3:2b), which is Paul's way of referring to the concrete ways in which he continues to live and suffer for the Corinthians as their "father through the gospel" (1 Cor 4:15).[27] Hence, for the Corinthians to deny Paul's apostleship would be tantamount to denying their own conversion, on the one hand, and the objective evidence of Paul's own way of life, on the other.

In 3:3b Paul puts these experiences in historical-redemptive context. Paul's ministry of bringing the gospel to Corinth (διακονηθεῖσα ὑφ᾽ ἡμῶν) centered on the pouring out of the Spirit in their hearts in fulfillment of Ezek 11:19 and 36:26-27, rather than being an extension of the ministry of Moses centered on the tablets of stone (cf. Exod 24:12; 31:18; 32:15-16; 34:1; Deut 9:10). Thus, the Corinthians' experience testifies that Paul's ministry of suffering is not in conflict with his ministry of the Spirit. Indeed, suffering and the Spirit are the twin pillars of Paul's apostolic defense. While the latter supports the former, both are incontrovertible evidence of his sufficiency as an apostle. For in both cases, the results are not only manifest in Paul's personal life but are also manifest for all to see in the new spiritual life of the Corinthians. The Corinthians cannot deny that they received the Spirit through Paul's ministry *and* that Paul's ministry was, at the same time, a ministry of suffering.

The polemic nature and implicit admonitions to the Corinthians throughout this section are now clear. In view of the Corinthians' own verifiable experience, neither the Corinthians nor Paul's opponents can argue that "weakness" and the power and glory of the gospel in the Spirit (i.e., "strength") cannot coexist in the genuine apostolic ministry (cf. 2 Cor 12:10). On the other hand, as I have concluded elsewhere,

> If Paul's suffering and his ministry of the Spirit are, in fact, convincing evidence for the validity of his apostolic authority and

27. For the various implications of the fact that Paul has the Corinthians in his "heart," cf. 1 Cor 4:14-16; 2 Cor 6:11-13; 7:3; 11:1-2, 7ff. in light of 11:28; 12:14-15. In each case, to have them in his "heart" does not refer merely to some interior and subjective feeling, but also includes the outward and objective actions of Paul on their behalf. And note once again how much of these actions revolve around his willingness to suffer on their behalf. Thus, in 3:2, Paul is again alluding, for the most part, to his suffering.

ministry, a ministry that he attributes directly to God (cf. 2:14, 17b; 3:5-6), then the Corinthians' decision to reject that ministry becomes, from Paul's perspective, a rejection of God as well.[28]

THE SUFFICIENCY AND BOLDNESS OF PAUL'S APOSTOLIC MINISTRY (3:4-18)

At this point in the argument, Paul has established two fundamental points concerning his apostolic ministry. First, rather than calling his apostleship into question, Paul's suffering is the vehicle through which God in Christ is revealing himself to the world. As an apostle of the new covenant, Paul stands between God and his people as the revelatory agent of the glory of God in the cross of Christ. Second, Paul has supported this claim by reminding the Corinthians that the content of his mediation is the very Spirit of God himself. As an apostle of the new covenant, Paul is the "Spirit-giver" who suffers on behalf of God's people as the "ambassador for Christ" (cf. 5:20). In view, then, of how God is now revealing himself through Paul's suffering, Paul does not shrink from declaring his sufficiency to be an apostle (2:16b).

In making and supporting these claims Paul has implicitly raised the subsidiary question of the relationship between his central role as a mediator of the "new covenant" and that of Moses as the mediator of the "old." What is the parallel and contrast between Paul's ministry of the Spirit and Moses's ministry of the law? Before Paul resumes the central argument of his letter in 4:1ff., he now pauses, parenthetically, to answer this crucial theological and redemptive-historical question in 3:4-18.

That Paul had this parallel in view is indicated already by his allusion in 2:16b to the call of Moses as found in the Septuagint version of Exod 4:10. Whereas Paul implied his sufficiency in the rhetorical question 2:16b, Moses responds to God's call with the confession, "I am not sufficient" (ἱκανός), only to be made sufficient by God himself. Then, in 3:3, Paul drew an explicit contrast between his ministry of the Spirit on human hearts and Moses' ministry of the law on tablets of stone. In doing so, Paul made the implicit assertion that his ministry is an essential part of the dawning of the new age as promised in Ezek 11; 36. In 3:4-6, Paul now reintroduces the theme of his sufficiency in order to make it clear that his sufficiency, *like that of Moses*, derives from God, since God is the one who has made Paul a minister of the new covenant of the Spirit. Here too, however, the contrast

---

28. Hafemann, *Suffering and the Spirit*, 221.

between Paul's ministry of the Spirit and the ministry of the "letter" is made explicit, this time with a reference to the other classic Old Testament passage on the new covenant, Jer 31:31-34 (2 Cor 3:6). To unpack the "letter/Spirit" contrast, Paul turns his attention in 3:7-18 to an extended discussion of the nature and effects of the giving of the law in contrast to the ministry of the Spirit.

This section of 2 Corinthians is one of the most difficult passages in all of Paul's writings for two reasons. On the one hand, the historical and theological backdrop to Paul's thinking must be carefully delineated. It is obvious that Paul is deriving his points in this passage from the Old Testament promise of the new covenant in Jer 31:31-34 (cf. 2 Cor 3:6) and the narrative of the "second giving of the law" in Exod 34:29-35 (cf. 2 Cor 3:7, 11, 13 and the direct quote of Exod 34:34 in 2 Cor 3:16). But the interpretation of these texts, both in their original contexts and in Paul's adaptation of them here, is a matter of great dispute. On the other hand, Paul's own argument has spawned a wide number of conflicting interpretations. The various views of 3:17a alone ("The Lord is the Spirit") would take a tome to discuss, not to mention Paul's view of the function of the law as introduced in the "letter/Spirit" contrast of 3:6 and then explained in 3:7-14. It must suffice for our purposes here merely to present a brief overview of the six interpretive pillars needed for approaching this difficult passage.[29]

First, Paul's introduction of the terminology of the "new covenant" in 3:6 forces us to take Ezek 11:19; 36:26; Jer 31:31-34 seriously as the backdrop to understanding the letter/Spirit contrast in 3:6-18. As an apostle of the Messiah, Paul is an agent of the "new age" of the Spirit in which the law will be written on the hearts of God's people as the foundation of the universal knowledge of YHWH within the covenant community. The perspective that guides Paul throughout this section, as well as the undergirding presupposition of Paul's self-understanding, is that his ministry is an integral part of the inauguration of the eschatological "age to come," which, from Paul's point of view, is the age of the Spirit.

Second, if Jeremiah and Ezekiel are taken seriously as the starting point for understanding this passage, then Paul's view of the law *per se* in 3:6-18 is not to be interpreted as a negative evaluation, either of its structure or its nature. Indeed, in 3:7-11 the expressed foundation of the *a fortiori* argument for the glory of the new "ministry of the Spirit" (3:8) and "righteousness"

---

29. The detailed exegetical support for and application of these perspectives are the subject of my monograph on 2 Cor 3:4—4:6, *Paul, Moses, and the History of Israel.* Again, these six basic perspectives have been outlined in my previous work, *Suffering and the Spirit,* 221-25. In support of the following points, see the summary of my exegesis of 3:7-14 in chapter 5 below.

(3:9) is the unassailable glory of the old covenant "ministry of death" (3:7) and "condemnation" (3:9). The truth of the former depends on the validity of the latter. That which makes the glory of the ministry of the Spirit so overwhelming for Paul is that it even outshines the most glorious revelation of God previously known to his people, the law (3:10). Hence, when Paul says that "the letter kills" and characterizes the giving of the law as a "ministry of death" and "condemnation" he is not referring to the nature of the law (which is glorious), but to its *function and result* within the life of Israel. The problem in the "old covenant" was not, therefore, the *nature* of the law, but the fact that from its beginning the hard hearts of the people had remained, for the most part, unchanged, even after the revelation of the glory of the law (cf. Jer 31:32; Ezek 36:16–21).

In Israel's history this point is perhaps most forcefully seen in the account of the giving of the law itself, especially as it reaches its climax in the incident of the golden calf, the second giving of the law, and the veil of Moses in Exod 32–34. In the past, commentators have assumed that Paul ripped the motifs surrounding Moses's veil out of this context and simply reinterpreted them according to his Christian presuppositions. But if they are read within the fuller context of Exod 32–34, it becomes apparent that Paul's argument in 3:7–18 follows closely the original contours of this passage in its canonical form. For as the exodus narrative demonstrates, the reason the Israelites could not gaze at the glory of the Lord as it shown on the face of Moses (cf. 3:7, 13; cf. Exod 34:30) was, as Paul put it in 3:14, because their minds were hardened. The incident with the golden calf was a clear sign that, despite the exodus and the giving of the law, Israel was still a "stiff-necked people" (cf. Exod 32:9, 22; 33:3–5; 34:9). Consequently, if God's glory were to remain in their midst, even for a "single moment" (Exod 33:5), the people would be destroyed. In fact, the first result of Israel's encounter with the law was the judgment and death of three thousand idolaters as a graphic illustration of the fact that the "letter kills" (cf. Exod 32:25–29). This explains why the people were *afraid* when they saw Moses returning with the glory of God on his face (cf. Exod 34:30): they feared the ensuing judgment of God.

Viewed from this perspective, Moses's veil was not an attempt to deceive the people by covering up the fact that the glory on his face was fading in order to preserve his authority. There is no indication either in Exod 32–34 or in 2 Cor 3:7–18 that this glory was fading. The passive verb usually translated "fading" throughout this passage (καταργέω) is better rendered in its usual sense, "to be made ineffective" or "powerless" or "to be removed" or "nullified."[30] Hence, rather than an act of deception, Moses's veil was an expression of God's grace and mercy: it allowed Moses to mediate God's glory in the midst of the people without destroying them (cf. Exod 34:35).[31] As Paul puts it in 3:13, the veil stopped this goal (τέλος) from taking place. The veil of *Moses* therefore becomes for Paul a metonym for the fact that *Israel's* hearts were hardened, since it was Israel's sinful condition that necessitated its use. This explains why Paul can switch from the literal use of the veil in 3:13 to its metaphorical use as a symbol for Israel's condition in 3:14–15.

In 2 Cor 3:7, 11, 13 Paul's point is that the glory on Moses's face was rendered ineffective by the veil in that it stopped the destruction of the people that would otherwise have resulted. In 3:14 Paul is simply stating that this "veil" itself ("veil" now used metaphorically) is removed or nullified in Christ, since it is the cross of Christ that makes it possible for the Spirit to be poured out on all mankind in order to remove its hard hearts. Hence, throughout 2 Cor 3:6–13 Paul follows Ezekiel, Jeremiah, and most directly Exod 32–34 in pointing out that the "problem" under the "old covenant" was not in the law itself but in the fact that the hearts of the people remained hardened to God's will. As a result, God's presence could not remain in their midst without destroying them, and even the mediator of God's presence, Moses, had to veil his face to keep the people from being judged. In describing the law as "letter" in 3:6, Paul is thus introducing a shorthand way of referring to the law in its old covenant context as the objective revelation of the will of God. Devoid of the accompanying Spirit to change Israel's heart under the old covenant, however, the "letter" brought about only judgment and death.

The third interpretive pillar is the stark contrast Paul makes between the *function* of the law and that of the Spirit. While the law kills, the "Spirit makes alive" (3:6). What was needed in Israel's history was not a new structure or nature of revelation, but the power of God poured out to change the hearts of his people. The "Spirit makes alive" because it is the Spirit who changes the hearts of people. So what is "new" in the new covenant is not a new law *per se*, but the commitment of God to pour out his Spirit in conjunction with the preaching of the Christ. This is why Paul is so "bold" in contrast to Moses (cf. 3:12). Paul knows that as a servant of the new covenant his gospel will encounter people in whom the Spirit is at work to change their hearts. Unlike Moses, Paul has no need, therefore, to veil the glory of God, but is bold to proclaim it everywhere and to everyone. Both

---

30. See BDAG, 526. The authors offer no other evidence for the translation "transitory" suggested for 2 Cor 3:11, 13.

31. For the veil motif elsewhere in Scripture, see Lev 21:23; Num 18:7; Isa 25:7; Lam 3:65 (?); Mark 15:38par.

Paul's sufficiency and his boldness thus derive from the centrality of the Spirit in his apostolic ministry (cf. 3:6, 12, 17).

Fourth, according to 3:14, the work of the Spirit under the new covenant also has hermeneutical significance. The veil, now as a symbol for the hard heart or mind, continues to exist upon the "reading of the old covenant." This means, above all, that the barrier to understanding the law in relationship to the Christ is not intellectual but moral. Those who refuse to accept that Jesus is the Messiah in fulfillment of the old covenant do so not because they lack some esoteric "Christian" hermeneutic, but because they are morally inclined against it.

Fifth, it must be kept in mind that Paul's boldness as an apostle (3:12; 4:1) is based on his conviction that the renewed access to the glory of God made possible by the Spirit results in the transformation of those who encounter it (3:18). Paul wants to assure his readers that Moses's past experience of encountering the Lord described in Exod 34:34, quoted in 3:16, is not qualitatively different from that of those believers who are presently encountering "the glory of God in the face of Christ" through his own ministry (cf. 4:6). The Lord encountered by Moses in the tent of meeting is the same Lord Christians encounter in the Spirit (3:17a). For "where the Lord is, there is freedom" from the hard hearts that formerly separated God from Israel. Freed from their hardened hearts, those who have their "faces unveiled" are able to contemplate the glory of the Lord in the glory of (the) Christ, since he is the "image of God" (cf. 4:4). As a result, they are being transformed into that same image "from glory to glory" (3:18).

Finally, if this view of 3:7–18 is correct, Paul is ultimately so confident (not *self*-confident!) of his sufficiency and so bold in his ministry because he sees around him the visible results of the pouring out of God's Spirit in the gospel of the Messiah (cf. 3:2–3 with 3:18). The glory of God is being revealed through Paul's ministry of suffering and the Spirit and as a consequence people's lives are being changed! Despite this detour into theological reflection in 3:4–18, Paul has therefore never left the controversy in Corinth. The issue throughout has been the validity of Paul's apostolic ministry. The question is whether his sufferings can be reconciled with the genuine ministry of the Spirit that characterizes the new covenant. And Paul's proof that they can, indeed must, be reconciled is still the same: the transformed lives of the Corinthians themselves. It is this "fruit of the Spirit" which demonstrates that the glory of God *is* being revealed in and through Paul's suffering. Nothing else can explain the transformation taking place among God's people.

Thus, Paul is not hesitant to assert his sufficiency and boldness as an apostle. He knows that whether it is in his own personal suffering (1:3–11), or in his suffering on behalf of others (1:15—2:13), God is at work to make his divine glory known through the comfort (1:6–7, 19–20, 23–24; 2:7–8) and power (1:9–10; 2:15–16; 3:3, 6, 14, 17–18) of the gospel that Paul preaches and embodies. It is always and only the work of *God* that is the basis of the minister's sufficiency and boldness, and never the minister's own talents or abilities. Paul's adequacy is the adequacy of the one who knows what it is like to be led to death (1:9; 2:14) so that the power and life of the Spirit might be made manifest through him (1:9; 2:14; 3:6).

5

The Glory and Veil of Moses in 2 Corinthians 3:7–14

An Example of Paul's Contextual Exegesis of the Old Testament[1]

As Morna Hooker expressed it over three decades ago, when modern readers of the New Testament encounter its adaptation of Old Testament texts, "often one is left exclaiming: whatever the passage from the Old Testament originally meant, it certainly was not this!"[2] Ever since the work of Hans Windisch (1924) and Siegfried Schulz (1958),[3] nowhere has this reaction been more universal than to Paul's interpretation of the glory and veil of Moses from Exod 34:29–35 in 2 Cor 3:7–14. The reason for this is readily apparent. According to the virtually unanimous opinion of biblical and postbiblical Jewish tradition, the glory on Moses's face as he descended from Mount Sinai after the second giving of the law was not only brilliant,

---

1. This chapter is a brief excerpt and summary of various sections of my monograph on this subject, *Paul, Moses, and the History of Israel*, esp. 189–334. The bulk of this project was written during a year's sabbatical at the University of Tübingen, which was made possible to a large degree by a generous research grant from the Alexander von Humboldt-Stiftung, to whom I am deeply indebted. Now from Scott J. Hafemann, "The Glory and Veil of Moses in 2 Corinthians 3:7–14: An Example of Paul's Contextual Exegesis of the Old Testament—A Proposal." In *Right Doctrine from the Wrong Texts? Essays on the Use of the Old Testament in the New*, edited by G. K. Beale, 295–309. Grand Rapids: Baker, 1994.

2. Hooker, "Beyond the Things," 295.

3. See Windisch, *Zweite Korintherbrief*, 113ff.; Schulz, "Decke des Moses," 1–30.

but permanent. The only possible divergence from this opinion is found in *L.A.B.* 19:16, though even this text probably supports the overwhelming consensus.[4] Opinions in early Jewish literature vary concerning exactly why Moses consequently veiled himself, but both the Masoretic Text and later tradition agree that it was to protect the people in some way, not to cover up some deficiency in Moses or the glory he reflected. In contrast, Paul is seen to assert both that the glory on Moses's face was "fading" (καταργέω; cf. 3:7, 13) and that Moses veiled himself to hide this fact and/or its implications from Israel (εἰς τὸ τέλος τοῦ καταργουμένου; 3:13). Read in this way, Paul's argument has been construed to be not only internally inconsistent (cf. 3:13 with 3:7), but also inherently anti-Jewish in its apparent attribution to Moses of duplicitous motives and deceptive activity, while Paul portrays himself as both forthright and honest.

The responses to this common conclusion by P. von der Osten-Sacken (1989), Stockhausen (1989), Hays (1989), and Hofius (1989) vary greatly in their approaches and conclusions.[5] Nevertheless, all of these studies share the conviction that Paul's argument, though perhaps not an expression of a willful misreading of the Old Testament, can nevertheless be justified only on the basis of his own distinctively Christian presuppositions. Moreover, it has become common in recent discussions to suggest that, although Paul's interpretation of Exod 34:29-35 is not acceptable by modern historical-critical standards, it can be justified on the basis of the exegetical practices of his day. Such an assumption has led Brevard Childs to posit, against the lack of evidence, that, since Paul read Exod 34 in this way, there must have been some prior Jewish tradition that also did so; and Belleville has tried to rediscover such a trail of thought in order to provide a necessary backdrop to Paul's thinking conceptually or methodologically.[6]

Against this backdrop, the thesis of this essay is that Paul's argument in 2 Cor 3:7-14 takes Exod 34:29-35 seriously within its original context (Exod 32-34) and that it is precisely this context—not Paul's apostolic experience or Christian convictions *per se*—that provides the background and key for Paul's "exegesis" of the glory and veil of Moses. In contrast, the vast majority of students of Paul have been content to look merely at the one verse that Paul quotes from Exod 34:29-35, Exod 34:34 in 2 Cor 3:16, or at the allusions to Exod 34:30, 33, 35 in 2 Cor 3:7, 13, rather than taking Exod 34:29-35 seriously as part of the larger biblical narrative in which it is

---

4. For an argument in favor of reading this text to refer to the fading of the glory on Moses's face, see Belleville, *Reflections of Glory*, 40-43.

5. Osten-Sacken, "Decke des Moses," 87-115; Stockhausen, *Moses' Veil*; Hays, *Echoes*, 122-53; and Hofius, "Gesetz und Evangelium," 75-120.

6. See Childs, *Exodus*, 621; and Belleville, *Reflections of Glory*, 13-79.

anchored.⁷ The implications of a critical, atomistic reading of biblical narratives have thus inadvertently carried over into the interpretation of Paul's own reading of the biblical tradition.

THE THEOLOGICAL MEANING OF EXODUS 32–34

Unfortunately, we do not have the space here to summarize the entire narrative of Exod 32–34, so we will jump in at the climax to the story, which is found in the text Paul cites in 2 Cor 3, namely Exod 34:29-35. At this juncture in the account, the turning point of the narrative, which was reached with the granting of Moses's petition in 33:19–23, finds its fulfillment in Moses's descent from the mountain. For as 34:29 makes clear, Moses returns as the "answer to his own prayers" in that he both brings the reestablishment of the covenant and unknowingly becomes himself the *means* of its continuation.⁸ The former is underlined by the emphasis in the text on Moses as the one who brings the two tablets "in his hand" (בְּיַד־מֹשֶׁה, v. 29a), an allusion to the fact that Moses was also the one who earlier broke the tablets by throwing them "from his hand" (מִיָּדוֹ, 32:19). The one who mediated the breaking of the covenant is the one who also mediates its restoration. The latter, and now more important, theme is expressed in the reference to Moses's not knowing that his face was "shining" (קָרַן) because he had been speaking with YHWH (34:29b).

The translation of קָרַן has been a matter of much debate. But regardless of its etymology or use elsewhere, the present context, with its emphasis on Moses's role as the mediator of YHWH's presence, together with the explicit reference to the "skin of [Moses's] face" (עוֹר פָּנָיו) as its subject, demand that it be rendered "shine."⁹ Moreover, this

---

7. For this same critique of past scholarship and a similar call to reinvestigate the content and function of Exod 34:29–35 within the "thematic covenant unit, Exod 19–34" as the backdrop to 2 Cor 3:7–18, see now Dumbrell, "Paul's Use of Exodus 34," 179–94, 180. Recently, Stockhausen, *Moses' Veil*, 96, has also emphasized the importance of remembering that Exod 34:29–35 is a narrative so that Paul's "verbal echoes call to mind the whole *story* and not just isolated snatches of it" (emphasis hers; see p. 101n30 for the same point). It is surprising, then, that she limits her reading to Exod 34:29–35, which has serious implications for her understanding of 2 Cor 3:7–18.

8. Brichto, "Golden Calf," 36, suggests that the role of Moses as the one who will mediate God's presence in the midst of the people is already expressed in 34:10 with YHWH's statement that he will perform his wonders for the people "in whose midst Moses is." Brichto interprets this to mean that YHWH will be present in Moses "and will thereby be present in the midst of the people." But Brichto's further attempt to identify Moses with the angel promised in Exod 23:20–24 remains unconvincing to me.

9. So too Moberly, *Mountain of God*, 107; and Childs, *Exodus*, 609. The attempt to

is certainly the way it was understood in the LXX, where קָרַן in 34:29-30, 35 (MT) is rendered by δεδόξασται, ἣν δεδοξασμένη, and δεδόξασται respectively. This meaning is further highlighted in the LXX by its use of ἡ ὄψις ("the appearance") and χρώματος ("color") in reference to Moses's face, which have no equivalents in the MT, but call attention to the fact that Moses now appeared glorified. Some image of a shining or radiance upon his face thus lies close at hand, as indicated by the direct reference to the glorification of Moses's face in 34:35, rather than to the "skin of the face of Moses" (עוֹר פְּנֵי מֹשֶׁה) as in the MT.[10] The use of the perfect tenses and periphrastic construction in 34:29-30, 35 to describe the glorification of Moses's face as a permanent condition and the explicit reference in 34:34-35 to the repeated action of removing and replacing the veil (cf. ἡνίκα δ' ἂν, ἕως ἂν, and the use of the imperfect tense in vv. 34-35) further highlight this emphasis on the

---

render it as a reference to "having horns" (of a priestly mask) is based on the verbal form מקרן in Ps 69:32 and the corresponding noun form throughout the OT. For an insightful study of the issue in support of the position taken here, see Jaros, "Des Mose 'Strahlende Haut,'" 275-80, and Haran, "Shining of Moses' Face," 159-60, 163-65; for the opposing view, see esp. Anton Jirku, "Die Gesichtsmaske des Mose," 347-49. The article by Propp, "Skin of Moses' Face," 375-83, provides an extensive bibliography of sources and literature for both basic interpretations spanning from antiquity to the present and a helpful analysis of the Hebrew text and its reception in the LXX, Targumim, and other early Jewish literature. Propp's own thesis is that Exod 34:29 should be translated "the skin of his face was burnt to the hardness of horn" (386), so that the text refers to an injury or disfigurement suffered by Moses (i.e., "some kind of light or heat burn," 385). For Propp, the Israelites thus fled from Moses because of his disfigured face, while the veil functioned "to spare the people the gruesome sight" (following B. D. Eerdmans, 384). But Moses's glimpse of YHWH's back not only disfigured him by hardening his skin, it also rendered him "invulnerable to divine radiance" (386). Moses can therefore take the veil off in YHWH's presence to "renew ... his immunity" (386). Exodus 34:29ff. "has no ritual significance," rather, "the story honors Moses as the human most intimate with Yahweh, but it also specifies the price he paid" (386). However, just as Propp accuses those who advocate that Moses was wearing a horned ritual mask with a "disregard for the present form of the biblical text" that "diminishes the plausibility" of their theory (383), so may it be said of Propp's own suggestion. For in addition to the fact that there is no direct evidence of קרן being used metaphorically of a skin disease, Propp's view also fails to do justice to the cultic role of Moses in the context of Exod 32-34, where, in addition to Moses's role as mediator of God's presence in 34:29-35, the narrative also stresses in 33:18-23 that YHWH hid Moses to protect him, not to disfigure him. And, as we shall see, Israel's fear in 34:29-35 is to be understood against the backdrop of 33:3, 5.

10. Contra ibid., 377, who takes the lack of an explicit reference to radiance and the wide semantic range of δοξάζω/δόξα to be a sign of a lack of clarity concerning this point. But the context alleviates this ambiguity. For his explanation of the origin of the LXX rendering of 34:30a as a result of reading the MT עוֹר ("skin") as אוֹר ("light") and a possible redivision of כִּי קָרַן, see ibid., 379-80. The simplest solution, however, is to see the LXX as an interpretation of the MT in terms of Moses's skin shining.

glorification of Moses's face. Finally, within the context of Exod 32–34, the choice of δοξάζω throughout 34:29–35 naturally recalls the theme of God's glory introduced earlier in 33:5, 16b, 19 and the thematic parallel in 33:13.

Hence, as the LXX makes explicit, Moses becomes the vehicle through which the presence of the glory of God, lost by the people as a result of their sin with the golden calf, is restored, albeit now in a mediated manner. The shining on Moses's face in 34:29–35 is the shining of God's glory itself that Moses reflects as a result of his theophanic experience in Exod 34:5–8 (cf. 33:19). The point of 34:29 is thus made by way of contrast. Although Moses had earlier been in the presence of God on several occasions, never before did his face shine as a result. Now, however, as a result of the unique experience of God's glory in 34:1–9, Moses himself bears the glory of God with him back to camp. This becomes the means by which YHWH will place his presence in the midst of his people. Moses is now the mediator not only of the covenant law, but also of the covenantal presence of God.[11]

The fact that Moses now mediates the very glory of God in the midst of the people becomes the key to explaining both the reason and nature of the people's fear in 34:30 and the purpose of the veil in 34:33–35. At the first theophany and giving of the law in Exod 19:16—20:18a the people also responded with fear at seeing the revelation of YHWH on the mountain (cf. 20:18b–21). But this fear was interpreted *positively* as the sanctifying means employed by YHWH to keep the people from sinning (Exod 20:20).[12] Moreover, Moshe Greenberg has shown that, according to Exod 20:20, the purpose of the original Sinai revelation was not only to legitimize Moses's authority (cf. Exod 19:9), but to accomplish this sanctifying purpose by giving Israel a "direct palpable experience of God."[13] Moses thus commands the people not to be afraid because of God's terrifying presence, but to accept it as part of the ratification of the covenant itself (20:22; cf. Exod 24:9–11).

---

11. Contra Coats, "Opposition," 105, who interprets the glory on Moses's face not in terms of the reflection of the glory of God, but as a symbolic expression of the authority of Moses. But although Moses's speaking with the glory of God on his face certainly substantiates his authority, when read against the backdrop of the problem of God's presence in 33:1ff., this is a secondary motif.

12. So too Childs, *Exodus*, on Exod 20:18–22.

13. Greenberg, "נסה in Exodus 20:20," 275. His argument is based on the structural parallels between Exod 20:20 and Deut 4:10; 5:29 and the use of נסה elsewhere to mean "to have/cause to have an experience" (cf. 1 Sam 17:39; Deut 28:56; 2 Chr 32:31; Judg 3:1–3). Israel is thus not being "tested" at Mt. Sinai, but being brought into the presence of God (276). Even if Childs, *Exodus*, 344n20, is correct that this factitive use of the verb has not been demonstrated, Greenberg's basic view of verse 20 seems to hold inasmuch as the giving of the law and the theophany, by "testing" Israel, would lead also to their obedience. Childs is thus right in emphasizing that there is no need to separate the giving of the law from the theophany, as Greenberg seems to do (372).

Of course, the people as a whole cannot approach God's presence directly, but are represented by Moses and the elders (cf. Exod 19:24; 20:21; 24:1–2, 9–11). This restriction, however, is not because of a broken relationship with YHWH, but because of their mortal nature. Still, the people are encouraged to remain as close as possible to the theophany and to hear YHWH's voice directly as an integral part of their covenant relationship with him (Exod 20:22).

In stark contrast, the people's fear in response to Moses's shining face in 34:30–55 must be interpreted in view of the effect of YHWH's presence after their idolatry with the golden calf. Rather than sanctification, God's presence in the midst of his people now entails judgment for the people (cf. Exod 33:3, 5). While earlier the people feared YHWH because of their mortality, now they must fear him because of their sinful condition. Even though YHWH can no longer speak to the people directly, but only through Moses as mediator, and in spite of the fact that the radiance of God can now only be seen "second hand" on Moses's face, the people's response in 34:30 testifies to the genuine nature of Moses's role, on the one hand, and to their own *altered* relationship to YHWH, on the other. From this point on, YHWH only comes to them mediated through Moses. But even this is still too much for the people to bear in their hardened condition.

Moses therefore responds with two acts of gracious mercy in view of their stiff-necked nature. He first calls the leaders (34:31a) and then the people (34:32a) to himself in order to deliver YHWH's covenant commands. In this way, the legitimacy of the message and the authority of the messenger are again authenticated through a "tangible confirmation of the fact that it is God's word that is being spoken to them when they see the light radiating from Moses's face"[14] (cf. 34:31–32 with Exod 19:9). Then, after speaking the words of YHWH to the people, Moses veils himself. He does so not to make up for some deficiency in God's glory or in himself,[15] not as an expression of his humility and modesty,[16] not to keep the glory of God from being

---

14. Haran, "Shining of Moses' Face," 162. Haran is thus correct in emphasizing that it is not the veil *per se* which is the main point of the text, but the fact that the glory of God can now be seen once again. Coats, *Moses*, 131, misses this point when he suggests that the veil itself functions, like Moses's rod, as "a visible and concrete symbol of Mosaic authority derived from his intimacy with God" (see too ibid., 138, 190). It is the shining, not the veil, which results from Moses's experience of the theophany. The veil results from Israel's hardened condition.

15. Contra Brichto, "Golden Calf," 37; there is no indication that the veil exists to hide the fact that the glory was fading or to compensate for Moses's own human "concerns and aspirations." On the permanent nature of the glory on Moses's face, see Morgenstern, "Moses," 4–5.

16. Contra Cassuto, *Exodus*, 450.

wasted,[17] nor even to keep it from being profaned.[18] Rather, the veil makes it possible to bring the glory of God into the midst of the rebellious people. Against the backdrop of the explicit statements of Exod 32:9, 22; and 33:3, 5 and the function of the tent of meeting itself in 33:7–11, the veiling of his face should therefore be seen as a second act of mercy on Moses's part, this time keeping the people from being destroyed by the reflected presence of God.[19] The veil of Moses makes it possible for the glory of God to be in the midst of the people, albeit now mediated through Moses, without judging them. In view of the people's "stiff necked" idolatry with the golden calf, Moses's veil is thus the final expression of the theme of YHWH's judgment and mercy, which runs throughout this narrative and from the theological perspective ties it together.

THE SIGNIFICANCE OF MOSES'S VEIL

As the theological corollary to the sinful nature of Israel, the veil of Moses is the demonstration of the character of YHWH declared in 34:6–7. Moreover, the switch to the frequentative nature of the action regarding the veil in 34:34–37 indicates that the protective function of the veil continued as the people moved on in their wilderness wanderings. Throughout the rest of his life Moses mediates God's presence among his people and, not only as an act of divine judgment, but even more so of divine mercy, veils himself in their midst. It is not saying too much, therefore, to conclude with Wilms that as it now stands the theology of the "*Mittleramt*" of Moses determines the main points of chapter 34,[20] and, beyond that, of chapters 32–33 as well. The restoration of the covenant in Exod 32–34 finds its climax, possibility, and means of fulfillment in Moses as the mediator of both the law and the glory of God. Moreover, from the perspective of the narrative, the eventual filling of the tabernacle with the glory of God in Exod 40:34, behind the curtain(!), is the logical extension of Moses's experience in the tent of meeting and of his role as mediator between YHWH and Israel.[21]

17. Contra Haran, "Shining of Moses' Face," 162.

18. Contra Eissfeldt, "Gesetz," 210.

19. Thus, though Moberly, *Mountain of God*, 108, is correct that "no reason is given" for the purpose of the veil in the text, the context indicates its function clearly enough that we need not merely "speculate" concerning its function.

20. Wilms, *Bundesbuch*, 183.

21. The historical relationship between the tent of meeting and the tabernacle is a matter of much dispute; for their identification in the final redaction of the text, see Haran, *Temple*, 271–72. In support of this he points to Exod 38:21; Num 1:50, 53; 9:15; 10:11; 17:23; 18:2; and esp. Exod 39:32, 40; 40:2, 6, 29.

This is the key to understanding the theological significance of Moses's veil: Just as Moses had to be kept from God's direct presence in 33:22 because of his mortality, now the Israelites must be veiled even from God's indirect presence because of their sinful state (34:33–35). Due to her "stiff neck," Israel cannot bear to see the radiance of God's glory (cf. 32:9, 22; 33:3, 5 with 34:30). Hence, in both cases, the barrier is an expression of YHWH's protection and mercy, the first in regard to mankind's finitude, the latter in regard to Israel's sin. But in Israel's case, the veil on Moses's face also embodies the theme of God's judgment, which together with his mercy runs both implicitly and explicitly throughout the narrative (cf. 33:19; 34:6–7). Whereas Moses experiences protection from God's direct presence as an act of mercy in response to the favor he has found before YHWH, Israel is kept from gazing at the glory of God as an act of both mercy and judgment in response to her sinful nature.

The problem of God's presence dwelling in the midst of a rebellious people is finally solved because God's mercy overshadows his judgment. For within the flow of the narrative, the answer to the problem of God's presence is Moses himself as the mediator of the will and splendor of God in anticipation of the establishment of the tabernacle. This is reflected in the fact that in Exod 39:33–14 the articles for the tabernacle are first presented to Moses, who then inspects them and blesses the people prior to the tabernacle's establishment (39:42–43).[22] Israel is hereby reminded, above all, of her cultic obligations (as in 34:10–26), while the theological significance of Exod 32–34 as a whole is embodied in Moses's descent from the mountain with the light of God's glory shining on his face, a glory that must then be veiled from the people due to their stiff-necked condition. In this context, the veil on Moses's face is not only part of YHWH's judgment against his people; but more importantly, it is an expression of his grace.[23]

With these specific themes from Exod 32–34 in mind, we now turn our attention to Paul's argument in 3:7–18 in order to posit a thesis for consideration. What does Paul's argument in 2 Cor 3:7–18 look like against this backdrop?

---

22. For this point and the chiastic relationship between Exod 25–31 and 35–40, as well as the loss of the structural role of the creation motifs in chapters 35–40, facts which can only be explained by the influence of chapters 32–34, see Kearney, "Creation and Liturgy," esp. 380–81.

23. Though it is beyond the scope of this paper to develop this, in the LXX this reading of Exod 32–34 is not only supported, but strengthened.

THE ARGUMENT FROM SCRIPTURE IN 2 CORINTHIANS 3:7-14

First, Paul's references to the "fading" glory of Moses's face in verses 7, 13, and the Sinai covenant that it represents in 3:11 must be rethought. The use of καταργέω in the ancient world apart from the New Testament and the literature dependent upon it is rare. A partial search of the stem καταργ- in the literature from the fourth century B.C. to the fourth century A.D. provided by *TLG* produced over 1,300 occurrences of the verb.[24] Of these occurrences, only sixteen are found in literature outside the New Testament and its circle of influence.[25] In particular, the vast majority of other references throughout the literature are dependent either by allusion or quotation on Paul's writings, especially his statements in Rom 3:3, 31; 6:6; 1 Cor 1:28; 2:6; 15:24, 26; Eph 2:15; and 2 Thess 2:8. This is not surprising in view of the fact that of the twenty-seven times the verb appears in the New Testament, twenty-five are found in the Pauline corpus.[26] The only exceptions are Luke 13:7 and Heb 2:14. Hence, as the lexicons testify and the *TLG* search confirms, our evidence for these meanings must largely be drawn from Paul's use itself.[27]

Yet there is little, if any, doubt concerning the semantic field encompassed by the *active* forms of the verb καταργέω in these non-Christian sources. The few sources that we do have outside the Christian sphere in ancient literature, including the LXX, all testify to the meanings "put to an end," "abolish," or "destroy" as adequate equivalents for καταργέω.

The same lack of uncertainty is true for Paul's writings. Paul uses the active forms of καταργέω figuratively in the sense of "to cause something to lose its power or effectiveness" (Rom 3:3, 31; 1 Cor 1:28; Gal 3:17; Eph 2:15; cf. Luke 13:7); and in a related sense they can mean "to abolish, wipe out,

---

24. Because of the focus on the present passive form of the verb, the aorist and perfect indicative forms were not included, but have been surveyed in the LXX and NT. See Polybius, *Fragmenta* 176, for the use κατηργηκέναι. The papyri have not been surveyed.

25. Besides the texts explicitly cited below, see *Scholia in Homerum, Scholia in Iliadem* 19:157–58, scholion 3 (no canon yet available) and the *Cyranides* (ante first/second cent. A.D.) 10:101 (designations, dates, and references to editions given according to *TLG*).

26. Six times in Romans, nine times in 1 Corinthians, four times in 2 Corinthians, three times in Galatians, and one time each in Ephesians, 2 Thessalonians and 2 Timothy. See Aland, *Konkordanz*, 2:148–49.

27. Including the LXX, BDAG, 525, now includes *Mart. Ascen. Isa., T. Sol.*, two papyri, and Justin Martyr (second cent. A.D.) and also the four non-Christian citations found in LSJ (Polybius, Euripides, POxy, and PFlor). *Mart. Ascen. Isa.* 3:31, however, is part of the Christian addition to the composite work sometimes called the *Testament of Hezekiah* found in *Mart. Ascen. Isa.* 3:13—4:22; see Knibb, "Martyrdom and Ascension," 143.

set aside something" (1 Cor 6:13; 13:11) or "bring (something) to an end" (1 Cor 15:24; 2 Thess 2:8; 2 Tim 1:10; cf. Heb 2:14).[28] This is confirmed not only by the larger contexts in which these occurrences are found, but also by the specific verbs that are used in parallel constructions in several of the passages.[29]

Furthermore, in the case of Rom 3:3; 1 Cor 1:28; 13:11; 15:24; Gal 3:17; Eph 2:15; and 2 Thess 2:8 this act of nullification is explicitly linked to the abolishment of the *effects* of that which has been brought to an end. In Rom 3:3 the fact that the faithfulness of God is not nullified results in the continuation of the truthfulness and justice of God in judgment in 3:4-8. In 1 Cor 1:28 God nullifies the things that are "so that [ὅπως + subjunctive] no one may boast before God" (1 Cor 1:29). The abolishment of "childish things" in 1 Cor 13:11 results in the putting away of speaking, thinking, and reasoning as a child. According to 1 Cor 15:24-25, Christ abolishes every rule, authority, and power in order to eliminate the rebellion that still remains against the Father and as a result turn the kingdom over to God. The fact that in Gal 3:17 the law does not nullify the promise means that the effects of the promise remain valid—that is, that the inheritance of God still comes "from the promise" (ἐξ ἐπαγγελίας, 3:18). As the modal use of the participle καταργήσας indicates, the point of Eph 2:15 is that Christ establishes peace *by means of* abolishing in his death the enmity that existed between Jew and Gentile. The result of this destruction is the creation of Jews and Gentiles into "one new man," which in turn establishes peace on the basis of their mutual reconciliation to God through the cross (Eph 2:15b-16). And finally, in 2 Thess 2:8 the Lord will bring to an end "the Lawless One," which in the context means bringing to an end the corresponding false power, signs, and wonders and the deception that these things caused among those who are perishing (2 Thess 2:9-10). From these texts it is important to see that in developing his use of καταργέω Paul intends not simply to call attention to the fact that something has been definitively abolished, but to raise the question of the consequences of these acts of nullification.

---

28. So accurately now BDAG, 525-26; and Bauer, et al., *Worterbuch*, 848-49, give the same three basic meanings: "außer Wirksamkeit, Geltung setzen, entkräften," and from this, "wirkungslos machen, zunichte machen"; "vernichten, vertilgen, beseitigen" and "aus d. Verbindung mit jmdm. oder mit etw. gelöst werden." LSJ, 908, supplies the basic meaning, "leave unemployed or idle."

29. See the contrast between καταργοῦμεν and ἱστάνομεν in Rom 3:31; the parallel between οὐχ ... κληρονομήσουσιν and ὁ θεὸς καταργήσει in 1 Cor 6:10, 13; the use of παύσονται as a parallel to καταργέω in 1 Cor 13:8, 11; the parallel between ἀκυροῖ and καταργῆσαι in Gal 3:17; the synonymous use of λύσας and καταργήσας in Eph 2:14-15, and of ἀνελεῖ and καταργήσει in 2 Thess 2:8; and finally, the antithetical use of καταργήσαντος and φωτίσαντος in 2 Tim 1:10.

In those texts where no explicit result is mentioned, as in 2 Cor 3; Rom 3:31; 1 Cor 6:13; and 2 Tim 1:9–10, it is thus consistent with Pauline usage elsewhere, and confirmed by their immediate contexts, that here too Paul is directing his attention to the ramification of the act of abolishing. In asserting that the gospel does not "nullify" (καταργοῦμεν) the law in Rom 3:31, Paul is also implying that its past failure among the Jews and its continuing validity among Christians must be explained (cf. Rom 7:1—8:4; 9:30—10:4; 13:8–10). Similarly, though not explicitly stated in 1 Cor 6:13, the implications of the fact that God will "abolish" (καταργήσει) food and the stomach for the ethical admonitions and warnings of the impending judgment in the surrounding context are clear. Christians are to act in the present as if the future effects of the lure of appetite have already been destroyed (cf. 6:9–20). This is also the point of 2 Tim 1:9–10, though now applied to the willingness to suffer with Paul for the sake of the gospel (2 Tim 1:8).

Hence, when Paul speaks of "abolishing," "nullifying," or "bringing something to an end," he also consistently speaks, either explicitly or implicitly, of the corresponding effects of that which has or has not been made ineffective. The active sense, "rendering something inoperative," thus captures both the act and the effect expressed by the verb καταργέω.[30] In no case, however, is it appropriate to translate καταργέω with the sense of a gradual "fading away" of that which is said to be brought to an end. Of most significance for our study is the fact that these same three observations also hold true of the *passive* use of καταργέω in Paul's writings. Of the twenty-five appearances of the verb in Paul, fourteen are passive, including the four occurrences in 2 Cor 3:7, 11, 13, 14. And in each of these cases, a rendering equivalent to the active force of the verb captures the meaning well: "to be brought to an end, made powerless, or rendered inoperative in regard to its effects." Once again, in no case, either active or passive, does καταργέω refer to the gradual "fading away" of some aspect of reality.

In returning to the argument of 2 Cor 3:7–11, the question before us is whether this consistent use of καταργέω found throughout the Pauline corpus is also found in 2 Cor 3:7, 11 and 13, or whether Paul has in fact, as past students of Paul have assumed, introduced a distinctive meaning for the verb in this one passage. Clearly, the burden of proof will now be on those who wish to render it in any way different from the range of meaning established by Paul in the rest of his writings. The presumption must be that the use of καταργέω in 2 Corinthians 3 is consonant with Paul's consistent use of the verb elsewhere. Read in this way, Paul is referring to the fact that

---

30. See Clark, "*ENERGEO* and *KATARGEO*," 190–91, who suggests that it ought to be translated "render powerless" as the antonym of ἐνεργέω.

the veil of Moses brought the glory of God to an end in terms of that which it would accomplish if not veiled—that is, the judgment and destruction of Israel. As we have seen, this meaning corresponds exactly to what we find in the Exodus narrative. The result clause in 3:7 can thus be rendered in this way: the ministry of death came in glory, "so that as a result, the sons of Israel were not able to gaze into the face of Moses because of the glory of his face, which was being rendered inoperative as to its effects." Paul's statement in 3:7 reflects the point of Exod 34:29–35 concerning both the fear of the Israelites in response to the glory of God after their sin with the golden calf and Moses's response. Correctly translated, Paul's interpretation of Exod 34:29–35 corresponds to its original context and none of the various attempts to "redeem" his reading by recourse to contemporary exegetical methods or by taking the attributive participle to refer to some time other than that of the Exodus narrative are necessary.

Second, contrary to the overwhelming consensus, the purpose of the veil in 3:13 also corresponds to its function in Exod 34:29–35 once καταργέω is understood correctly and the Exodus narrative is read within its original context. Moses must continually veil himself "in order that (taking πρὸς τό + the infinitive to indicate a final rather than a result clause, in contrast to Paul's use of ὥστε + the infinitive in 3:7) the sons of Israel might not look into the τέλος of that which was being rendered inoperative as to its effects." Moses's purpose is not to hide something from the Israelites, either intentionally or unintentionally. In Exod 34:29–35, Moses veils himself in order that the glory of God might not produce its intended result—the judgment of the people because of their "stiff necks." In 2 Cor 3:13 Paul is simply repeating this point. As such, τέλος ought to be rendered, "goal" or "result" as a reference to what the glory would have brought about had it not been veiled.

Furnish is right in objecting that those who argue that τέλος means "aim" or "outcome" in 2 Cor 3:13 "have in general not been persuasive in their explanations of *why* Paul thought Moses wanted to hide the aim of the old covenant—that is Christ—from Israel . . . or *how* the veil could have done that."[31] Furnish's objection itself, however, points to the heart of the problem, *since the problem with past attempts to read τέλος in this way has been their assumption that its referent in this context is Christ*, either the pre-existent Christ or the coming of Christ in Paul's day. Yet the parallel between τέλος in 3:13b and "the face of Moses because of the glory of his face" in 3:7b indicates that in 3:13b Paul is simply summarizing in one word what he described at length earlier. Though not to be preferred, the introduction

---

31. Furnish, *II Corinthians*, 207.

of the textual variant τὸ πρόσωπον as an attempt to relieve verse 13b of its ambiguity is an indication that this was the case.[32]

Hence, Moses is not keeping Israel from seeing either that the glory is fading or that the law really points to Christ as its goal. In 3:13, as it was in 3:7, the imperfect verb ἐτίθει in 3:13a indicates that the time reference is still that of the Exodus narrative. From this perspective, 2 Cor 3:14a provides the theological rationale for Moses's action as implied in Exod 34:29–35. Paul is merely making explicit the tie between Exod 32:9; 33:3, 5; 34:9 and 34:29–35 that is so crucial in the original context of the narrative. Only in 3:14b does Paul switch back to his present situation, and he indicates this overtly. Again, Paul's exegesis proves to be a sober and careful contextual interpretation of the Scriptures, rather than a paradigmatic example of Paul's supposedly presuppositional re-reading (or mis-reading) of his tradition in which he "starts from Christian experience and expounds Scripture in the light of that experience, quarrying the Old Testament where he will."[33]

The "how" and "why" of Paul's statement in 3:13 now become apparent. In turning his attention in 3:13 from the glory on Moses's face to the purpose of the veil that it made necessary, Paul is calling explicit attention to the presupposition that undergirded his earlier statement in verse 7b. Specifically, Moses veiled himself in order that the sons of Israel might not gaze "into the outcome or result" (τὸ τέλος) of that which was being rendered inoperative—that is, the death-dealing judgment of the glory of God upon his "stiff necked" people as it was manifested in the old covenant.[34] For *unlike* Rom 10:4, the τέλος in 2 Cor 3:13b takes place within the time frame of *Moses's* activity, rather than referring to the time of Christ, since in 3:13, as in 3:7, the time reference is *still* that of the Exodus narrative. For this reason, in 3:13 Paul does *not* identify the τέλος of the old covenant with Christ as he does in Rom 10:4, even though the two statements are related theologically within Paul's overall history-of-salvation perspective. It is precisely because Moses had to veil the purpose (τέλος) of the glory of the old covenant due to Israel's hard hearts (2 Cor 3:13b) that Christ eventually must become the τέλος of the law, whatever τέλος means in Rom 10:4. The τέλος kept from Israel's view in 2 Cor 3:13 was the outcome or consequence of the glory of God as it encounters a rebellious people had it not been veiled, which is one piece with the purpose of the old covenant as a whole (cf. 3:7, 9). Far from duplicity, Moses's merciful *intention* was to keep Israel from being judged

32. See A *pc* b f* vg (bomss).

33. Hooker, "Beyond the Things," 305.

34. This use of τέλος in 2 Cor 3:13 to refer to the outcome or consequence of a given action corresponds to Paul's undisputed use of τέλος with this same meaning in Rom 6:21–22; 2 Cor 11:15; and Phil 3:19. Cf. too 1 Tim 1:5; Jas 5:11; 1 Pet 1:9; 4:17.

by the glory on his face, which was the τέλος of that glory in response to the continuing hardened nature of the people.

Once again, Paul's meaning in 3:13 is best recaptured when read in the context of Exod 34:29–35. There is no compelling exegetical basis for concluding that it is the expression of a foreign, specifically "Christian" re-reading of the text, whether based upon Paul's supposedly negative view of Moses and the old covenant, his introduction of the idea of a "fading" glory not found in the biblical account, the postulating of some hidden referent in Exod 34:29–35 imported into the present context on the basis of Rom 10:4 or, in the case of those who argue for the veiling of the preexistent Christ, from 1 Cor 10:4.

Moreover, Paul has not ignored or reinterpreted the fact that Israel could in fact see the glory of God on the face of Moses during those periods of revelation in which Moses removed the veil, as is often maintained. Rather, his careful choice of ἀτενίσαι in verses 7 and 13 indicates that it is precisely this periodic and limited access to the glory of God that Paul presupposes as indicative of Israel's problem. They were not able "to gaze" (ἀτενίσαι) into the glory of God, but could only encounter it briefly. When seen in this light, rather than being in tension with, or even a contradiction of verse 7, verse 13 is its natural complement, just as verse 12 is Paul's equally natural response to his own ministry of the glory of God. Again, Paul's exegesis proves to be a sober and careful contextual interpretation of his tradition.

Against this backdrop, it may not be surprising if the rest of Paul's argument in 3:7–18 can also be shown to derive from his understanding of Exod 34:29–35 within its original context. Paul can be bold, where Moses had to veil himself (3:12–13), precisely because Paul can expect that, instead of destruction, those whose hearts have been changed will be *transformed* by their encounter with the glory of God on the face of Christ (3:18; 4:4–6). Paul's reason for this confidence and boldness (3:4, 12; 4:1) is clear. In the preaching of the gospel God is at work through his Spirit to change people's hearts (3:8, 17–18; 4:2–6). In contrast to Moses, Paul need not "veil himself" before a people whose disposition toward God and his will has been radically changed. For where the Spirit is, there is freedom (3:17), not from the law, or the old covenant, or from judgment *per se*, but from the veil as a metonym for the hardheartedness that continues to characterize those outside of (the) Christ. For now, through Christ, God's people once again are brought near to God so that, with unveiled faces, they too, like Moses before them, may see the glory of God, albeit still dimly (3:18). This transformation, as the promises of the new covenant in Jer 31:31–34; and Ezek 11; 36 make clear, is a moral transformation in accord with the commandments of the Torah as the stipulations of both the old and new covenants. The dawning of the new covenant brings the beginning of that obedience to God which is brought about by the merciful redemption and restoration that characterizes the new creation (2 Cor 3:18; 5:17).

6

The Sum of the Matter

Paul's Understanding of Perseverance[1]

In fulfillment of the reality of the new covenant (Jer 31:31–34), the apostle Paul is convinced that those who have been redeemed by Christ *will* continue to "fight the good fight" and "finish the race" by "keeping the faith" (2 Tim 4:7). For to Paul, this statement of confidence concerning the believer is first and foremost a conviction about God's grace. The doctrine of "perseverance" is a statement about the surety of God's merciful commitment to his people, not a reflection of their commitment to God (1 Cor 1:7–9). Believers persevere in their faith not because of their own decision or fortitude, but because of *God's* self-generated eternal decree, which unleashes a chain of consequences that begins with God's foreknowledge and predestination and climaxes with their glorification (Rom 8:29–30). In short, believers persevere because of *God's* historical activity of working all things together toward this good end (note that Rom 8:29–30 functions to support 8:28 and 8:31–39).

If perseverance is the expression of God's grace, the surety of God's grace is rooted in his character. God's commitment to sanctify and glorify those whom he has predestined and justified, and to orchestrate all things together to that end, means that *God's* glory is being displayed in the perseverance of those whom he "chose before the foundation of the world, that [they] should be holy and blameless before him in love" (Eph 1:3; cf. Col 1:21–22; 1 Thess 5:9; 2 Thess 2:13–14). Conversely, the "hope in sharing the

[1]. From Scott J. Hafemann, "Paul's Understanding of Perseverance." *SBJT* 2/1 (1998) 68–71.

glory of God" (Rom 5:2) honors not those who are hoping but "the *God of hope*" (Rom 15:13), since it reflects their confidence in the perfection of *his* character (i.e., his integrity to do what he says he will do) and in the strength of *his* might (i.e., his ability to do what he says he will do) (Rom 4:20). Those to whom God is committed will therefore remain committed to God because God's ultimate commitment is to display his glory, one means of which is ensuring the perseverance of his people in accordance with his promises (Rom 11:36; 16:25–27; 1 Cor 15:28; 2 Cor 1:20; Eph 1:6, 12, 14; Phil 2:11, etc.). For this reason, Paul is convinced that "he who began a good work [in the Philippians] will bring it to completion at the day of Jesus Christ" (Phil 1:6). This is why those who do not persevere show, by their very lack of perseverance, that they were never called by God.

So, given his theocentric perspective, Paul's crucial question concerning perseverance is not whether one has made a "decision" for God, but whether God has called someone to himself. Paul's first consideration as a pastor was therefore whether genuine evidence existed that the grace of God had been poured out in a person's life. This was not because Paul wanted to be a "spiritual cop." Rather, he wanted to comfort God's people in the midst of their personal and circumstantial adversities by pointing to that evidence in order to assure them that God was present and powerfully at work in their lives for their good (note, e.g., the evidence for Phil 1:6 in 1:5, 7; for 1 Thess 1:4 in 1:3, 5–10; for 2:13 in 2:14; for 3:7 in 3:6; for 1 Cor 1:4 in 1:5–7, with the promise of 1:8, because of God's faithfulness as declared in 1:9; for Col 1:3 in 1:4–8, etc.). For Paul is sure that where the Spirit is present, he will produce "fruit" (Gal 5:22–23). Where the glory of God is encountered, it will produce transformation into the image of God (2 Cor 3:18). Where God has called his people, they will follow with faith, hope, and love, even though this may entail suffering for the sake of the gospel (1 Thess 1:3, 6; 3:3; 2 Thess 1:3–4; Eph 3:14–19; Rom 8:37; 2 Tim 3:12).

In sum, the sign that the Spirit poured out through the gospel has taken root in one's life is "obedience [as the organic expression of faith itself]," which, in order to glorify God, was the purpose of Paul's apostolic ministry as a servant of the new covenant to the Gentiles (Rom 1:5; 15:18; 16:26; cf. 2 Cor 3:3–6). For Paul, perseverance in "the obedience of faith" is thus *visible* in a real change of life in real people in the midst of the real world (Titus 2:14). Persevering faith is not a continuing mental assent to the truth of data from the past; it expresses itself in a continuing and active obedience to God's will as the expression of a growing trust in his promises for the future. Hence, as the inextricable expression of dependence on God's promises, Paul's imperatives are not options or good advice, but the necessary embodiment of the indicative reality upon which they are based (cf.

Phil 2:12-13; 2 Thess 2:14-15). Within this context, perseverance is not the experience of the Christian elite, but the promise to all those who belong to God. Paul demands what he demands because he is convinced that God has granted what he has granted. "How can we who have died to sin still live in it?" (Rom 6:2). Because we *are* saved we must therefore exhibit "endurance with regard to good work" in order *to be* saved (Rom 2:7; cf. 2:10-13; Gal 6:9; 2 Tim 4:7-8).

Of course, Paul recognizes that perseverance in sanctification is a matter of progress over a lifetime, not perfection overnight (cf. Phil 1:25; Col 1:10; 1 Thess 4:1; 2 Thess 1:3). Consequently, for example, Paul gives the Corinthians, despite their involvement in the strife of 1 Cor 1:11-12, the benefit of the doubt that they are Christians (cf. 1 Cor 1:2, 4-9). But if so, then they are still "babes in Christ" inasmuch as they are not acting spiritually, but as "men of the flesh" (1 Cor 3:1, 3). And if they *are* "spiritual," then Paul fully expects them to grow up (1 Cor 1:10; 3:18-22; 4:7, 16; 5:1-2; 6:4-8, 18; 11:17-22; 14:20)! Indeed, since the Corinthians had shown signs that God had in fact "washed," "sanctified," and "justified" them (1 Cor 6:11), Paul expects them not to be classified any longer among the morally wicked who will not inherit the kingdom of God (1 Cor 6:9-10; cf. Gal 5:21; Eph 5:3-11). And he anticipates that those in Corinth who are already strong in the faith will get even stronger (1 Cor 8:11; 10:24, 31; 11:1; 14:1, etc.; cf. Rom 14:13-21), just as he later expected those who had repented to demonstrate it by giving away their money (cf. 2 Cor 8:7-8, 24; 9:3, 13).

First Corinthians 3:1-3 is therefore not a word of comfort ("relax, the issue is not your salvation, but your growth"), but of chastisement ("be on your guard, the issue of your growth is a matter of your salvation"). Moreover, 1 Cor 3:15 is not the loophole in the doctrine of sanctification that denies the necessity of spiritual growth. Paul's concern there is with evaluating the work of his fellow ministers, not with their personal, salvific status in Christ (cf. 1 Cor 3:9-10). Nor does the "burning up" of some work turn obedience into a striving for rewards, as if there are other things that we do earn with our efforts. Finally, the "carnal Christian" of 1 Cor 3:1-4 is not a third class of humanity that exists somewhere between being a non-Christian and being a "Spirit-filled Christian." Just as the designation "Spirit-filled Christian" is a needless tautology (Rom 8:9, 14), so too "carnal Christian" is an oxymoron that cannot endure for long, for in 1 Cor 3:3 Paul places the behavior of the "men of the flesh" who are still "babes in Christ" in the category of those who do not have the Spirit at all! From Paul's perspective, to claim to be a Christian, while at the same time willingly and gladly remaining in baby-like states of immature sin, is a contradiction in terms that must be resolved in one direction or the other (cf. Rom 6:15-19).

The natural outworking of Paul's understanding of the divine foundation and human necessity of perseverance is the fact that whenever he encounters those who claim to be Christians, but show no interest in repenting from sin and becoming more like Christ, he *warns* them that they may be deluded about their salvation (1 Cor 15:2; 2 Cor 6:1; Gal 1:6). The fear of God is God's gracious gift granted to those who believe in order to keep them persevering (2 Cor 5:11; 7:1; cf. Rom 3:18). The warning of peril is thus God's instrument of perseverance (cf. 2 Cor 5:10; Rom 2:1–29; 14:10–12; and chapter 12 below). Hence, Paul's initial word to those Corinthians who were tearing the church apart with their boasting was the warning that "if any one destroys God's temple, God will destroy him" (1 Cor 3:16). In the same way, after doing everything in his power to win them back to Christ, Paul's last word to those Corinthians still in rebellion against him and his gospel was that they were to test themselves to see if they are "holding to [their] faith" (2 Cor 13:5). If those still in rebellion do not finally repent, he will have to conclude that they were never part of God's people. God's commitment to perfect his people is conditioned by their continuing in the faith, since that is what he enables them to do (Col 1:22–23).

In calling others to account for themselves, Paul is simply preaching what he practices. Like a boxer, Paul's constant admonition to himself was "to pummel my body and subdue it, lest after preaching to others I myself should be disqualified" (1 Cor 9:27; cf. 1 Tim 4:7–10; 6:11–12). For Paul, these warnings are real, since God's work is effective. Those who will not believe them cannot be considered "believers." Perseverance in repentance, not persistent nonchalance in the face of sin, is the sign that the Spirit is at work. For where the Spirit is at work, "*godly* grief," not comfort, will be the response to the recognition of sin (2 Cor 7:1, 9–12). Since God cannot go back on his word nor be thwarted in his purposes, perseverance in the obedience of faith is *the* evidence of a genuine conversion.

So, if only perseverance signals salvation, can "believers" ever be sure of their redemption? Paul's answer is a resounding "yes" (cf., e.g., Rom 5:6–11). But true assurance exists only when we need it: in the present, based on the reality of perservance in the present! The problem with the doctrine of "eternal security" ("once saved, always saved, no matter what you do!"), which is based on a passive view of saving faith as a one-time "decision" regarding the message of the gospel, is that its "faith" focuses on what the believer has "accepted as true" in the past without regard for the present or the future. In so doing, it misconstrues the nature of faith, failing to see it as an active, ongoing dependence on God that expresses itself in obedience to God's commands, and separates it from God's prior provisions and subsequent promises, thereby removing faith from that which both creates and sustains it. This leads to a false assurance. In stark contrast, Paul's understanding of perseverance is focused squarely on continuing to trust God in the present and the future (Phil 3:12–16).

As a pastor, Paul therefore comforts the contrite and encourages the confident, but confronts the complacent with the judgment of God, no matter what his or her past track record in the church. Although Paul never establishes any "degree of holiness" that must be reached to be assured of one's salvation (God is the author of sanctification!), he does paint a picture of what perseverance looks like: *increasing* conformity to the image of Christ as the image of God (Rom 8:29; 2 Cor 3:18; 4:4; Eph 5:1).

Finally, and most importantly, since God is the author of our sanctification, the pathway to perseverance is prayer and the power of the Spirit. For this reason, perseverance is itself an expression of utter dependence on God (cf. 1 Thess 3:11–13; 2 Thess 1:11–12; Eph 1:15–23; 3:14–19; Col 1:9–14). Hence, the end of perseverance is praise (Rom 11:36; Eph 1:6, 12, 14).

PART TWO

Paul's Ministry

7

Paul's "Jeremiah" Ministry in Reverse and the Reality of the New Covenant[1]

It is a great honor for me to dedicate this essay on Paul's self-understanding as a missionary-apostle to George Chavanikamannil on the occasion of his sixtieth birthday, since it represents his own visionary commitment to serious biblical and theological studies as a key to the global mission of the church. It is a small tribute to his pathbreaking work in the establishment of the Luther W. New Jr. Theological College, Dehradun (Uttarakhand, India), as an educational center for pioneer mission. It is also fitting to offer such an essay on Paul, since the apostle Paul and the missionary statesman George Chavanikamannil share several rare but significant things in common. Both understand that reaching the nations with the gospel of Jesus Christ is an essential expression of the dawning of the kingdom of God and the establishment of the new covenant. Both share the God-given "ambition to preach the gospel, not where Christ has already been named" (Rom 15:20). Both have been called to do that in difficult, extremely pluralistic settings.[2] As a result, both have built their ministries squarely on a living devotion to Christ and a serious study of the Scriptures, valuing the centrality of know-

---

1. From Scott J. Hafemann, "Paul's 'Jeremiah' Ministry in Reverse and the Reality of the New Covenant." In *Remapping Mission Discourse: Festschrift for Rev. George Kuruvila Chavanikamannil*, edited by Simon Samuel and P. V. Joseph, 72–83. Dehradun/Delhi: NTC Publications and ISPCK, 2008.

2. Savage, *Power through Weakness*, 52, points out that no less than thirty-four different deities have been found among the ruins of Corinth, all existing within an emphasis on the harmony of all religions.

ing both intimately for the mission of the church. Both have given their lives to fulfilling the mission of the church by building churches and raising up leaders for them. Both have been blessed by God as strategic leaders and mission strategists for their era. Both have counted "everything as loss because of the surpassing worth of knowing Christ Jesus [as] Lord" (Phil 3:8).

The goal of this essay, therefore, is to set forth the purpose of the ministry of the gospel as seen in Paul's own ministry, and exemplified in that of George's, by examining the context, content, and two consequences of Paul's argument in 2 Cor 10:7–8: "Look at what is before your eyes. If anyone is confident that he is Christ's, let him remind himself that as he is Christ's, so are we. Therefore,[3] even if I boast a little too much of our authority, which the Lord gave for building you up and not for destroying you, I shall not be put to shame."

THE CONTEXT OF PAUL'S ARGUMENT

In this text Paul is responding to the criticism in Corinth that he suffers too much to be an apostle of Christ! The use of "anyone" in 10:7b is a generic designation that most likely refers not to people in general, but either to Paul's opponents, or to all in Corinth who are questioning his integrity as an apostle and, hence, his legitimacy as a Christian (cf. this same use in 1 Cor 3:12, 18; 8:2–3; 14:37). The two were one for Paul. To question Paul's apostleship was to call into question Paul's very status as a believer.[4] In response, Paul points to the Corinthians' own confidence that they belong to Christ. If the Corinthians are children of God in Christ, then Paul, too, must be, since he is their father in the faith (1 Cor 4:14–15). If they deny Paul, they will be denying their own standing in Christ (cf. 10:7; 3:1–3). Paul is therefore not ashamed of his continued boasting, even if it is a bit strong at times, for in doing so he is merely underscoring both his legitimacy and their own.[5] Paul's mediation of the Spirit, through his lifestyle of suffering, verified by their own belonging to Christ, is ample proof of the legitimacy of his ministry, and, hence, of the fact that he, too, belongs to the Lord (cf. 1:1;

---

3. Taking the γάρ in 10:8 not to introduce a ground or causal clause, with the meaning "for" (as in the NIV), but to be inferential, with the meaning "therefore" (cf. the NRSV's rendering, "now"); cf. BDAG, 190. Paul's confidence before God does not logically *support* his confidence in belonging to Christ, but is *derived from it*.

4. See now Harris, *Second Corinthians*, 690: "The issue at stake was not Paul's status as a genuine Christian but his position as a true apostle with authority. Yet the one ultimately involved the other, for a false apostle hardly belonged to Christ."

5. For the theme of boasting in chs. 10–13, see 10:13, 15–17; 11:12, 16, 18, 30; 12:1, 5–6, 9.

3:2–3; 4:7; 6:4; 13:5–6). In verse 7 Paul thus summarizes his argument from *experience*, his and theirs.

In verse 8 Paul turns to an argument from Scripture, specifically from the history of redemption. This movement from experience to Scripture and vice versa is common in Paul. So, as further support for his confidence as Christ's apostle, Paul alludes in 10:8 parenthetically to the call of Jeremiah in order to underscore that his boasting concerning his authority is not an empty self-commendation, like that of his opponents (see 10:12 and the discussion of 2 Cor 3:1–3 above). Rather, it derives from his call to be a servant of the new covenant; that is, like Jeremiah, the Lord gave Paul authority "for building you up rather than pulling you down" (10:8). For in calling Jeremiah, the Lord declared: "Behold, I have put my words in your mouth. See, I have set you this day over nations and over kingdoms, to pluck up and to break down, to destroy and to overthrow, to build and to plant" (Jer 1:10).[6]

Note, however, that in Jeremiah the emphasis clearly falls on Jeremiah's "negative" ministry of divine judgment and destruction, which is given first and in a double set of negative descriptions ("to pluck up and to break down, to destroy and to overthrow"), followed by a single set of positives ("to build and to plant"). Paul, on the other hand, simplifies the point of Jer 1:10 by summarizing both of its points in one description each, *reverses their order*, and then draws an explicit contrast between his own ministry and that of Jeremiah's ("our authority, which the Lord gave for building you up and *not* for destroying you")!

To underscore the importance of this comparison to Jeremiah's ministry, Paul returns to this same theme to close the final section of his letter in 13:10, where he reiterates that he is giving the rebellious minority in Corinth yet one more opportunity to repent before he returns to enforce God's judgment over the community. He is doing so because, as a verbatim inclusio to 10:18, he is acting "in accordance with the authority that the Lord gave me, for building up and not for tearing down" (13:10).

Students of 2 Corinthians have often recognized Paul's allusion to Jeremiah's calling in these verses,[7] though without drawing out its broader

---

6. Cf. Jer 24:6; 38:27–28; 42/49:10LXX; 45:4/51:34LXX for the continuation of this theme, and esp. 38:27–28LXX, 49:10LXX; 51:4LXX, where the related vocabulary of καθαιρέω ("to destroy/tear down") and οἰκοδομέω ("to build up") found in Paul is used. The LXX in this passage reflects the basic sense of the MT. It simply reduces the symmetry of a double set of negatives ("to pluck up and to break down, to destroy and to overthrow") followed by a single set of positive designations ("to build and to plant") to a sequence of three negatives followed by two positives ("to root out, and to pull down, and to destroy, and to rebuild, and to plant").

7. See Furnish, *II Corinthians*, 467; Barnett, *Second Corinthians*, 472; Harris, *Second Corinthians*, 694–95; etc. This allusion is strengthened by Paul's often-recognized

implications for Paul's argument. Furnish even states that "it is unclear why Paul adds that this authority is not for your destruction."[8] Yet against the backdrop of 2 Corinthians as a whole, I suggest that 10:8 and 13:10 reflect Paul's conviction that his *apostolic* authority "for building you up rather than pulling you down" is a fulfillment of Jeremiah's promise of the new covenant to come, whereas under the old covenant the emphasis of Jeremiah's *prophetic* ministry was just the opposite. In other words, the language from Jeremiah signals that the substance of Paul's argument comes from Scripture, now spoken *to* Paul's context rather than derived *from* it.

THE CONTENT OF PAUL'S ARGUMENT

The first observation, of course, is that Paul contrasts his ministry with that of Jeremiah. The reason is equally clear: the focus of Jeremiah's calling and subsequent ministry was on the divine judgment to be meted out in Israel's exile. As Dempster points out,

> This note of doom is sounded at the beginning of Jeremiah's call with four of the six verbs that describe his task as a prophet . . . "to uproot, to destroy, to tear down, and to smash" . . . (1:10). . . . Jeremiah, whose call resembles those of Moses and Samuel, had a mission that was largely negative. . . . The prophetic task of destruction constitutes the main theme of Jeremiah's activity. It was a wrecking ministry, a ministry of demolition.[9]

Moreover, God's uprooting what he had planted in Judah, now beginning to take place through his prophet, functions in Jer 45:4–5 as an introduction to the oracles against the *nations* in chapters 46–51. Thus, "this judgment of Judah, expressed in tearing down and uprooting, has been a prelude to *universal* judgment."[10]

Yet, in view of this coming judgment, the promise of a new covenant is also intimated in Jeremiah's call. Jeremiah's ministry was indeed,

---

appeal in Gal 1:15–16 to the call of Jeremiah in Jer 1:4–5 to explain his own call as an apostle; see Sandnes, *Paul—One of the Prophets?* 48–69.

8. Furnish, *II Corinthians*, 477. Furnish suggests that perhaps the imagery of Jeremiah "is explanation enough," though he prefers to see the reference as a response to criticism that his teaching has been destructive (477). Barnett, *Second Corinthians*, 473, focuses on the "authority" given to Paul as an allusion to his call on the Damascus Road and its use in 1 Cor 9 as the key concept. In other words, Paul's *language* may come from Scripture but the *substance* comes from Paul's own context, the former merely providing the container for his polemic.

9. Dempster, *Dominion and Dynasty*, 160.

10. Ibid., 163, emphasis mine.

a wrecking ministry, a ministry of demolition. . . . But it was clearly more than that, since a constructive set of verbs—"to build and to plant"—follows the double set of destructive ones. This sequence shows that even the destruction is positive, since it clears the way for a new building to be constructed from the rubble of the old. Moreover, the scope of the prophetic activity extended beyond the borders of Judah to the world (Jer 1:10).[11]

In short, "looking back on the failure of the covenant at Sinai, which has led to the judgment of exile, Jeremiah announces a new covenant."[12]

Though the wording is not exactly the same in both passages, Paul's call in 10:8 "to build" and "*not* to tear down" may therefore reflect the repetition of the positive side of Jeremiah's call in Jer 24:6LXX ("I will build them up and *not* pluck them down; and I will plant them, and *not* pluck them up"), which refers explicitly to the future restoration of Israel, when they will be given "a heart to know me, for I am the Lord; and they will be my people, and I will be their God, for they will return to me with their whole heart" (Jer 24:7; cf. too Jer 38:27–28LXX; 49:10LXX).

Against this backdrop, Paul's statement in 10:7-8 reflects his conviction that this new covenant restoration of God's people, begun by Jeremiah by way of prophetic sign (cf. his buying land during the Babylonian siege: Jer 32:14–27), has now taken an eschatological step forward in its fulfillment, including its extension to the nations, as in Corinth. Paul's role as a "*servant*" of the new covenant, detailed in 2 Cor 3:1–18 (see chapters 3–5 above), is now explicitly tied to Jeremiah's role as the *prophet* of the new covenant by way of the contrast between their ministries necessitated by the fulfillment of Jeremiah's own promise. In 2:16—3:18, Paul argued that he was called like Moses, but with a distinctively different ministry than Moses (i.e., a new covenant ministry of the Spirit, which brings life due to

---

11. Ibid., 160. Dempster, *Dominion and Dynasty*, 161, based on Jer 1:10; 18:9; 24:6; 29:5, 28; 35:7; 42:10; 45:4; Ezek 28:26; 36:36; Isa 5:2; 65:21, 22 and Amos 9:14–15, goes on to point out that it is therefore not coincidental that "the last close coincidence of the two verbs 'to build and to plant' in the canon occurs in Nathan's oracle to David, in which it is stated that Israel would be planted in the land, David's son would build a house for God, and God would return the favor to David by building him a royal house (2 Sam 7:10, 13). The final coincidence of these two verbs in the Prophets is in the Twelve, where Amos states that in the future the Lord will build David's fallen house, raising its ruins from the dust. The people will rebuild the desolate cities, and Israel will be replanted in the land, never to be uprooted again (Amos 9:11–15). . . . If there is destruction, it is simply paving the way for building and planting. God's 'No!' is followed by his 'Yes!' In fact, these words linguistically dominate the book of Jeremiah and also occur, less frequently, in the prophets following Jeremiah. But the meaning of these words, if not their precise phraseology, pervades these prophets."

12. Ibid., 159.

the effecting of righteousness, rather than a ministry of the "letter"—that is, the law without the Spirit—which brings death and condemnation). Here he affirms that he was consequently also called like Jeremiah, but with the distinctively different ministry that Jeremiah himself announced. In this way, both the Law and the Prophets find their goal in Paul's ministry, made possible by the inauguration of the new covenant brought about by the coming of the Messiah.

This is why Paul's role as a minister of the new covenant is to mediate the Spirit, since, as Christ's apostle, Paul's primary purpose is the salvation of God's people, not their judgment (cf. 1:11, 23–24; 2:3; 3:6–11, 17–18; 4:6, 13–15; 5:13–15; 6:2). Though both Jeremiah and Paul were called to save *and* to judge, their *primary* purposes within redemptive history—that is, the accents of their respective ministries—have been reversed. As the introduction to the promise of the new covenant in Jer 31:27–28 puts it: "'The days are coming,' declares the Lord, 'when I will plant the house of Israel and the house of Judah with the offspring of men and of animals. Just as I watched over them to uproot and tear down, and to overthrow, destroy and bring disaster, so I will watch over them to build and to plant,' declares the Lord."

This is also why Paul exercised patience and restraint in meting out the judgment of God in church discipline, even when it cost him his own reputation. By giving the Corinthians multiple opportunities to repent before he returned for his third visit to judge those still in rebellion, Paul was extending Christ's own patience toward them in anticipation of the "day of our Lord Jesus" (cf. 1:14, 19; 13:1–4). The delay of the Parousia as the period of God's patience for the sake of the repentance of God's people was Paul's model for his own ministry—a first-century example of Christ-determined ethics.

Nevertheless, Paul will not hesitate to be bold when the time comes (10:2, 11; 13:2, 10), and even now in his letter he is destroying the obstacles being raised up against the knowledge of God (cf. 10:4–5 with 10:8). Hence, as he contemplates returning to Corinth, Paul is "ready to punish all disobedience [of the false apostles and those who persist in following them[13]]" (10:6). Just as Jeremiah declared twice that the temple would be destroyed if the people's idolatry continued (chs. 7; 26 in view of 2:10–13), in 6:14—7:1 Paul too pronounces divine wrath on the Corinthians as God's temple if they do not purge the idolatry of the false teachers from their midst, indeed, all the more so in view of the new covenant reality of the Spirit. Thus, just as in 1 Cor 3:16–17, here, too, in 2 Cor 6:14—7:1 the temple image is used to support a warning of divine destruction against those within the com-

---

13. So now Harris, *Second Corinthians*, 685.

munity who would destroy it, since the Corinthians, as God's temple, are "holy" (cf. 1 Cor 3:17 with 7:1). For given their redemption in Christ, Paul is stunned that believers would consort with idolatry and wickedness (2 Cor 6:16). The righteous who belong to the Messiah have been delivered from their idolatry and wickedness and brought back into the presence of God's glory. To act otherwise is a simple contradiction in terms. As James Scott has demonstrated, this new covenant argumentation is then amplified in the collage of passages quoted in 6:16c–18, which focus on the new covenant restoration of Israel after the exile, now applied to the Corinthians.[14]

However, as a minister of the new covenant Paul's *first* expectation is not for judgment, but for repentance in response to the work of the Spirit; that is to say, he will only judge the unbelievers in Corinth "whenever [the repentant ones'] obedience is complete" (10:6).[15] Like the cross itself, the apostle, as the "fragrance of Christ," is both the aroma of life to those who are being saved *and* the aroma of death to those who are perishing (cf. 2 Cor 2:15–16a with 1 Cor 1:18). But as in 1 Cor 1:18, the chiasm in 2:15–16a places the emphasis on life, not death (saved . . . perishing . . . death to death . . . life to life). In fulfillment of Jeremiah's promise, Paul therefore declares in 12:19, "Everything we do [including Paul's self-defense!] . . . is for your strengthening [= building up]."

Because of the new covenant context and content of Paul's ministry as Christ's apostle, the Jeremiah-theme of "building up" becomes a common Pauline description of the call to plant churches and to strengthen the faith of believers (cf. 1 Cor 3:9–10, 12, 14; 8:1; 14:3, 5, 12, 26; Rom 14:19; 15:2, 20; 1 Thess 5:11). The establishment of Israel and the intended restoration of the nations, both "torn down" under God's judgment in the past, are now being "built up" as a result of the divine "yes" to God's promises in Christ (1:20). It is of note, however, that whereas Paul adopts Jeremiah's language of building up Israel and of restoring the temple and applies them *both* to the church

14. Scott, "Use of Scripture," 73–99.

15. Contra Harris, *Second Corinthians*, 694, who argues that Paul contemplates "'destruction' as a legitimate, intermediate technique that may be used in the shaping of his convert's conduct," like God's judgment against Israel, though God's aim "was always their ultimate restoration to obedience and right relations with him (e.g., Jer 30:3–22; Hos 6:1–2)." However, this confuses the history of Israel as a disobedient people under the old covenant and the promise of their future redemption with the church as the beginning fulfillment of this restoration under the new—for Paul, the exercise of destruction and upbuilding is directed to two *distinct* groups, namely, to the unbelievers and believers respectively. Harris views 13:10 as Paul's contemplating punishing some of the Corinthians in order to prepare them for the day of the Lord, as in 1 Cor 5:5; I view 13:10 as the prospect of finally being forced to judge some of the Corinthians as unbelievers—i.e., as an inauguration of the day of the Lord itself because their hardened refusal to repent has put them outside the realm of God's people.

in Corinth, he does not pick up the language of God's once again planting Israel in the land after the exile, although this too is inextricably linked to the new covenant promise of Jer 31:31–34 (cf. Jer 31:1–26; 31:38–40; 32:36–44). This may reflect Paul's conviction that the church is the inauguration but not yet the consummation of the new covenant promises. The coming of the Christ and Paul's ministry as his apostle are not the "climax of the covenant" but its penultimate anteclimax.

Clearly, then, 2 Cor 10:7–8 summarizes the implications of Paul's earlier arguments concerning the nature of his new covenant ministry detailed in 2:14—4:6 and 6:14—7:1. Paul's boast in his authority and his expectation that those who are truly believers in the real Christ will respond to his calls to repentance are based on Paul's fulfillment of Jeremiah's ministry in reverse as outlined in the first nine chapters of Second Corinthians. Indeed, chapters 8–9 detail what "godly grief that produces repentance leading to salvation" (7:10–11) looks like: those who have come back to Christ and his apostle will once again support the collection as the capstone of Paul's new covenant ministry.

TWO CONSEQUENCES OF PAUL'S ARGUMENT

First, the *priority* and *sequencing* of these prior arguments are essential to and assumed by Paul's allusion in 10:7–8. The parenthetical reference to Paul's Jeremiah-like ministry "in reverse" in 10:7–8 consequently supports both the compositional unity of the letter and its canonical ordering as original. Second Corinthians 10:7–8 would make much less sense if placed before 1–9, and to excise 6:14—7:1 as an interpolation would remove one of the key pillars to its argument. Chapters 10–13 extend to the rebellious minority the same warning Paul has given to the repentant majority in 6:14—7:1. If the rebellious are in fact part of God's "replanted people," they too will pass the test of faith by turning from the idolatry of spiritual adultery that currently characterizes their lives (13:5). That is to say, they too will tear down the "other Jesus" and "different Spirit and gospel" in their lives (11:4), repudiate the false apostles who preach them (11:13), and turn with repentance back to Paul as the true servant of the Messiah (11:23ff.). And such "godly grief" will evidence itself in a renewed participation in the collection.

Second, Paul's self-understanding as an apostle of (the) Christ in terms not only of Jeremiah's *new* covenant *promise* but also of Jeremiah's *old* covenant *ministry* demonstrates that the contrast in contemporary scholarship between apocalyptic and covenantal conceptions as competing frameworks for understanding Paul and his message is misguided.[16] As a servant of the new covenant who belonged to the Messiah, Paul was called to mediate the dawning of the eschatological, apocalyptic "hour" of God's deliverance in Christ (2 Cor 6:2; cf. Gal 1:4; Col 1:13; Rom 7:24), a deliverance that brought as its main accent the restoration of God's people, but, as its secondary motif, must therefore also bring God's wrath. The apocalyptic Christ establishes the history-altering new covenant between God and his people, now mediated to the nations by the Spirit through the apostle Paul. If, as Käsemann drilled home, apocalyptic is "the mother of Christian theology,"[17] then Paul's equally revered nanny is the contrast between the old covenant ministry of the law without the Spirit (γράμμα ["letter"]) and the new covenant ministry of the Spirit (πνεῦμα). In this contrast, the believing remnant under the old covenant provides the paradigm for understanding the believer under the new covenant, as the parallel in 2 Cor 3:18 between Moses and the Christian makes clear.

Like Paul, George's ministry of the apostolic gospel is establishing the world-redeeming reality of the kingdom of God in the midst of this evil age. And in fulfillment of this same apostolic gospel, it does so by establishing communities of new covenant believers who are being built up, not torn down, by his ministry. May the Lord continue to bless his ministry (with Leela!) for many days to come.

16. For a programmatic statement of the issues, see Martyn, *Theological Issues*.

17. The conclusion to Käsemann's now-classic essay, "Primitive Christian Apocalyptic," 137.

8

"Because of Weakness" (Gal 4:13)

The Role of Suffering in the Mission of Paul[1]

The starting point of this presentation is the claim that I once read: "Paul was no theologian; he was a missionary"—a claim that is false both in principle and in fact. In principle false, because there is no Christian theology that is not in the broad sense kerygmatic theology; factually false, because the historical Paul wrote as a theologian and worked as a missionary.[2]

C. K. Barrett's starting point is my own. Indeed, Paul's kerygmatically driven theology and his missionary endeavors as a theologian are nowhere more

---

1. From Scott J. Hafemann, "'Because of Weakness' (Galatians 4:13): The Role of Suffering in the Mission of Paul." In *The Gospel to the Nations: Perspectives on Paul's Mission; In Honour of Peter T. O'Brien*, edited by Peter Bolt and Mark Thompson, 131–46. Leicester: InterVarsity, 2000. A passionate heart for God's glory in the mission of the gospel, matched by a keen mind in service of the Scriptures, in a humble spirit submitted to Christ—Professor O'Brien has been an example to me of what it means to worship God in Spirit and truth. It is a gift to know him.

2. "Ausgangspunkt dieses Vortrags ist die Behauptung, die ich einst gelesen habe: 'Paulus war kein Theologe; er war Missionar'—eine Behauptung, zugleich prinzipiell und sachlich falsch. Prinzipiell falsch, weil es keine christliche Theologie gibt, die nicht im breiten Sinne kerygmatische Theologie ist; sachlich falsch, weil der historische Paulus als Theologe geschrieben und als Missionar gearbeitet hat" (Barrett, "Paulus," 18). This essay is part of a larger paper presented at the "Symposium on the Mission of the Early Church to Jews and Gentiles," 28–29 April, 1998, at the School of Mission and Theology, Stavanger, Norway. I am indebted to the members of the symposium for their helpful interaction with it.

apparent than in those key passages where Paul delineates the missiological significance of his suffering for his proclamation of the gospel. And nowhere is this significance more striking than in Paul's sudden shift from his direct theological arguments in Gal 2:15—4:10 to the implications of his apostolic suffering in 4:12-20, and then back again to theology in 4:21—5:26. It is surprising, therefore, as Ernst Baasland pointed out sixteen years ago (now thirty!), that Paul's recounting of his suffering in Gal 4:13-14 and the argument he builds from it in 4:12-20, as well as his passing references to his persecution in 5:11; 6:12, 17, have long been a neglected feature of his apologetic in this letter.[3] Though understandable in view of the law/gospel contrast that has dominated the church's engagement with this letter ever since the Reformation, this lack of attention is especially striking in regard to 4:13-14. For within Paul's overall argument this reference to Paul's suffering functions to support Paul's first direct command in the letter (4:12a), which rhetorically marks out a (*the?*) key turning point in the epistle. The letter's other commands can all be seen to be specific explications of Paul's general admonition in 4:12a (cf. Gal 5:1, 13, 16, 25-26). Far from being simply an emotional aside in Paul's argument,[4] Paul's reference to his suffering in 4:13-14 provides the immediate, evidential support for his leading appeal to the Galatians. In so doing, it presupposes a theological perspective and follows an apologetic pattern that is pervasive throughout Paul's letters. Thus, rather than rendering it *less* important than the more overtly "theological" arguments that surround it, the distinct personal nature of this "highly enigmatic paragraph" (4:12-20)[5] actually calls *more* attention to its importance.

---

3. Baasland, "Persecution," 135–50. But see now the major studies of Goddard and Cummins, "Ill or Ill-Treated?," and T. Martin, "Whose Flesh?"

4. So, e.g., Black, "Weakness," 26, who suggests that "the obscurity of this passage perhaps cannot be explained in a purely logical way; it is possible that Paul was so overwhelmed by emotion at this point in writing that he simply lost his train of thought. For this reason many scholars are of the opinion that Paul has ceased argumentation and has turned to emotional begging and appealing" (referring to Lagrange, A. Oepke, Burton, and Mussner as examples). Black himself rightly cautions that such psychological interpretations fail to recognize the rhetorical character of this passage, pointing to Betz's analysis of the unit as a Hellenistic "friendship" topos (26–27). But if Betz's analysis holds, this still means that Paul's appeal is primarily personal, based on earlier bonds of friendship, rather than theological.

5. So Black, "Weakness," 25.

THE PAULINE GOSPEL: BECOME LIKE PAUL![6]

The personal nature of Paul's argument in 4:12-20 is manifest already in the imperative of 4:12a, which is the main point of Paul's argument in this paragraph: Paul begs the Galatians to become *like him* because *he* also has become like them (the tenses of the implied verbs of the two clauses are naturally present and past respectively).[7] Within the larger context of Paul's argument, this is best taken as a reference to Paul's own conversion-call (Gal 1:13-24) and its consequence: "The one who was once persecuting us is now preaching (εὐαγγελίζεται) the faith that he was once trying to destroy" (Gal 1:23; cf. 4:13). This "faith" is the gospel that Paul received "through a revelation of Jesus Christ" (Gal 1:12) and preached to the Galatians (Gal 1:8). And it is the same gospel that is now being called into question by the "Judaizers," who argued that one had to keep the stipulations of both the old *and* new covenants in order to be a fully fledged, Spirit-filled member of God's eschatological people (Gal 1:6-9; 2:21; 5:2-4). For this reason, Paul begs the Galatians in 4:12 to resist the Judaizers by becoming like him in his freedom from the "works of the law" as Israel had encountered them in slavery to this world while under the old covenant (Gal 4:1-7; 5:1). Paul's desire is that they continue to join him in the Spirit-empowered obedience that now truly fulfils the law (5:13-26; 6:8), since, like Paul, God has freed the Gentile believers from this same slavery (Gal 4:8-11). In other words, in 4:12 Paul is calling the Galatians to the freedom in Christ that characterizes his own life because of Jesus's death on the cross (2:20; 3:13-14; 6:14). For the cross of Christ that initially caused Paul to persecute the church had now become the centerpiece of his own life and ministry as an apostle. As

---

6. For the exegetical support behind this section, see my "Paul and the Exile," 329-71. This present essay expands the basic point made in the sketch of 4:12-20 found on 354-55.

7. Goddard and Cummins, "Ill or Ill-Treated?" 97-99, reject this common reading as "a convoluted and inexplicable shift from that which Paul has in view in the first clause (the Galatians as Judaizers or about to judaize) to that in view in the second clause (the Galatians as Gentiles)" (97). In their view, this shift is impossible, since, according to Gal 4:8-11, the Galatians' former state was "a negative existence in pagan enslavement" (98). But as Paul's argument in 4:12-20 makes clear, Paul is referring to becoming like them in their conversion (cf. 4:9!), not in their pre-conversion state. Certainly Paul is not saying that in Christ he became a pagan! Goddard and Cummins argue that we should simply leave the verbs omitted and take the comparison to be a general one to "the whole history ... of his relationship with the Galatians and to their shared identity within that relationship" (99). However, quite apart from the fact that the dependent clauses require verbs (their omission does not signal their actual absence [!]; Goddard and Cummins actually presuppose two present-tense verbs), Paul's argument rides on a comparison between the present and the point of their conversion in the past (cf. 4:8-9 with 4:14-16).

a result, the persecutor had now joined the ranks of those being persecuted for their faith in the crucified Messiah (cf. 5:11; 6:17).

THE ROLE OF PAUL'S SUFFERING IN SUPPORT OF HIS GOSPEL

This brings us to the specific question of how Paul's suffering relates to the gospel he now preached, since in Gal 4:13 Paul reminds the Galatians that it was "*because* of a weakness of the flesh" (δι'[8] ἀσθένειαν τῆς σαρκός) that he first preached the gospel (εὐηγγελισάμην[9]) to them. As David Black has rightly argued, the general consensus is correct that here ἀσθένεια "refers to a physical condition of the apostle, and not to an unimpressive appearance, timidity, the emotional scars from persecution, sexual desires, human frailty in general, or some other figurative meaning."[10] Paul's "weakness" in 4:13 is best seen as a sickness, with the genitive τῆς σαρκός most likely descriptive—that is, a "bodily infirmity." Paul hereby coins a phrase that would locate his weakness in his "body" (σάρξ), while at the same time creating a play on his own theological concept of the "flesh" (σάρξ).[11] He did

---

8. The most natural reading of διά + accusative here is causal, since purpose cannot fit the context; see BDF §222, 223 (3). The meaning "by force of," suggested for Rev 12:11; 13:14, may also fit here. See T. Martin, "Whose Flesh?" 73–74, for a proper rejection of the common attempt to take this prepositional phrase as modal (as if it were διά + genitive), which occurs because commentators have recognized that a causal reading makes Paul's suffering the ground of his preaching in Galatia, when they desire a "more noble reason." Martin too seeks such a reason, but finds one only by denying that 4:13 refers to Paul at all (see below). But once Paul's suffering is seen to be his missiological corollary to the cross of Christ, this cause for his preaching is certainly "noble" enough.

9. That Paul's twenty-one uses of εὐαγγελίζω usually refer not to preaching in general, but specifically to preaching the *gospel*, even when the cognate noun is not present as in Gal 4:13, has been argued by O'Brien, *Consumed by Passion*, 62.

10. Black, "Weakness," 29; cf. his arguments in favor of this consensus against its few detractors on pp. 29–31. For uses of the ἀσθένεια word group to refer to physical sickness within the Pauline corpus, he points to Phil 2:26–27; 1 Tim 5:23; and 2 Tim 4:20.

11. Following T. Martin, "Whose Flesh?," 69, whose extensive survey of the use of σάρξ in relationship to ἀσθένεια uncovers the fact that "the phrase 'weakness of the flesh' (ἀσθένεια τοῦ [sic] σαρκός) as a reference to illness does not occur in ancient non-Christian Greek authors before the seventh century A.D. Nor do these authors refer to sickness with the adjectival construction 'weak flesh' (σάρξ ἀσθενής)." Instead, the references all speak of the "weakness of the flesh," whether in a healthy or sick body, in terms of its "weak" nature as porous or susceptible to the influences of fluids and temperature, etc. (67–69). Thus, the evidence points to the fact that Paul probably coined this phrase, throwing us back on Paul's own argument for its meaning. But given its uniqueness, Martin rejects the consensus view that ἀσθένεια τῆς σαρκός refers to Paul's

so in order to call special attention to the fact that he was sick *with regard to* his "flesh," rather than being sick *because* of his "flesh" (cf. Gal 3:3; 4:29; 5:13, 16–17, 19–21, 24; 6:8). Attempts to interpret it as a reference to Paul's persecutions (cf. Acts 13:50; 14:19; 2 Tim 3:11) fail to account adequately for this descriptive use of σάρξ and for the fact that Paul's being persecuted was a *result* of his preaching, not its underlying *cause* (cf. 5:11; 6:12, 17).[12]

---

illness, taking it instead to be a reference to the Galatians' pre-gospel fleshly condition and consequent need for the gospel as that which drove Paul to evangelize them (78–79, 82–86; pointing to Jerome as an advocate of the view that the Galatians were the referent of the phrase and to Gal 2:16, 20; 5:24; and Rom 5:6–8; 6:19; 15:20–21). However, in 4:13 the noun being modified is ἀσθένεια, not σάρξ, and σάρξ carries the adjectival function, not ἀσθένεια. Thus, Martin's lexicography is helpful, but in itself could be misleading, since in the relevant texts outside of Paul ἀσθένεια is being used adjectivally, rather than as the lead noun. Thus, in comparing these texts at the conceptual level we are, in fact, comparing apples and oranges. Furthermore, in terms of the evidence itself, the sample is small. Martin observes that only eight non-Christian passages before the seventh century even connect the two nouns, of which only four use σάρξ as a genitive modifier. Here too one must be careful with the evidence. Of these four, two use the plural of σάρξ (i.e., "fleshly parts") and another a derivative of ἀσθένεια (i.e., "weak thing" [ἀσθενής]; 66–68). In the only other use, Eustratius refers to "the soul's being fettered on account of the weakness of the flesh (δι' ἀσθένειαν τῆς σαρκός) if the soul does not do praiseworthy things" (68), which is also clearly not a parallel to Paul. So even at the linguistic level, these parallels are of little relevance for determining the meaning of Paul's phrase one way or the other, and they certainly do not rule out interpreting ἀσθένεια as illness in 4:13 in accordance with one of its common meanings. It is therefore overstating the case to conclude, as Martin does (71n25), that "since no authors before Paul and no non-Christian authors after him use this phrase to refer to illness, exegetes would probably not have either were it not for the link with 2 Cor 12:7." Indeed, Martin suggests that if Paul were referring to his illness in 4:13, this new modification "would have confused the Galatians, who viewed illness as a problem of the body, not of the flesh. They would have found Paul's newly coined phrase a strange and unusual reference to illness" (70). But to be "strange" and "unusual," or even idiosyncratic, is far from being incomprehensible, especially if Paul is following the common linguistic convention in his use of ἀσθένεια as a reference to sickness (Martin, *2 Corinthians*, 66, himself admits that the absolute use of ἀσθένεια is a frequent way to designate illness). Evidently such confusion did not exist in the early church (Martin finds 154 uses in Christian literature!), since from the beginning Christian tradition readily took Gal 4:13 as a parallel to 2 Cor 12:7, and understood both as a reference to Paul's illness (see Heckel, "Dorn," 76–77, 83–85, referring to Tertullian on 2 Cor 12:7, who relies already on oral tradition available to him, and Jerome on the parallel between 2 Cor 12:7 and Gal 4:13)! Hence, while Martin's lexicography demonstrates the unusual nature of Paul's construction, in so doing it merely highlights Paul's idiosyncratic and theologically motivated description of his sickness as that which is located *in his flesh*. And the close parallel between δι' ἀσθένειαν τῆς σαρκὸς in 4:13 and ἐν τῇ σαρκί μου in 4:14 makes it difficult to accept Martin's thesis that the former refers to the Galatians, not Paul, with its implication that verse 13 "no longer informs the interpretation of the succeeding phrase 'your temptation in my flesh' in v. 14" (86; see below).

12. This is the central problem with the thesis of Goddard and Cummins, "Ill or

"Because of Weakness" (Gal 4:13)   121

In Galatians Paul's weakness *grounds* his preaching, whereas persecution is its *consequence*. In addition, Ulrich Heckel has convincingly demonstrated that Paul's parallel reference to his "thorn in the flesh" (σκόλοψ τῇ σαρκί) or "weakness" (ἀσθένεια) in 2 Cor 12:7, 9-10 is also best understood not as a reference to his own inner temptations (as in the Latin tradition) or to persecution by his opponents (first found among the Fathers beginning in the fourth century A.D.), but to Paul's personal sickness.[13] Furthermore, Heckel has argued that Paul's silence concerning the nature of his sickness in 2 Cor 12:7 is intentional. Paul is not interested in the diagnosis of his weakness in a medical sense, but in its theological origin, cause, and purpose.[14] So too, Paul's silence in Gal 4:13-14 concerning the nature of his suffer-

---

Ill-Treated?" that Paul's "weakness" is a reference to some kind of "bodily weakness due to the trauma of persecution" (95), or some kind of "bodily trauma due to persecution which attended his original ministry in Galatia" (125). In their view, Paul is calling the Galatians once again to follow Paul's example of faithfulness in suffering for the sake of the gospel in the line of the suffering righteous and as exemplifying the suffering of Christ (99, 103, 107), rather than join the Judaizers in order to avoid persecution (cf. 6:11). For although they too argue strongly that διά + accusative must provide the ground or reason for Paul's preaching, in order to make their thesis work, they must posit that it also includes not only attendant circumstances, but even consequences of Paul's preaching (103n29). Though there is no doubt that Paul suffered as a regular *consequence* of his preaching, this is simply not Paul's point here. Moreover, even if Paul's persecution were in view here, Paul's persecution cannot be equated with his weakness itself, but must be seen as another source for it. In reality, Goddard and Cummins are not offering another interpretation of 4:13, but another hypothesis for the cause of Paul's weakness, which is hidden in history. Is it also problematic for their view that Paul is not calling the Galatians to suffer persecution (though that might become necessary), but to return to the gospel Paul preached and embodied in his life. Hence, Goddard and Cummins ultimately reject a reference to illness in 4:13 because they fail to see the significance of Paul's suffering as that which embodies and reveals the gospel (see 101, 116; for my view of this significance, see below).

13. Heckel, "Dorn," 66-77, 83-85. Heckel (84) points out that Paul could have already been suffering under the same illness mentioned in 2 Cor 12:7 at the time of Paul's preaching in Galatia, since the "thorn in the flesh" was given to Paul fourteen years earlier, ca. A.D. 42. Contra T. Martin, "Whose Flesh?" 71-73, who, rejecting that 4:13 refers to Paul's weakness, consequently denies the link between Gal 4:13 and 2 Cor 12:7. In addition to his view of 4:13, Martin does so because in 2 Cor 12:7 the messenger of Satan affects Paul, whereas in 4:13 the temptation affects the Galatians; in 2 Cor 12:7 the explanatory phrase refers to the sickness itself, whereas in 4:14 it refers to the effect, and in 2 Cor 12:7 the sickness is a messenger of Satan, whereas the Galatians accept Paul as a messenger of God. For my own analysis of the reason for these differences, see below.

14. Heckel, "Dorn," 80. In view of Paul's silence in 2 Cor 12:7 and elsewhere, all attempts to determine the nature of Paul's sickness remain purely speculative. The main suggestions have been: epilepsy, an eye sickness, a speech impediment, malaria, leprosy, hysteria, or depression (see Heckel, "Dorn," 80-83, for the sources, and 84-92 for his evaluation).

ing demonstrates that the focus is not on the nature of his "weakness of the flesh" as such, but on its very existence and function. Indeed, the frontloading of δι' ἀσθένειαν τῆς σαρκός in 4:13 is most likely not merely stylistic, but emphatic (cf. the corresponding front-loaded position of τὸν πειρασμὸν ὑμῶν ἐν τῇ σαρκί μου in 4:14).

However, in spite of Paul's theological evaluation of his persistent "weakness" in 2 Cor 12:7 and the corresponding development of this theme elsewhere in his letters (see below), most have argued that Gal 4:13 is a reference only to the specific circumstance that led to Paul's being in Galatia. The assumption is that Paul's suffering had either forced Paul into Galatia or caused him to remain in this region longer than planned, during which time he preached the gospel to the Galatians.[15] In this view, Paul's "weakness" was merely the circumstantial means by which God, in his providence, brought the gospel to the Galatians logistically. Black even speaks of Paul's "physical condition that stranded him in Galatia," but "proved to be a blessing in disguise . . . thus accomplishing more than he had originally set out to do."[16]

But to my knowledge there is no evidence in Paul's letters or Acts that Paul's sickness or personal suffering ever influenced his chronology or travel plans. When Paul's plans change it is due either to the needs of others (cf. 2 Cor 1:15—2:4; 2:12-13; Rom 15:22-29), to persecution (cf. 2 Cor 11:32-33; Rom 15:30-33; 1 Thess 2:18), or to divine intervention (cf. 1 Cor 16:9). Moreover, the apologetic function of Paul's suffering elsewhere in his letters speaks against Gal 4:13 being a reference solely to the providential circumstances of his preaching. Rather, as in 2 Cor 12:7-10, Paul's suffering in Gal 4:13 is a matter of theological affirmation and interpretation. But whereas in 2 Cor 12:7-10 Paul relates his weakness to his personal character as a means to an end (see the purpose-clause *inclusio* of 12:7: ἵνα μὴ ὑπεραίρωμαι . . . ἵνα μὴ ὑπεραίρωμαι), in Gal 4:13-14 he relates it to his apostolic mission as a cause to its consequence (δι' ἀσθένειαν τῆς σαρκὸς εὐηγγελισάμην ὑμῖν τὸ πρότερον). In 2 Cor 12:7-10 the focus is on the implication of Paul's weakness for himself, since as an apostle he had been entrusted with private revelations in heaven (cf. 2 Cor 12:7a). In Gal 4:13-14 it is on the implication of Paul's weakness for the Galatians, since as an apostle he had been entrusted with a public revelation of Jesus Christ on the road to Damascus (cf. Gal 1:12, 16). Rather than being an unusual circumstance that occasioned Paul's preaching in Galatia, Paul's "weakness" was the very basis upon which Paul preached everywhere he was sent by God. While the function

---

15. See, e.g., Schlier, *Galater*, 210; Betz, *Galatians*, 84; and Black, "Weakness," 29, 35. Surprisingly, Heckel, "Dorn," 84-85, 91-92, also opts for a circumstantial reading of Gal 4:13-14 in which Paul's sickness held him up in Galatia.

16. Black, "Weakness," 35-36.

of Paul's weakness for himself was a private matter that he discussed only when forced to do so by the circumstances in Corinth, the role his weakness played in his preaching was a public affair well known to the Galatians, as it was everywhere Paul went (cf. 1 Thess 2:1; 1 Cor 4:9–13; Phil 1:12–14, 30; 2 Tim 1:11; 3:11). Instead of being a recourse to emotional, special pleading, Paul's return to his suffering in 4:12–20 is an essential aspect of his polemic.

The contrast established in 4:14 confirms that Paul's weakness was not merely the circumstance that brought the gospel to Galatia, though it may have been that as well. More importantly, Paul's suffering was the divinely ordained means by which the gospel itself was made clear to the Galatians. Given the cultural assumption of Paul's day that a deity's approval meant earthly blessing, and inasmuch as the desire for health, wealth, and status was the driving motive for participation in the Greco-Roman civic cults, Paul's suffering posed an immense barrier to his gospel.[17] And Ernst Baasland has pointed out the conceptual link between Paul's suffering as a "temptation" (πειρασμός) to despise Paul (4:14) and the Old Testament "curse" tradition that made a link between sin and suffering, of which "the most convincing evidence is found in the אָרוּר catalogue in Deut 27:15–26; 28:16–19," based on the warnings of Deut 27:26; 28:15.[18] The allusion to this Old Testament curse tradition in 4:14 no doubt reflects Paul's having taught it to the Galatians in order to explain the role of Christ's suffering in taking upon himself God's curse on sin (cf. Deut 27:26 in Gal 3:10 and Deut 21:23 in 3:13), as well as explaining his own willingness to suffer for the gospel as

17. For an investigation of the broad cultural values current in first-century Greco-Roman society, see Savage, *Power through Weakness*, 19–53. Contra T. Martin, "Whose Flesh?" 78, 87–90, who, in view of Gal 6:13, construes the temptation in 4:14 to be the fact that Paul himself was circumcised, since Gentiles disdained the practice. It is difficult to see how this could have tempted the Galatians to reject Paul, since a hallmark of his gospel was its explicit exclusion of the necessity of such "works of the law" (Gal 2:3–5, 16, 18; 3:2–5; 5:3–6; 6:12–15). Moreover, this reading of 4:14 does not fit as well with the argument of 4:12 and 15: if they were tempted to disdain Paul as a circumcised male, then in what sense are they to become like him?—to be circumcised but to ignore its significance? If what potentially offended the Galatians was Paul's circumcision, was this the stumbling block with Christ too (rather than the cross?), since Paul equates accepting him with accepting Christ? And would not Paul's emphasis here on their acceptance of Paul and Jesus as circumcised males play into the hands of the Judaizers? Moreover, Martin's position entails viewing the problem in Galatia to be the Galatians' desire to return to paganism rather than submitting to the Judaizers' demand for circumcision (which they now see to be a legitimate part of the Christian message), in contrast to the prevailing view that the problem was their being persuaded to join the Judaizers themselves (see T. Martin, "Apostasy," 437–61). Finally, Martin's reading finds no thematic support in the immediate context, which is based on the curse tradition from Deuteronomy (see below), not the issue of circumcision.

18. Baasland, "Persecution," 141.

a display of the sufferings of Christ (4:13-14). Neither Christ nor Paul (in this regard) is suffering for his own sins, but each is willingly taking up the cross for the sake of others. For Christ, this suffering was the centre of his calling as the messianic Son of God who was sent to atone for the sins of God's people. For Paul, it was the centre of his calling as an apostle, through whom the gospel of Christ was being mediated to the Gentiles (see below).

In theological hindsight, Paul's reminder in 4:14 therefore takes on great polemic significance within the contemporary context in Galatia: Paul's reference in 3:10 to Deut 27:26 (28:15) as an essential aspect of his dispute with the Judaizers points to the likely inference that they were probably now using this same tradition *against* Paul, arguing from Paul's own suffering that *he* was the one who was still under the curse of the law, not they. From their perspective, Paul's suffering was evidence that God's judgment or curse had fallen upon Paul for his failing to keep the Sinai covenant (cf. his fivefold punishment as a transgressor by the synagogue in accordance with Deut 25:1-3 [2 Cor 11:24]).[19] As in Corinth, in Galatia too Paul's suffering was being used to question the legitimacy of his ministry and message.

Nevertheless, although both Christ's death on the cross and Paul's weakness had initially posed a cultural and theological temptation to the Galatians, they had not rejected Paul's weakness out of contempt (ἐξουθενήσατε), nor disdained it (ἐξεπτύσατε[20]), but had rather received Paul "as an angel of God" (Gal 4:14). Given the contrast between the Galatians' refusal to reject Paul out of contempt and their acceptance of him as an "angel of God" (ἄγγελον θεοῦ), Paul's use of ἐκπτύω most likely signifies more than simply the transferred metaphorical meaning of "disdain."[21] It is best taken as a concrete reference to the practice of "spitting out" that signaled

---

19. So too ibid., 142. As Baasland points out, Paul's failure to require circumcision of his converts could be taken as "cursing Abraham," which results in falling under the curse of God (cf. Gen 12:3).

20. See s.v. ἐκπτύω, BDAG, 309: literally, "*spit* (out) as an expression of contempt . . . or to ward off hostile spirits . . . hence *disdain*"; and s.v. ἐξουθενέω, BDAG, 352, which suggests that, since the meaning "reject something" is well attested for both διαπτύω and περιπτύω, Gal 4:14 may be translated, "You neither treated me with contempt nor did you turn away from the temptation that my physical appearance might have become to you."

21. Contra Goddard and Cummins, "Ill or Ill-Treated?," 105-7, and T. Martin, "Whose Flesh?" 75, who, in line with their respective views of 4:13, take ἐκπτύω and ἐξουθενέω simply to be synonyms for scorn and disdain (cf. their use in Mark 9:12; 10:34; 14:65; Matt 26:27; Luke 18:32; 23:11; Acts 4:11; 1 Cor 1:28; 6:4; 16:11; Rom 14:3, 10, etc.).

the repulsion of sickness as a demonic threat.²² If so, then Paul's point is that when he first came to them the Galatians did not attribute Paul's weakness to demonic activity (i.e., he was not an ἄγγελος Σατανᾶς disguised as an ἄγγελος φωτός; cf. 2 Cor 11:14), but accepted it as the very basis of Paul's ministry as a messenger sent from God. In this light, the contrast between 2 Cor 12:7 and Gal 4:13 is maintained here as well: whereas in 2 Cor 12:7 Paul's weakness is explicitly attributed to Satan's "angel" (ἄγγελος) and hence may be resisted and prayed against, in Gal 4:14 Paul's weakness was the basis upon which God was speaking through Paul as if he were an "angel" sent to do God's bidding. Rather than falling prey to the temptation to reject Paul and his message because of his suffering, the Galatians saw the essential link between the two and had accepted Paul's life as an embodiment of the divinely authorized gospel that he preached. To quote Baasland again, "Paul insists that his sufferings are not the result of a curse, but they show that he belongs to Christ,"²³ who redeemed him from that very curse (3:13; 4:5).

The reason for the Galatians' earlier acceptance of Paul, in spite of his weakness, is given in the further appositional designation of verse 14c: ὡς Χριστὸν Ἰησοῦν. When Paul preached the gospel because of his suffering, the Galatians accepted him not only as if he were an angel sent from God, but as if he were Christ Jesus himself! This identification of the suffering Paul with Christ is best explained in view of the *missiological* (not ontological) identity between Paul's own suffering as an apostle and the cross of Christ that made up an essential aspect of Paul's early preaching among the Galatians. Paul's suffering was the instrument by which he "publicly portrayed" the crucified Christ "before [the Galatians'] eyes" (Gal 3:1).²⁴

In Gal 3:1 and 4:14 Paul is therefore alluding to a complex of ideas that he explicates in detail in 1 Cor 4:6–16; 2 Cor 1:3–11; 2:14–17; 4:7–12; 6:3–10; and 12:1–10. I have argued in the chapters above that in these passages Paul portrays his apostolic suffering as the revelatory vehicle through which the knowledge of God as made manifest in the cross of Christ and in the

---

22. See Schlier, "ἐκπτύω," 448–49, who is quite certain that this is its meaning here. So too Heckel, "Dorn," 84: "Für die Galater muß daher die Versuchung nahegelegen haben, in Paulus wegen seiner Schwäche einen dämonisch Befallenen zu sehen." Cf. Mark 7:33; 8:23; *T. Sol.* 7:3 and the references in Heckel, "Dorn," 85–86nn121–27.

23. Baasland, "Persecution," 146. The implication of this identification has already been given in the countercurse of Gal 1:8!

24. Here we are more emphatic than Goddard and Cummins, "Ill or Ill-Treated?" 110n62, who suggest that "the vivid and visual (rather than aural) language" of Gal 3:1 "might possibly suggest that Paul *himself* tangibly represented the crucified Christ before the Galatians—not least in the marks of persecution upon his body (cf. 6:17)" (emphasis theirs).

power of the Spirit is being disclosed.[25] The clearest direct statements of this point are found in the thesis-like affirmations of 1 Cor 4:9; 2 Cor 1:9-10; 4:10-11; 6:3-10; 12:9-10; and, by way of metaphor, 2 Cor 2:14.[26] In these passages Paul's suffering, as the corollary to his message of the cross, is the very instrument God uses to display his resurrection power (cf. too 1 Cor 2:2-5; 1 Thess 1:5). This revelation takes place either by God's rescuing Paul from adversity when it was too much to bear, as in 2 Cor 1:8-11 and Phil 2:25-30, or by the even-more-glorious means of God's strengthening Paul in the midst of adversity that he may endure his suffering with thanksgiving to the glory of God (cf. 2 Cor 4:7-12; 6:3-10; 12:9; 2 Tim 2:10).

---

25. For this thesis, with 2 Cor 2:14 as its centerpiece, see in addition to chapters 3-5 above my *Suffering and the Spirit*, slightly abridged as *Suffering and Ministry*. For the similarities and differences between 1 Cor 4:8-13 and 2 Cor 4:7-12 as these reflect the essential difference between the situations behind the two letters, together with the parallels between 1 Cor 4:9; 2 Cor 2:14; and 4:11 outlined below, see my *Suffering and the Spirit*, 65-76.

26. Though Paul's allusion to the Roman triumphal procession in 2 Cor 2:14 is widely granted, not all have agreed with me that the metaphor of "being led in a triumphal procession" (θριαμβεύω) should be decoded to picture Paul as a captured slave of Christ who is being led to *death* in Christ by God as the means by which the knowledge of God is being made known in the world. But the structural and semantic parallels between 1 Cor 4:9; 2 Cor 2:14; and 4:11 continue to convince me of my reading (see below). Furthermore, in the other passages within the Corinthian correspondence in which Paul discusses his experiences as an apostle, it is evident that for Paul "death" is a metonym for suffering (1 Cor 4:8-13 [cf. 4:9]; 2 Cor 1:3-11 [cf. 1:9]; 4:7-12 [cf. 4:10]; 6:3-10 [cf. 6:9]). For the two most substantive criticisms of my proposal, see Schröter, *Versöhner*, and Scott, "Triumph." But neither Schröter nor Scott deal seriously with the exact parallels between 1 Cor 4:9; 2 Cor 2:14; and 4:11 that support my reading. What is significant about these texts is that in 1 Cor 4:9 and 2 Cor 4:11 Paul is explicitly discussing the role of his *suffering* as an apostle in his ministry of the gospel, not merely his role in preaching the gospel *per se* (*à la* Schröter), nor his mystical experiences (*à la* Scott). Moreover, my view does most justice to its immediate context by explaining the transition from Paul's concern over Titus in 2:12-13 to his praise for God in 2:14. Finally, one must ask what the metaphor contributes materially to the discussion at hand. In Schröter's view, the metaphor becomes redundant, since the motif of revelation is already explicitly mentioned in the verse (see φανεροῦντι). In Scott's view, the metaphor contributes something unique to the text, since there is no other referent in the context to Paul's visionary experiences as the basis of his revelatory function. In fact, in 2 Cor 12:1-9 Paul explicitly denies that such personal and ecstatic visions of God's glory are the basis or subject of what we communicate to others. So in the first case, Schröter's view says too little. In the latter case, Scott's view says too much.

PAUL'S LIFE OF SUFFERING AS AN EMBODIMENT OF THE GOSPEL

In 2 Cor 4:7 Paul unpacks in a vivid way the identity between his suffering and the gospel of Christ affirmed in Gal 4:13–14 by reminding the Corinthians that he carried his gospel "treasure"—that is, "the knowledge of the glory of God in the face of Christ" (2 Cor 4:6)—in a "jar of clay," namely, in his sick and persecution-plagued body.[27] This is God's design in order to make it evident that the power of the gospel did not reside in Paul, but belonged to the God who was at work in and through Paul to reveal himself and to deliver his people (4:7b). The power of the gospel Paul preaches is so potent and its glory so great that it must be carried in a "pot," lest people put their trust in Paul himself (cf. 1 Cor 2:1–5). For although the purpose clause in 2 Cor 4:7b is often translated with the idea of "making manifest" or "demonstrating," formally it reads, "in order that the all-surpassing power might *be* (ᾖ) from God and not from us." As Savage points out, if we take the verb, "to be," seriously in this text, then Paul's point is even more striking: "it is only in weakness that the power may *be* of God, that [Paul's] weakness in some sense actually serves as the *grounds* for divine power."[28] When understood in this way, the parallels to 2 Cor 12:1–10, where this point is applied to Paul himself (Paul's "earthen vessel" keeps him humble and dependent on God), and to Gal 4:13, where it is applied to his public ministry (Paul's earthen vessel is a platform for preaching the gospel to others), are clear. Paul therefore goes on to use the categories of Jesus's death and resurrection in 2 Cor 4:10–11 to interpret his experience of suffering and sustenance from 2 Cor 4:8–9 because he is convinced that his experience mediates to the world the knowledge of God revealed in Christ. Yet 2 Cor 4:10–11 also makes clear

---

27. As Savage, *Power through Weakness*, 165, has pointed out, the idea of picturing humans as "jars of clay" ("earthen vessels") was common in the ancient world, including the Qumran writings, as a metaphor for human weakness (cf. the references to clay pots as weak and prone to break in Ps 30:13LXX; Isa 30:14LXX; and in 1QS 11:22; 1QH 9:23–24; 11:21–22; 12:30, etc. [The column/line numbering for 1QH here follows the new reconstruction found in DJD 40]). Read in this way, Paul's image points to a contrast between his own suffering and the power of God. Others, however, see it as metaphor of "cheapness," based on Lam 4:2LXX, thus establishing a contrast between Paul's lack of significance or worth and the surpassing value of the treasure. Some argue that both ideas of being "weak" and "inferior" are present here (as in Lev 6:21; 15:12LXX), so that 4:7 provides a contrast to both the "treasure" and the "power of God." In Savage's words, "the glorious gospel is borne about by those who are comparatively inferior, the powerful gospel by those who are weak" (66). This reading is possible, but the purpose clause in verse 7b seems to indicate that the point of contrast is God's power, and hence the intention of the image is to highlight the weakness of Paul.

28. Ibid., 166 (emphasis mine).

that Paul's suffering and his experience of God's deliverance are both always derivative, since Jesus's death and resurrection, not Paul's own love and fortitude, provide the pattern for Paul's experience and the content of what is mediated to others. Paul's endurance of faith in the midst of suffering is not a "second atonement," but a mediation of the reality and significance of the death (cross) and life (resurrection) of Jesus. In his preaching and suffering, Paul stands between the glory of God and the life of his congregation as an instrument in the hand of God to mediate the life of faith among God's people. As such, Paul's sufferings are not coincidental, but part of the divine plan for the spread of the gospel (cf. the "divine passive" in 4:11).

Just as Christ suffered and died to atone for the sins of his people in order to deliver them from the power of this present evil age (Gal 1:4), so too Paul is called as an apostle to "die every day" (1 Cor 15:31) as a means by which the significance of the cross is made real to those to whom the gospel is preached (Gal 4:13–14). Paul's willingness to suffer on behalf of his churches reflects and embodies Christ's willingness to consider the need of God's people for salvation more important than his own position in glory (cf. Phil 2:3–5 as supported by 2:6–11). The foolishness of Paul's "weakness" as a Spirit-filled apostle is the platform upon which God portrays the foolishness of the crucified Christ as the Son of God. Conversely, Paul's endurance in the midst of his suffering is the vehicle by which God displays the reality of the power of the resurrection. Thus, as the "aroma of Christ" (2 Cor 2:15), Paul's suffering embodies and extends the same twofold effect brought about by the cross of Christ itself. This is confirmed by the parallels between 1 Cor 1:17–18 and 2 Cor 2:14–16a:

1. Paul is sent to preach in a mode that corresponds to the cross of Christ (1:17)	1. Paul is "being led to death," which is a mode of existence that reveals the cross of Christ (2:14)
2. For (γάρ) (18a)	2. For (ὅτι) (15a)
3. the word of the cross (18a)	3. we are an aroma of Christ to God (15)
4. is foolishness to those who are perishing (18b)	4. among those who are perishing . . . to those a fragrance from death to death (15c, 16a)
5. to us who are being saved it is the power of God (18c)	5. among those who are being saved . . . to those a fragrance from life to life (15b, 16a)

Both the manner of Paul's life and the content of his message were determined by the cross of Christ. Due to its cruciform nature, Paul's ministry functioned to further the process of salvation ("life") and judgment ("death") in the lives of others. To reject Paul and his message of the cross as "foolishness" (1 Cor 1:18) or "cursed" (Gal 4:14) confirmed that one was already "perishing." To accept Paul and his message demonstrated that the power of God was already at work to save.

THE APOLOGETIC FUNCTION OF PAUL'S SUFFERING

We can now see why in Gal 4:12–20 Paul suddenly shifted from the theological and scriptural arguments in favor of his gospel to the personal circumstances of his suffering. The latter, no less than the former, provided a foundation for his past preaching in Galatia and for his present polemic against those who would preach a different gospel (cf. 1:6–9). Like Christ on the cross, Paul's coming to Galatia in the "weakness of the flesh" portrayed Christ's own participation in this evil age. But as a manifestation of the "new creation" inaugurated at Christ's resurrection, Paul's endurance and giving of himself to the Galatians demonstrated that already in this age the Spirit is powerfully transforming the lives of believers (cf. Gal 5:2–6, 16–26; 6:8, 15). This reality is reflected at this point in the structure of Paul's argument. The recounting in 4:13–14 of the Galatians' prior positive response to Paul's preaching, in spite of his weakness, serves a bilateral, bridging function between 4:12 and 4:15–16. Looking back, it supports Paul's assertion in 4:12c that the Galatians had done Paul no injustice in the past (οὐδέν με ἠδικήσατε). Rather, they had accepted his suffering as the ground of his preaching, since it was the means by which the significance of the cross was made evident in their midst. Looking forward, it supports Paul's rhetorical questions in 4:15a–16 concerning the present. Given their past acceptance of him "as an angel of God" who brought the message of "Christ Jesus," Paul is perplexed (4:20; cf. 1:6) that their past "blessing" (μακαρισμός), which they received from doing so, has apparently disappeared (4:15a). Instead, he has become their "enemy" for telling them the truth about those who are seeking to exclude the Galatians from being fully fledged members of the people of God (4:17). Paul's real goal, however, like a woman in travail, is to make sure that they stay alive to the gospel until they can mature enough in Christ to avoid such temptations (4:19, τέκνα μου . . . ὠδίνω; cf. 1:6–9; 5:7–8).

The structure of Paul's argument in 4:12–16 makes it apparent that Paul's reference in 4:15b to the Galatians' past willingness to pluck out their own eyes on Paul's behalf does not reflect the nature of his "weakness" as some sort of eye infirmity.²⁹ Rather, it is best taken to be a proverbial reference to the Galatians' past willingness to do whatever was necessary to support Paul's ministry. The Galatians had been so convinced of the gospel of the cross, and had so esteemed their consequent participation in the Spirit as *the* mark of the new age of the new creation under the new covenant (cf. Gal 1:6a; 3:3a, 4a; 4:6–7, 9a; 5:5, 7a), that they would have been willing to give up even their most precious possession, their "eyes," in exchange if need be.³⁰ Conversely, both Paul's preaching on the basis of his suffering and the Galatians' acceptance of it confirmed that the new age had in fact dawned and that the Galatians, like Paul, were indeed participating in it. Nothing else could adequately explain why Paul suffers as he does, both personally (2 Cor 12:7) and vocationally (Gal 4:13, etc.), and why he would be willing to live like a Gentile, all for the sake of the gospel (4:12a; cf. 1 Cor 9:21). Likewise, the Galatians' willingness to give their all for Paul is an example of precisely that "faith working itself out in love" which can only be attributed to the Spirit's work of bringing about a new creation (cf. 5:5–6). In other words, Paul's love for the Galatians, manifested in his suffering, and the Galatians' love for Paul, manifested in their acceptance of his suffering, are both expressions of a Spirit-induced freedom to serve one another as slaves (5:13; cf. Rom 15:7–9). In stark contrast, the Judaizers' attempt to exclude the Galatians reveals their own rejection of the gospel, lack of participation in the Spirit, and corresponding impure motives (4:17–18; cf. 2:13; 6:12). By way of implication, if the Galatians capitulate to their demands, they will be denying the reality of their earlier "blessing" of the Spirit as the children of Abraham (4:15a; cf. 3:1–5; 5:2–5), and Paul's labor will have been in vain (4:11; cf. 2:2).

---

29. Cf. already Lightfoot, *Galatians*, 301, who followed Theodore of Mopsuestia in arguing that the reference to writing with "large letters" in Gal 6:11 is not a consequence of Paul's bad eyesight, but a way of emphasizing "the force of the apostle's convictions" in that they will "arrest the attention of his readers in spite of themselves."

30. For the expression "to pluck out the eyes" as a reference to making the ultimate sacrifice, see Black, "Weakness," 32–33, who points, e.g., to Deut 32:10; Ps 17:8; Prov 7:2; Zech 2:8; and Horace, *Sat.* ii.5, 33, following the commentaries of Eadie and Andre Viard. Cf. Goddard and Cummins, "Ill or Ill-Treated?" 111n67, who also point to this background. The difficulty of applying this insight to their overall thesis is illustrated by their attempt (112–13) to go on to argue that this metaphor is an actual reference to the gouging out of the eyes as one of the cruelest tortures inflicted on the persecuted (see the experience of the martyrs in 4 Macc 5:29–30). As such, Paul is speaking of the Galatians' earlier willingness to suffer with Paul and for the gospel. The problem with this view is that the Galatians were willing to pluck out their *own* eyes for Paul's sake, which can hardly mean a willingness to persecute themselves.

BAPTISM ON BEHALF OF THE DEAD

Paul's argument in Gal 4:12–20 exemplifies again that the glue which united Paul's thought and life with the message he preached and the mission he conducted was his suffering as an apostle of Jesus Christ. Paul's suffering was the vehicle through which the saving power of God, climactically revealed in Christ, was being made known in the world. To reject the suffering Paul was therefore to reject Christ; to identify with Paul in his suffering was a sure sign that one was being saved by the "foolishness" and "stumbling-block" of the cross. For as Joel White has demonstrated, "to be baptized on behalf of the dead" (1 Cor 15:29) is not an *ad hominem* allusion to some long-lost cultic ritual.[31] Instead, it is a reference to the convert's identification with Paul's ministry as an apostle, which is once again pictured in terms of "death" as a metonym for the daily suffering that Paul endures in hope of the resurrection and the final reign of God in Christ (see 1 Cor 15:28, 30–32). In Paul's words, "For what will those do who are being baptized on account of the 'dead' [i.e., in response to the ministry of the apostles who suffer for the sake of the gospel]? If the truly dead are not being raised, why then are people being baptized on account of them [i.e., on account of the apostles, since their gospel offers no hope]?" (1 Cor 15:29).[32] Paul would not willingly suffer, and the Corinthian believers would not have accepted his suffering as legitimate, having been baptized as a result, were it not for the truth of Paul's gospel. To do so otherwise would be ludicrous. The same is true for the Galatians. Like the Corinthians, they too cannot deny that Paul, in and through his suffering, was indeed their father in the faith (1 Cor 3:5; 4:15; Gal 1:6–9; 3:1–2; 4:13). So they should not go back on Paul's gospel now. In short, 1 Cor 15:29 represents the same argument found in Gal 4:13–14.

In the end, if it is no longer adequate to speak of Paul as *either* a theologian *or* a missionary, it is also not adequate to speak of him as a theologian *and* a missionary. Paul's apostolic ministry of missionary suffering and his gospel theology were an inseparable unity. Hence, our study confirms what Peter O'Brien, himself a missionary-theologian like Paul, has observed regarding the fact that, although there has been a "paradigm shift" since the 1960s and

---

31. White, "Baptized," 488–91.

32. See ibid., 493–99. White argues that οἱ βαπτιζόμενοι is to be taken literally, ὑπέρ is to be understood in its causal sense, τῶν νεκρῶν is to be taken metaphorically as a reference to the apostles, and νεκροί refers to the literal dead, modified by ὅλως (i.e., "truly dead persons").

the notion that Paul was both a missionary and a theologian has gained ground among biblical scholars . . . yet Paul's theology and mission do not simply relate to each other as "theory" to "practice." It is not as though his mission is the practical outworking of his theology. Rather, his mission is "integrally related to his identity and thought," and his theology is a missionary theology.[33]

Paul was a theologically driven missionary and a missiologically driven theologian. His theology was missiological and his missionary endeavors were theological. May Paul's gospel of the crucified and risen Christ and his willingness to embody it through his own endurance of suffering on behalf of others be our "consuming passion" as well.

---

33. O'Brien, *Consumed by Passion*, xi–xii.

9

Pastoral Suffering

Recovering Paul's Model of Ministry in 2 Corinthians[1]

Though there are exceptions, the contemporary landscape of American evangelical churches is flat. Instead of rising above their surroundings, worship is anemic, filled with emotion but little life-changing gravity. Discipleship is wrongheaded, focusing on meeting the felt needs of the self, with little regard for meeting the real need to know God more profoundly. Goals are idolatrous, deriving from a health-and-wealth gospel of family life, social status, and retirement, with little thought of laying down our lives for the sake of the kingdom. For as David Wells rightly says, "The fundamental problem in the evangelical world today is that God rests too inconsequential upon the Church. His truth is too distant, his grace is too ordinary, his judgment is too benign, his gospel is too easy, and his Christ is too common."[2]

One of the central reasons we find ourselves in this crisis is that our pastoral leadership no longer has a clear conception of its calling. In place of the biblical portrait of the pastor as a shepherd who embodies the gospel by laying down his life for God's people, we have substituted models of the pastor as a teddy bear, CEO, coach, or therapist. The pastor has become

---

1. This essay is adapted from my work on 2 Corinthians as presented in my *2 Corinthians*. Now from Scott J. Hafemann, "A Call to Pastoral Suffering: The Need for Recovering Paul's Model of Ministry in 2 Corinthians." *SBJT* 4/2 (2000) 22–36. For a more detailed substantiation and development of these points and their application, see my *2 Corinthians*. If not otherwise indicated, Scripture references are to 2 Corinthians.

2. Wells, *God in the Wasteland*, 30.

someone who dispenses comfort without the cross, who "manages" the church rather than models Christ, and who helps us feel good about ourselves by giving "advice" rather than mediating the glory of God revealed in his Word. It is easy to see why this is the case, given the powerful cultural forces that are at work behind the contemporary redefinition of the pastoral office. As Hauerwas and Willimon insightfully point out,

> One can readily understand why pastors are so ready to take up the general description of being one of the "helping professions." After all, most of us professing Christians, from the liberals to the fundamentalists, remain practical atheists in most of our lives. This is so because we think the church is sustained by the "services" it provides or the amount of "fellowship" and "good feeling" in the congregation. Of course there is nothing wrong with "services" and "good feeling"; what is wrong is that they have become ends in themselves. When that happens the church and the ministry cannot avoid sentimentality, which we believe is the most detrimental corruption of the church today.
> Sentimentality, after all, is but the way our unbelief is lived out. Sentimentality, that attitude of being always ready to understand but not to judge, corrupts us and the ministry. This is as true of conservative churches as it is of liberal.... Without God, without the One whose death on the cross challenges all our "good feelings," who stands beyond and over against our human anxieties, all we have left is sentiment, the saccharine residue of theism in demise.[3]

WE ARE CORINTHIANS

This reconfiguration of the pastor is nothing new. Timothy Savage has shown that in Paul's day Greco-Roman society also stressed (1) a rugged individualism that valued self-sufficiency, (2) wealth as the key to one's status within society, (3) a self-display of one's accomplishments and possessions in order to win praise from others, (4) a competition for honor that viewed boasting as its natural corollary, and (5) a pride in one's neighborhood as a reflection of one's social location.[4] These values combined to create a populace for which self-appreciation became the goal and self-gratification the reward. Moreover, all of this was fueled by a drive for upward social mobility by advancing economically. For with wealth came other

---

3. Hauerwas and Willimon, *Resident Aliens*, 120–21.
4. Savage, *Power through Weakness*, 19–53.

significant markers of social advancement, such as reputation, occupation, neighborhood, education, religious status, political involvement, and athletic achievement. In short, the culture was openly materialistic in its quest for praise and esteem.

In such a milieu, the vast majority of religious people had no interest in theology. Their religion had little content, apart from the rituals needed to influence the deity. Consequently, the various cults and temples seldom clashed, since experience, not confession, drove religion. Since all religious experience was fundamentally equal, toleration was practiced. Most people, regardless of what religion they practiced, sought deliverance from suffering, power in daily life, and entertainment. As a group, first-century worshippers, regardless of their religious affiliation, wanted "health, wealth, protection, and sustenance, not moral transformation."[5] Religious services, like other social gatherings, were simply ways to gain fellowship, especially as they revolved around lavish banquets. Indeed, regardless of one's religion of choice, "the cults seemed to exact little appreciable change in a convert's manner of life . . . religion served not as a critic of, but as a warrant for, society. It uplifted, entertained, prospered and confirmed those it was designated to serve."[6]

As children of this culture, the Corinthians were easy prey for Paul's opponents. After all, his opponents came with flashy and entertaining rhetorical power, a track record of "success" in other churches testified to by letters of recommendation, and a stress on signs and wonders. Moreover, they promised "more" of the Spirit to those who would show their sincerity by giving them money!

THE ANTIDOTE TO PRACTICAL ATHEISM: A SUFFERING APOSTLE

As the antidote to this atheism of sentimentality, with its implicit health-and-wealth gospel driven by materialism and a search for social status, God sent Paul to suffer as an apostle of the crucified Christ, carrying his treasure in a "jar of clay" (4:7). Paul did not represent Christ, embody the gospel he preached, or mediate the power of the Spirit through great displays of rhetorical power, political savvy, and personal strength, but by *suffering* (cf.

---

5. Ibid., 34. The point of the cults was not based on the doctrine of the religion. As Savage puts it, "It mattered little who the gods were or what the cults taught. What was important was . . . whether everyday desires for health, wealth and safety and, more importantly, power and esteem, were being fulfilled" (52).

6. Ibid., 34.

Acts 9:16; 1 Cor 2:1-5). In calling Paul to be a minister of the new covenant (2 Cor 3:4-6), God sentenced Paul to *death* (2 Cor 1:9; cf. 1 Cor 4:9). Or in the words of Paul in 2 Cor 2:14, God was "*always* leading us *to death* in Christ like a prisoner in a Roman triumphal procession." As he said elsewhere, "I *die* every day" (1 Cor 15:31).

Paul's point is as simple as it is profound. Rather than calling his sufficiency into question, Paul's suffering, pictured under the metonym of "death," is the revelatory vehicle through which the knowledge of God, manifest in the cross of Christ and in the power of the Spirit, is disclosed (cf. 1:3-11; 2:14-17; 4:7-12; 6:3-10; 11:23b-33; 12:9-10; 13:4). God uses Paul's suffering,[7] an embodiment of the crucified Christ, as the instrument to display his resurrection power (cf. too 1 Cor 2:2-5; 4:9; 1 Thess 1:5). This revelation took place in two ways. Occasionally, God rescued Paul from adversity when it was overwhelming, as in 2 Cor 1:8-11 (cf. Phil 2:25-30). More often, however, God used these prior acts of deliverance to strengthen Paul's faith so that he might *endure* his suffering *with thanksgiving to the glory of God* (4:7-12; 6:3-10; 12:9; 13:4; cf. 2 Tim 2:10).

These texts illustrate that Paul's call to suffer as an apostle was theological, that is, it was the means by which God made his love and power known in the world *for the proclamation and praise of his glory* (1:3, 11, 20; 3:8-11; 4:4-6; 4:15; 9:11-15). If Paul's suffering is the means of God's self-revelation, then the manifestation of God's glory is its ultimate goal. Moreover, Paul affirms that whenever God's people, by trusting in God's love, power, and promises, endure the same sufferings to which he was called as an apostle, they too manifest the power and glory of God in the midst of their adversity (1:7).

Since the praise of God's glory is his ultimate purpose, God's goal in suffering is to teach his people that, in life and in death (as in all eternity), God himself is all they ultimately need. God never intends to destroy his people, nor will he allow anyone or anything else to do so. Nor can anything separate them from the love of God in Christ (Rom 8:31-39). In placing Paul in a situation in which he despaired even of life itself (1:8), the only

---

7. The words Paul chose to refer to his troubles in 2 Cor 1:3-11, θλῖψις and πάθημα, are general terms that could signify both physical and emotional distress, as well as the suffering caused by persecution. Paul's full-orbed definition of "suffering" speaks against those who, whether in Paul's day or our own, have attempted to limit the kinds of suffering that can legitimately be experienced by those who are filled with the Spirit. Indeed, Paul's own experiences of physical suffering, persecution, natural deprivations, economic hardships, and the emotional distress of anxiety make such a limitation impossible (see 1 Cor 4:11-13; 2 Cor 2:12-13, 17; 4:8-9; 6:4-10; 11:23-28; 12:7; Gal 4:12-16).

thing God destroyed was Paul's self-confidence. In return, Paul received God himself. In response, Paul gave God praise.

In the three thesis statements of 1 Cor 4:9; 2 Cor 2:14; and 4:11, Paul therefore gives the *theo*logical basis for his conviction that his suffering, like the "death of Jesus," mediates the resurrection power of God—that is, the "life of Jesus." Paul asserts that his sufferings are not merely coincidental, but are part of the divine plan for the spread of the gospel, since God's power is expressed *through* Paul's weakness. Moreover, with the cross of Christ as its backdrop, these passages portray Paul's suffering under the imagery of "death." In two of the passages this is done by means of a metaphor (1 Cor 4:9: being sentenced to death in the arena; 2 Cor 2:14: being led to death in the triumphal procession). In 2 Cor 4:11 Paul explicitly associates his suffering with the death of Jesus itself. In each case, Paul views his suffering to be a divinely orchestrated "death" that, like the cross of Christ, performs a revelatory function.

2 Cor 4:11a	2 Cor 2:14a	1 Cor 4:9a
1. Divine Passive	1. Thanks be to God	1. God
2. Constantly (cf. "always" in v. 10a)	2. always	2. (cf. "until the present hour," v. 11, and "until now," v. 13)
3. we the living	3. us	3. us apostles
4. are being handed over to death	4. leads us in a triumphal procession to death	4. exhibited last of all as those sentenced to death
5. on account of Christ	5. in Christ	5. (cf. "on account of Christ," v. 10)

2 Cor 4:11b	2 Cor 2:14b	1 Cor 4:9b
1. in order that the life of Jesus might be revealed	1. and reveals the fragrance of the knowledge of him	1. because we became a spectacle
2. in our mortal flesh	2. through us	2. ---
3. ---	3. in every place	3. to the world, that is, to angels and to men

These parallels make manifest that Paul's message and manner of life were one. For this reason, Paul could say about himself the same thing he said about the gospel. In accord with this identity, the additional parallels between 1 Cor 1:17–18 and 2 Cor 2:14–16a make clear that as the "aroma of Christ." Paul's *suffering* also brings about the same twofold effect caused by his *proclamation* of the cross of Christ!

1. Paul is sent to preach in a mode that corresponds to the cross of Christ (1:17; cf. 2:1, 4)	1. Paul is "being led to death," which is a mode of existence that reveals the cross of Christ (2:14)
2. For (γάρ) (18a)	2. For (ὅτι) (15a)
3. the word of the cross	3. we are an aroma of Christ to God (15a)
4. is foolishness to those who are perishing (18a)	4. among those who are perishing . . . to those a fragrance from death to death (15c, 16a)
5. to us who are being saved it is the power of God (18c)	5. among those who are being saved . . . to those a fragrance from life to life (15b, 16b)

For Paul, the cross of Christ determined *both* the manner of his life *and* the content of his message. Paul recognized as a result that his life and ministry functioned to further the process of salvation ("life") and judgment ("death") in the lives of others. To reject Paul and his message as "foolishness" was a confirmation that one was already "perishing." To accept Paul and his message was a demonstration that the power of God was already at work to save.

THE MESSAGE OF THE GOSPEL IN THE LIFE OF THE APOSTLE

In Asia, God brought Paul to what Paul thought was the end of his life and then delivered him from his adversity (1:10a) *in order that* (note the ἵνα + subjunctive in 2 Cor 1:9) from then on Paul would not rely on himself, but only "on God, who raises the dead." This replay of Christ's "death" and "resurrection" in Paul's life led Paul to be confident that God could be trusted to deliver him in the future (1:10–11a). In both cases, the experiences of Christ and Paul became "video clip" illustrations of God's trustworthy purposes, power, and promises. From the experience of Christ and the apostle, God's people are to be comforted by knowing that what God did for Christ and Paul, he will do for them as well if they follow in their footsteps of faith (1:6–7).

The series of four adversative contrasts in 2 Cor 4:8–9 then illustrate *how* this divine power comes to expression in Paul's life:

The dying of Jesus	The life of Jesus
hard pressed	but not crushed
perplexed	but not in despair
persecuted	but not abandoned
struck down	but not destroyed

In spite of Paul's being "hard pressed," *nevertheless* he is not "crushed"; he is "perplexed, *but* not in despair," etc. Together these adversatives picture through the experience of suffering and sustenance the way in which Paul mediates the knowledge of God to the world by embodying Jesus's death and resurrection. Given Paul's weakness, his perseverance in the midst of these adversities can only be attributed to God's resurrection power. These four contrasts confirm experientially that the "power" manifested in the "treasure" of the gospel ministry must belong to God (2 Cor 4:7).

Moreover, the verb translated "[not] in despair" in 2 Cor 4:8 (ἐξαπορούμενοι) is the same word found earlier in 2 Cor 1:8, where Paul recounts that in the past he *did* despair of his life. The transition from 2 Cor 1:8 to 4:8 shows that Paul learned his lesson in Asia! God proved himself faithful. And God's faithfulness to Paul in the *past* gave him confidence that God could be trusted in the *future*, so that this hope enabled Paul to endure in the *present* (cf. 1:8–10). Paul's deliverance in Asia (1:8–10) leads to the daily endurance pictured in 4:8–9. Within this framework, the reference to not being "abandoned" (ἐγκαταλειπόμενοι) in 4:9 is especially significant. Its background in the LXX indicates that this is a "divine passive" that speaks of being abandoned *by God* (cf. Gen 28:15; Deut 31:6, 8; 1 Chr 28:20; Pss 15:10; 36:25, 28; Sir 2:10).[8] Just as God did not ultimately abandon Jesus in the grave, so too God's resurrection power sustains Paul in his own experiences of "death." The contrasts of 4:8–9 underscore that during this evil age it is endurance *in the midst of* adversity, not immediate, miraculous deliverance *from* it, that most profoundly reveals the power of God.

Anyone can worship the "Santa Claus" of the health-and-wealth gospel (if you are nice and not naughty—i.e., if you have enough "faith"—he will give you what you really want: a good family, material security, and a long life that is free of sickness!). But Paul's willingness and ability to endure in the midst of adversity for the sake of Christ and on behalf of Christ's people demonstrate the surpassing worth of knowing Christ now (Phil 3:8–11) and the incomparable value of life with Christ in the age to come (2 Cor

---

8. I owe this insight to Savage, *Power through Weakness*, 169.

4:16-18; Rom 8:18). Though counter-intuitive from the perspective of this age, the believer's praise that arises in the midst of affliction is testimony to this reality. This praise arises from the eyes of faith, which can see that God is at work through the suffering of his people for a future in his presence in comparison to which all present suffering seems merely "light and momentary" (4:13, 17-18). If Paul's suffering is a sign that the kingdom of God has *not yet* been consummated, his endurance is evidence that it *has been* inaugurated. The power of the new creation (4:6) is being mediated in the midst of this evil age (4:3) through Paul's suffering (4:7-11), which is itself an expression of God's triumph over Satan. Indeed, the power of the Spirit unleashed in the preaching of the gospel is so great and its glory so profound that it must be carried in a "pot," lest people put their trust in Paul himself (cf. 1 Cor 2:1-5).

This is why, in 2 Cor 6:3-10, Paul declares that it is not his suffering itself, but his endurance in the graces of 2 Cor 6:6-7a, in the midst of every kind of adverse and positive circumstance (2 Cor 6:4), that commends him as a servant of God. It is not the "death" of Paul's suffering *per se*, but his "life" as an apostle that reveals God's "resurrection" power and presence (cf. the references to the "Holy Spirit" and the "power of God" in 6:6-7). Paul's catalogues of suffering in 2 Cor 6:3-10 and 11:23-33 merely delineate the *platform* from which Paul "works together" with God in making the appeal of the gospel to be reconciled to God (2 Cor 5:18- 6:2).

It is crucial to keep in mind, therefore, that Paul's call to suffer as an apostle was not a call to a joyless, second-rate existence marked by having to "give up things" for God. Paul's call to suffer was not to a self-pitying sacrifice, but a call to follow Christ's path into the joy and glory of God's kingdom. Self-denial for Christ's sake is the pathway to gaining life itself (cf. Mark 8:34-38). That Paul held this conviction is borne out by the parallels between 2 Cor 1:8 and 4:17. Just as Paul had grown to trust God to sustain him under the "weight" of his afflictions (cf. ἐξαπορέω in 1:8 with 4:8), so too Paul has come to see that the "weight" of God's glory far surpasses that of his afflictions (cf. καθ' ὑπερβολὴν ... βαρέω in 1:8 with καθ' ὑπερβολὴν εἰς ὑπερβολὴν ... βάρος in 4:17). "The affliction that once felt like a lethal weight round his neck now seems weightless in comparison to his eternal load of glory."[9]

---

9. Ibid., 183.

THE CALL TO TAKE UP THE CROSS

Jesus's words in Mark 8:34-35, in the context of Jesus's own call to the cross, make it clear that trusting in the gospel of the kingdom (Mark 1:14-15) expresses itself in a cruciform life of discipleship. But "taking up one's cross" does not mean putting up with hassles and suffering in life. It refers to following in Jesus's footsteps by considering the needs of others more important than one's own. In Jesus's case, this led him to give his life as a ransom for the lives of his people (Mark 10:45). In the case of his followers, based on what Jesus has done for them (note the grounding function of Mark 10:32-34 and 45), it means seeking to be great in the kingdom by becoming a slave to the needs of others (Mark 10:35-44).

This is why Paul could commend himself as an apostle by pointing to the fact that he preached "Jesus Christ as Lord" and himself as the Corinthians' "slave" for Jesus's sake (4:5). For both of these only come about as a result of the Spirit's work of transforming one into the image of God as revealed in Christ (1 Cor 12:3, 7; 2 Cor 3:4-6, 18; 4:4-6). In response to the Spirit's work, having been called, like the Christ, to suffer as an embodiment of the gospel, he had learned, like the Christ, that trusting God in the midst of that suffering is the pathway to his own resurrection joy and deliverance. As a result, Paul was not dissuaded from following Jesus by his circumstantial suffering. Rather, Paul took up the cross *himself* by *willingly* considering the needs of others for Christ more important than his own needs for sustenance and peace, although this meant, as a by-product, even more suffering in his life. For Paul's greatest sufferings were not the illnesses he suffered or the dangers he encountered on his worldwide missionary travels. Rather, Paul's greatest afflictions, like those of Christ, were the result of his *voluntary suffering of love*. Paul endured his most severe hardships and scorn because of his willingness to give up his right to financial support for the sake of his churches (1 Cor 4:12; 9:15-23; 15:10; 2 Cor 2:17; 11:7-9, 23, 27; 12:14; 1 Thess 2:9; 2 Thess 3:8). He received additional persecution because of his commitment to preach the gospel to Jews and Gentiles alike (see below). And worst of all, he was plagued by daily anxiety because of his concern for his churches (11:28).

It is indeed striking that in 2 Cor 11:23-33 Paul's catalogue of affliction reaches its climax not with any of his circumstantial sufferings, but with a reference to the "daily ... pressure of [his] anxiety for all the churches" (v. 28). This too is part of Paul's apostolic suffering, since the pressure Paul feels is brought about by his identification with the weak and by his indignation over those who lead others into sin (v. 29). Normally such concern or anxiety (μέριμνα) is considered negative in the New Testament, since it expresses a lack of confidence in God's care and a lack of satisfaction in God's provision (cf. Phil 4:6; 1 Cor 7:32-34; Mark 4:19; Matt 6:25-34; 1 Pet 5:7). In these cases, however, the anxiety is directed toward *oneself*. Paul's anxiety in 2 Cor 11:28, in contrast, is not for himself, but for the welfare of others as an expression of his love (cf. the expressions of concern in Phil 2:20; 1 Cor 12:25). Moreover, the Corinthians must have realized that he was talking about them! And Paul is emphatic in stressing that his continual concern over the Corinthians, which has been a recurrent theme throughout the letter, is more difficult than any of his physical sufferings (cf. 1:6; 2:4; 2:12-13; 4:12, 15; 7:3, 5; 11:2; 12:20-21; 13:9).

In addition to carrying this emotional burden, Paul, like Christ, also considered the needs of his people for the gospel more important than his own physical comfort and personal reputation (cf. Phil 2:1-11). So Paul gave up his status as a Jew, his right to be paid, and his concern for his own physical welfare for the sake of proclaiming the gospel of the kingdom, and to remove any possibility that the gospel could be misconstrued as something he sold as part of his career as a public speaker (1 Cor 9:15-23; 2 Cor 2:17). Paul did not want his churches to base their faith on his performance and persona, but on the power of God (1 Cor 2:1-5). Paul consequently labored day and night in order to support himself while he preached (cf., e.g., Acts 20:9-11, 31), though the uncertainties of his work and travel meant days of homelessness, hunger, and thirst. To put it lightly, the social status of such artisans was less than desirable (cf. 1 Cor 4:11-13). Paul's "sleeplessness" in 2 Cor 11:27 could therefore refer to the late nights he spent writing and studying after working all day to support himself, as well as to the consequence of his pressing concern for his churches.[10] And Paul's reference to his being "naked" in 11:27 is probably a metaphor referring to the consequent social shame of being afflicted and disgraced, which Paul certainly was in the eyes of the world (1 Cor 4:13; 2 Cor 6:8; cf. Gen 2:25; 3:7-11; Ezek 16:8; Nah 3:5; Mic 1:11; Rev 3:18).[11] But here too, what others considered shameful Paul *boasts in* as authenticating signs of his calling and commitment to the ministry.

Likewise, the various arrests, imprisonments, and punishments referred to in 2 Cor 11:23-26 were suffered as an apostle for the gospel (cf. 6:5; Acts 16:23-30). Paul's more severe beatings (v. 23) refer both to the Jewish punishment of "thirty-nine lashes" (v. 24) and to the Gentile punishment

---

10. Plummer, *Second Corinthians*, 328, points to the prologue to Sir and to 2 Macc 2:26, where the word for "sleeplessness" in 11:27, ἀγρυπνία, is used of sitting up at night writing, while Sir 38:26-30 uses it to refer to laborers working at night. In Sir 36(31):1, 2, 20; 42:9 it is used of sleeplessness caused by anxiety or discomfort.

11. Pointed out by Martin, *2 Corinthians*, 380.

of being beaten with rods (v. 25a). Five times Paul received this synagogue punishment, which, among other things, was inflicted for false teaching, blasphemy, and seriously breaking the law. It was the most severe beating Scripture allowed (cf. Deut 25:1–3). The frequency of the beatings attests to Paul's continued strategic focus on the synagogues. Indeed, he was even stoned at Lystra (cf. Acts 14:5–19), the most common form of execution in the Bible.[12] At the same time, Paul's ministry as the Jewish apostle to the Gentiles caused tears within both the Jewish and Gentile social fabric. Hence, three times the Romans punished Paul for disturbing the peace by beating him with rods, a form of punishment usually reserved for non-citizens and slaves (11:25a; cf. 1 Thess 2:2; Acts 16:22–23, 35–38; 22:25–29).

These public punishments reveal yet another way in which Paul *willingly* suffered as a result of considering the needs of others more important than his own. God's leading Paul into situations of "death" was matched by Paul's own taking up of the cross. Paul repeatedly went to the Jews first with the gospel, even though they often convicted him of false teaching and/or breaking the law for his witness to Jesus as the Messiah and for his ministry among the Gentiles (cf. Acts 9:20; 13:5, 14–43; 14:1; 17:1–3, 10–21; 18:4, 19; 19:8).[13] That Paul submitted to these punishments rather than separating himself from the Jewish community is itself an indication of his self-understanding as an apostle and of his amazing love for his people (cf. Rom 1:16; 9:2–3). Because he took up the cross on behalf of both Jews and Gentiles, Paul suffered both for his mission to the Gentiles and for his continued commitment to his own people (cf. 1 Cor 9:19–23).

BOASTING IN WEAKNESS

Since Paul was called to embody his message of the cross and resurrection in a "jar of clay," Paul's argument for the legitimacy of his apostolic ministry concludes with the principle stated in 2 Cor 11:30 and then repeated in

---

12. I owe this observation to Scott, *2 Corinthians*, 218. Scott points out that stoning was used for apostasy (Lev 20:2; Deut 13:10–11; 17:2–7), blasphemy (Lev 24:14, 16, 23; 1 Kgs 21:10), sorcery (Lev 20:27), Sabbath violations (Num 15:35–36), misuse of the devoted things (Josh 7:25), a disobedient son (Deut 21:21), and adultery (Deut 22:21–24). Cf. Acts 5:26; 7:58; John 8:5; 10:31–33; 11:8; Heb 11:37.

13. Of the three most probable crimes worthy of such a lashing—doctrinal heresy, blasphemy, and serious offenses against Jewish customs—Harvey argues that most likely Paul was whipped for either profaning the Sabbath, working on the Day of Atonement, or committing offenses against food and ritual purity regulations (cf. *m. Mak.* 3:2; 3:15; *m. Ker.* 1:1). These are the Jewish crimes that would have come about because of his ministry among the Gentiles; see Harvey, "Forty Strokes," 84.

12:9–10: if forced to boast, Paul will do so concerning his weaknesses, since they are the platform for God's power.

At first, the subsequent recounting of Paul's experience in Damascus in 2 Cor 11:32–33 seems out of place. But Paul recounts this story to ground his commitment to boast only in his weaknesses because it was the initial and foundational example of his newly granted weakness as an apostle. Paul's ignominious flight *from* Damascus stands in stark contrast to the strength in which he had originally left *for* Damascus to persecute the believers. The one who left for Damascus to persecute Christians left Damascus as a persecuted Christian! Given the fact that Paul's weakness is now his strength, this experience also provided the platform for his "power" in preaching Jesus as the Christ (cf. Acts 9:16; 22). Paul's narrow escape in Damascus, like his despairing even of life (cf. 1:8–11), served as a stage for highlighting God's deliverance and sustenance. From the very beginning of his new life as an apostle, the experience of escaping from Damascus thus formed a foundation for Paul's calling to suffer for the sake of Christ and the gospel. Paul's litany of suffering in 11:23–29 is nothing new; weakness was the contour of Paul's calling from the start.[14]

In the same way, Paul buttresses the restatement of his commitment to boast only in his weakness in 2 Cor 12:9b–10 by recounting in 12:1–9a his experience with the "thorn in the flesh." Because of the great magnitude and magnificence of his revelations,[15] Paul knew that to boast in his visions, like his opponents were doing, would lead to exalting himself in a way that would cut the very heart out of the gospel (12:7a). Yet Paul's restraint was not the result of his own moral willpower. In 12:7b Paul makes it clear that God himself kept Paul from such conceit by granting him "a thorn in (or against) his flesh"—that is, "a messenger of Satan"—that was sent to batter or torment him. Strikingly, Paul uses the divine passive in this verse: "there was given me [*by God*] a thorn in my flesh." Paul's point is that both his

---

14. So already Schlatter, *Paulus*, 657: Paul gave this memory from the first period of his ministry in more detail than all the others "because it was an especially clear illustration of the way in which weakness and strength, danger and deliverance were bound together in his work from the very beginning."

15. 12:6b–7 should read as follows: "I refrain, so no one will think more of me than is warranted by what I do or say, and [= that is to say] because of these surpassingly great revelations. Therefore [διό], in order to keep me from becoming conceited, there was given me a thorn in my flesh, a messenger of Satan, to torment me, to keep me from becoming conceited." This reading follows the punctuation represented in the Nestle Aland Greek text (28th ed.), which rightly takes the beginning of verse 7 ("and because of these surpassingly great revelations") with verse 6 and begins a new sentence with the "therefore" of 7b. Keeping Paul from being conceited is derived directly from the granting of the thorn and the tormenting of Satan, which in turn are derived from the magnitude of Paul's revelations.

rapture *and* his thorn are the work of God! As Ralph Martin observes, "The importance of the passive verb, ἐδόθη, 'was given,' can hardly be exaggerated. God is the unseen agent behind the bitter experience."[16]

The exact nature of this "thorn" or Satanic messenger (literally: "angel of Satan") has been a matter of much debate. Though I am convinced that the "thorn" refers to Paul's physical illness, not his opponents, for our purposes its exact nature need not detain us. Indeed, Paul's own silence in 2 Cor 12:7 concerning the nature of his "thorn" is intentional. What concerns Paul is the "thorn's" theological origin (i.e., it is sent by Satan, but given by God), its cause (i.e., it is given because of Paul's great revelations), and its purpose (namely, to afflict Paul in order to keep him from becoming conceited). Hence, rather than calling his divinely granted authority into question, Paul's ongoing weakness is *itself* proof of the revelations granted to him as an apostle, since they are the *ground* for his receiving a thorn in the flesh. In 2 Cor 12:7, Paul therefore turns his opponents' argument on its head. The more they call attention to the severity of Paul's weaknesses as a "sick charismatic," the more they themselves point to the exalted nature of his revelations!

At first, Paul reacted to his "thorn in the flesh" as would be expected from one who knew the twin realities of God's sovereignty over evil and of God's love for his children: he prayed that the Lord would remove the "thorn" (12:8). Paul is no Stoic who sees the thorn as an opportunity for self-mastery and endurance. Nor is he a theological masochist who glorifies in suffering itself. When suffering hits, Paul prays for deliverance. That Paul did so "three times" may simply be a conventional way to emphasize that the prayer was repeated (cf. Ps 55:17, where the psalmist utters his complaint three times a day).[17] In this case, Paul is simply saying that he prayed repeatedly about the matter. The problem with this reading is that Paul *stopped* praying after the third time! The reference to "three times" is therefore better taken as signaling an event that is now over and done with, having gone through its beginning, middle, and end.[18] Read in this way, Paul's threefold prayer parallels Jesus's threefold prayer in the Garden of Gethsemane, which also culminated in Jesus's confidence that his prayer had been answered, *even though* the cup of suffering would remain (Mark 14:32–41).

God's answer to Paul's prayer as recounted in 2 Cor 12:9a and Paul's response in 12:9b–10 form the conclusion both to Paul's experience of his thorn in the flesh (vv. 7b–8) and to his refraining from boasting in his own

---

16. Martin, *2 Corinthians*, 416.
17. So Scott, *2 Corinthians*, 229.
18. Heckel, *Kraft in Schwachheit*, 84.

"surpassingly great revelations" (vv. 5–7a). Instead of removing the thorn, Christ declared that his own grace will be sufficient for Paul in the midst of his suffering, since it is Paul's weakness itself that provides the platform for perfecting the Lord's power (v. 9a). Paul's sufferings can never outstrip God's supply (cf. 1:8–11). For this reason, Paul will "all the more gladly" boast in his weaknesses, instead of his revelations, in order that the power of Christ might dwell upon him (v. 9b; cf. 1:9–10; 11:30; 12:5).

The promise of Christ's grace and power being perfected in his weakness leads Paul to be pleased in his sufferings (v. 10a), rather than continuing to pray for their removal, because he now knows that "when" he is weak, "then" he is strong (v. 10b). *Thus, the revelation of Christ's power in Paul's weakness (v. 9b), and Paul's consequent contentment (v. 10a), form the high point of Paul's argument in this passage and, in doing so, provide a summary of the theological substructure of 2 Corinthians as a whole.* Here we see the depth of Paul's experience and the breadth of his theological understanding. My sense is that even to comment on these verses is to risk detracting from their profundity. Suffice it to say that Paul's use of temple imagery in his reference in 2 Cor 12:9 to "Christ's power resting on him" (literally: dwelling or making one's abode; ἐπισκηνόω) recalls Paul's earlier affirmation in 3:7—4:6 that, under the new covenant, the glory of God is being revealed in Christ without a veil. Christ's declaration and Paul's response in 2 Cor 12:9 are yet another affirmation that Paul is a mediator of God's transforming presence under the new covenant ministry of the Spirit.

Here, however, Christ himself takes the place of the revelation of YHWH's glory in the temple, which is now being made known not in a theophany in heaven, but in and through Paul's suffering on earth. For whereas Paul was forbidden to speak about what he saw in heaven (12:4), he can quote Christ verbatim concerning what his life on earth is to be like (12:9). While Paul's personal revelations are irrelevant for establishing his apostolic ministry, his suffering plays a strategic role. That which he sees in heaven is matched by what Paul suffers on earth. His silence over his revelations is broken only by his boast in his weakness. The strength of Paul's visions in heaven remains "weak" when it comes to revealing God, while Paul's weakness on earth becomes the place of God's power.

Once again Paul hits the point he has been hammering in throughout 2 Corinthians. Instead of calling his ministry into question, Paul's various weaknesses, listed in 11:23b–33 and now summarized in 12:10, are therefore his only legitimating boast as an apostle, since they are the means by which God is making known his glory in Christ among the Corinthians (cf. 1:3–11; 2:14–16a; 3:7—4:6, 13–18; 6:3–10). For this reason, Paul boasts in the very things that cause others to slander him. Paul's "strength" in 12:10b is not his personal strength, but the strength that derives from his divinely granted ability to endure adversity for the sake of the gospel (cf. 4:7–18). This means that to boast in his weakness (11:30; 12:5, 9–10) is to boast in what the Lord is doing by his grace and power (Jer 9:22–23; cf. 2 Cor 10:12–18). This then is Paul's strongest argument for the legitimacy of his apostleship: his weaknesses are the very ground of Christ's power.

LESSONS FROM THE CHARACTER OF THE PASTOR

What recommended Paul as a true representative of Jesus Christ was his life of suffering as the means for mediating the transforming work of the Spirit, not his personality or his "success" in growing larger churches. Paul's understanding of the nature of Christian ministry strikes a piercing blow against all attempts, whether in Paul's day or our own, to fashion ministries and messages around celebrities, techniques, and public performance.

Paul's portrayal of his ministry in terms of his own suffering *and* the Spirit (not suffering *versus* the Spirit) also calls into question ancient and contemporary images of the "Spirit-filled" Christian. The "health-and-wealth gospel" of Paul's opponents, with its promise of God's physical and financial blessing for the faithful, remains virulent down through the ages. In our age of materialism, like that in the Corinth of Paul's day, it appears ludicrous to accept that God would not only use suffering as the vehicle for manifesting the presence and power of his Spirit, but also "lead someone to death" for the sake of revealing his glory and spreading the gospel (2:14). In its place, it makes "sense" that Christians are a people who overcome suffering and want, rather than those who find Christ strong in their very evident weakness. As Paul also experienced, this "health and wealth" assumption is even more evident in regard to pastors, both in terms of the church's expectations for them and in regard to their own self-understandings. The "natural" assumption is that the handsome and healthy are "strong" in the Lord, especially if they are skilled rhetorically. Yet, from Paul's perspective, the dominant characteristic of those in whom God is mightily at work is their confident endurance *in the midst of* adversity. Pastors are to model perseverance, not personality; Christ-like morality, not miracles.

At the same time, it must be emphasized that suffering in and of itself is not the revelation of God's power. Paul never glorifies in affliction *per se*. Paul has no romantic notion of suffering. So it would be a mistake to conclude that suffering and oppression in themselves are the marks of a representative of Christ in the world. Indeed, by itself, suffering is the consequence of sin. To experience suffering is to be impacted by the evil of our fallen world. Left to itself, suffering is not a noble and purifying virtue. There is no evidence that Paul sought suffering or encouraged others to do so as if it were a sign of special spirituality. Hence, the emphasis among some of the early church fathers on actively seeking martyrdom as the highest form of Christian witness is a dangerous *misapplication* of Paul's view of suffering.[19] Believers are to avoid circumstantial suffering and persecution whenever such avoidance does not hinder or compromise their calling, and to pray for healing and deliverance when sick (cf. Rom 12:17-18; 1 Cor 7:15; Phil 4:4-7; 1 Tim 5:23). But the righteous do suffer (Ps 116:10 in 2 Cor 4:13). And some, like Paul and those who minister the gospel as representatives of Christ, are even *called* to do so for the sake of the gospel (1 Cor 4:9; 2 Cor 1:3-11; 2:14; 4:7-15; cf. Gal 6:17).

Finally, the consequence of Paul's experience as an apostle is the conclusion that those called to proclaim and embody the kingdom of God are also called to a unique role within the church. Through their lives of trust (1:9), integrity (see 1:12—2:4), and mercy (2:5-11), *in the midst of adversity*, the "saints" entrusted to their care will see displayed before them the reality of Christ's death and resurrection. This implies that the life of the pastor will normally be characterized by a quality (and quantity?) of suffering not usually expected in the lives of those gifted for other equally important roles within the church (see esp. 11:28).

If the goal of Paul's ministry was to bring about the endurance of faith in the lives of God's people, the means to that end was for Paul to live his own life of faith as a servant of the new covenant publicly before them (3:4-6; 4:7-15; 6:3-10). The "one way" movement in 1:3-11 *from* God *to* Paul *to* the Corinthians illustrates that God calls those in ministry to be an example to the church in a way that cannot be said of the church as a whole. It was by watching their apostle that the Corinthians could see the comfort of God fleshed out, inasmuch as the suffering of the pastor or missionary functions as a primary vehicle through which the truth of the gospel is mediated to God's people (cf. 2:14—3:3; 12:9-10). To quote Barnett,

> Paul's experience of suffering and comfort in the course of his ministry is replicated in every generation in the lives of godly missionaries and pastors in their interrelationships with their congregations. While both minister and people suffer as they bear witness to Christ in an alien culture, there remains a distinctive role and therefore a distinctive suffering to the Christian leader.

---

19. See, e.g., the desire of Ignatius (died ca. A.D. 115) to be devoured by the wild beasts in Rome so that he might "truly be a disciple of Jesus Christ," quoting 1 Cor 15:32 in his letter *To the Romans*, 4-5.

> As the comfort of God is experienced in the life of the leader,
> so it will be passed on through ministry to the people.[20]

One of the central messages of 2 Corinthians is the significance of the pastoral office. Paul's message in 2 Corinthians reminds us that just as redemption took place through the coming of the Christ, so too God's plan for strengthening the faith of his people is not ultimately a program, but a person. The life and proclamation of the pastor, replicated in the faith of his people in the midst of their own sufferings, is the primary way God grows his church. And at the heart of the pastoral office is the suffering of the pastor, even as Christ came as the suffering servant who was obedient to the point of death.

---

20. Barnett, *Second Epistle*, 80.

10

The "Temple of the Spirit" as the Inaugural Fulfillment of the New Covenant[1]

One can hardly imagine a more diverse collage of concerns than those contained in the short span of 1 and 2 Corinthians. The topics range

- from the problems of factionalism, incest, prostitution, and idol meat, to celibacy, tongues, and veils;
- from baptism, the cross, final judgment, and the resurrection, to the appropriateness of using rhetorical flair in preaching and the question of payment for pastors;
- from suffering to love;
- from Paul's visions in the third heaven and the signs and wonders of a true apostle to an unrelieved anxiety that forced him to turn back from an open door for ministry;
- from Paul's divine comfort in the face of death to his comfort in meeting Titus;
- from the grief that leads to repentance to the grief that leads to punishment;
- from boasting in the Lord to boasting as a fool;

---

1. From Scott J. Hafemann, "The 'Temple of the Spirit' as the Inaugural Fulfillment of the New Covenant within the Corinthian Correspondence." *ExAud* 12 (1996) 29–42.

- from the gift of a second chance to the threat of the last chance;
- and from the change in Paul's travel plans for the sake of the Corinthians to the change in plans for the collection for the sake of others.

Yet in spite of all of this diversity, and in honor of the Latin title of the esteemed journal, *Ex Auditu*, one may assert that just as ecclesiology *intra nos* is the overriding concern of 1 Corinthians, so too ecclesiology *extra nos* is the overriding concern of 2 Corinthians. But to assert that ecclesiology, inwardly and outwardly focused, is the overarching concern within the Corinthian correspondence is merely to assert that Paul's burden in these letters is to keep the Corinthians from destroying the church and from being destroyed by God as a result (1 Cor 3:17). For in Paul's view, the Jerusalem temple provides a template for understanding the covenant blessings and curses that now pertain to the church as God's temple, since *the Spirit of the living God now dwells within/among her* (cf. 1 Cor 3:16; 6:19; 11:27–32; 2 Cor 5:10; 6:14—7:1; 13:2–5).

This explains why Paul is preoccupied in 1 Corinthians with the threat to the church posed by the sinful character of the Corinthians' interrelationships. Their spiritual experiences have led to a pseudospiritual one-upmanship, their knowledge to an arrogant lack of regard for those who are still "weak in faith," and their newfound freedom in Christ to an eschatology that expressed itself in ethical laxity, on the one hand (cf. 1 Cor 5–6), and in an undue asceticism, on the other (cf. 1 Cor 7). In response, the purpose of the letter we call "1 Corinthians" is first and foremost instructional. For in addressing the various factions that constitute the church, Paul counts on the fact that his apostolic authority is still accepted by the Corinthians (cf. e.g., the anticipated answers to his rhetorical questions and their support in 1 Cor 9:1f.). After all, the letter has its origin to a large degree not only in the recent factions in the church (cf. 1:10—4:21), but also in the recent correspondence from the Corinthians in which they have asked Paul to clear up misunderstandings from his previous instructions (1 Cor 5:9–13; 7:1, 25; 8:1; 11:2ff.; 12:1ff.; 15:1ff.). Thus, Paul's apostolic standing as their spiritual "father" provides the presupposition for Paul's arguments (1 Cor 4:6–7, 14–21).

But by the time of the writing of 2 Corinthians, things have changed dramatically. The arrival in Corinth of Paul's opponents had fueled the flames of discontent into a direct assault on Paul's legitimacy as an apostle. To stem the tide, Paul had already made a "painful visit" (2 Cor 2:1) and wrote a "tearful letter" (2 Cor 2:4) in an attempt to win back his church. Though to Paul's great joy the result was largely successful, a hardened minority still rejected him and his gospel (cf. 2 Cor 2:5–11; 7:5–16; 10–13). In response to this mixed situation, the purpose of the letter we call "2 Corinthians" is apologetic rather than didactic. Paul must now address those who have reaffirmed their allegiance to him as their apostle in order to support their decision both theologically and pastorally against those who would still oppose him (the main thrust of 2 Cor 1–9), while attempting for the last time to win back those who are still in rebellion against his authority before he returns in judgment (the main thrust of 2 Cor 10–13; cf. esp. 13:1–10).

In the midst of the diversity of themes, occasion, and purposes that consequently make up the Corinthian correspondence, the unity of theological rationale that pervades these letters is therefore remarkable. Instead of offering *ad hoc* responses to the issues before him, Paul replies to the concerns in Corinth out of an integrated perspective built upon his theology proper, his Christology, his understanding of redemptive history as revealed in the Scriptures, and his view of the work and significance of the Spirit. Moreover, although Paul's dominant recourse thematically is to his theology and Christology, whenever he turns his attention to ecclesiology directly, it is Paul's understanding of the significance of the Spirit's presence in the church that plays the strategic role (see below).[2] Thus, in view of Paul's overriding ecclesiological concerns in the Corinthian correspondence, Paul's conception of the Spirit becomes decisive for understanding the force of his arguments in these letters.[3] Furthermore, the centrality of the Spirit in Paul's ecclesiology does not derive from his Christology, as if the Spirit were viewed simply as another manifestation of the presence of Christ among his people. In this common view, Paul's references to the Spirit are treated as if they were references to the person and work of Christ incognito. However,

---

2. In 1 Corinthians and 2 Corinthians Paul refers to the Spirit or spiritual matters using the term πνεῦμα/πνευματικός seventy-three times in sixty-nine assertions spread over fifty-seven verses. This is slightly over 40 percent of the 142 total verses in which they occur in the Pauline corpus. By way of comparison, in 1 and 2 Corinthians, Paul refers to "God" (θεός) in 156 verses and Jesus Christ in 155 verses. Of these, Paul uses the title "Christ" in ninety-nine verses (with and without a reference to Jesus and/or the Lord) and "Jesus" as the "Lord" (κύριος) in nine verses. Paul refers to the "Lord" without further definition sixty-two times, forty-four of which by context most likely refer to Jesus, rather than to YHWH, though this involves several judgment calls. Interestingly, Paul refers to Jesus without a messianic title only three times in this literature, twice in 2 Cor 4:10–11 and once in 2 Cor 11:4. In the former text, Paul is referring to his death and resurrection, and in the latter to what the false teachers preach—i.e., "a different Jesus."

3. For a full-length treatment of the role of the Spirit in Paul's writings, see the major work of Fee, *God's Empowering Presence* (967 pages!).

rather than being interchangeable, it is the person and "work" of Christ that makes the new covenant presence of the Spirit possible. When Paul talks about the Spirit, he is not simply substituting one reality for another. Instead, Paul's understanding of the Spirit and its implications for the life of the congregation are predicated on his conviction that the prophetic promise of the new covenant from Jeremiah 31 has been fulfilled in Christ.

Before we look at Paul's new covenant understanding, it will therefore be helpful to review the main points of Jer 31:31–34 itself.

THE MEANING OF THE "NEW COVENANT" IN JEREMIAH 31:31–34[4]

The argument of Jer 31:31–34, separated into its constituent propositions, runs as follows:

31:31	"Behold, the days are coming," declares the Lord, "when I will make a new covenant with the house of Israel and with the house of Judah.
32a	*Specifically,* I will not make it like the covenant that I made with their fathers . . .
32b	*since* they broke this covenant of mine
32c	*even though* I was a husband to them," declares the Lord.
33a	"*The reason the new covenant will be different in this regard* (כִּי) *is that* this is the covenant that I will make with the house of Israel after those days," declares the Lord, "I will put my law within them, and I will write it on their heart.
33b	*The result of this new covenant will be that* I will be their God, and they shall be my people.
34a	*The ultimate consequence of this new covenant relationship in which I am their God and they are my people is that* they shall not teach again each man his neighbor and each man his brother saying, 'Know the Lord,'
34b	*because* (כִּי) they shall all know me, from the least of them to the greatest of them," declares the Lord.
34c	"*The basis for all of this* (כִּי) *is that* I will forgive their iniquity, and I will remember their sin no more."

The significance of this text may be outlined in four main points. First, the "new covenant" in Jer 31:31–34 is the divinely promised answer to the

---

4. For the detailed presentation and support of these points and those that follow, see my *Paul, Moses, and the History of Israel*, 92–186. My modest purpose in this essay is to digest and highlight some of the relevance of this previous work for the present topic.

perennial problem of Israel's hard-hearted rebellion against YHWH, which according to Jeremiah has always and still continues to characterize the people.[5] What is needed is nothing less than a new beginning, a "new covenant," in which Israel's relationship with God will be decisively changed. But as the wider context confirms, the adjective "new" in Jer 31:31 points to an eschatological reality yet to be fulfilled, which Jeremiah holds forth as Israel's only ultimate hope after the destruction of the exile (cf. 31:1-30, 35-40). Thus, with Jer 31:31-34 as its climax, Jeremiah's own prophetic call in 1:10 "to break down and destroy" as well as "to plant and build up" is being fulfilled in his preaching of destruction in the present and in his promise of God's restoration in the future, a restoration that centers on the establishment of a "new covenant" between God and his people (cf. Jer 1:10 with its promised fulfillment in Jer 31:28).[6]

Second, the nature of this "new covenant" is described in Jer 31:32-33 by *contrasting* it to the Mosaic/Sinai covenant (cf. Jer 11:1-11; 22:9f.), a covenant that both the fathers "in the day that I brought them up from the land of Egypt" (11:7) and the Israel and Judah of Jeremiah's own day (11:9-10; cf. 22:9-10) have broken "in the stubbornness of their evil heart" (11:8). Hence, according to verse 32, the essential difference between the Sinai covenant and the new covenant is that the latter will not be broken (though of course under the Sinai covenant God had already remained faithful to *his* covenant commitments; the problem was with *the people*, not God; cf. Jer 2:5-8). The new covenant is an "everlasting covenant that will not be forgotten" (Jer 50:5). Verse 33 then gives the reason for this confidence (note the כִּי ["because"] in v. 33a; ὅτι in 38:33aLXX). Unlike the Sinai covenant, in this new covenant God will place his law (the preferred LXX manuscript tradition reads the plural "laws") "within them" or "in their mind" and "write it on their heart." In so doing, God will bring about an eschatological reversal of the present situation in which, instead of the law, the *sin* of Judah is being "written down with an iron stylus; with a diamond point it is engraved upon the tablet of their heart" (Jer 17:1). In view of Jeremiah's emphasis on Israel's stubborn rebellion from the exodus onward, this implies that in the new covenant Israel's rebellious nature will be fundamentally *transformed*

---

5. For the motif of the "stubbornness" of Israel's evil heart and her hardened condition in relationship to the perpetual disobedience of the people within Jeremiah, see Jer 2:21-22; cf. 22:9-10; 3:17; 5:20-25; 7:24-26; 8:7; 9:12-16; 11:14; 13:10, 23; 14:11, 22; 15:1; 16:12; 17:1, 23; 18:12-15a; 19:15; 23:17, etc. For the corresponding point that the covenant people and their leaders have continued to break the covenant, see Jer 2:8; 5:31; 6:13, 17; 10:21; 14:18; 23:13-14; 27:16; 28:2, etc.

6 For Paul's understanding of the relationship between Jeremiah's ministry under the old covenant and his own under the new, see chapter 7 above.

so that her hardened disobedience is replaced by an open compliance with God's covenant stipulations in his law. When read against the backdrop of Jeremiah as a whole, this is the point of God's declaration in verse 33 that he will "put (his) law within them" and its synonymous expression in verse 33 that he will "write it on their heart."

The promise of the new covenant in Jer 31:31–34 is therefore God's response to Israel's inability to heed the call in Jer 4:4 that they "circumcise [themselves] to the Lord and remove the foreskins of [their] heart." Apart from this divine work, Israel will suffer God's punishment against "all those who are circumcised and yet uncircumcised," since "all the house of Israel are uncircumcised of heart" (Jer 9:25–26; cf. 4:4b; Deut 10:16). For in describing the law as being "within" and "written on the heart," Jeremiah is picturing a people who accept God's law as their own and obey it willingly, rather than merely obeying it grudgingly or spurning it altogether (cf. Deut 6:4–5; 10:16; 11:18; Ps 40:8; Isa 51:7). This divinely enabled acceptance of God's law as his covenant stipulations ensures that covenant faithfulness to YHWH will be maintained, rather than continually broken. In the words of the typical covenant formula, YHWH "will be their God, and they will be [his] people" (31:33c).

Third, the movement of thought from Jer 31:32 to 33 makes clear that the covenantal relationship between God and his people is maintained by keeping the law in *response* to God's prior acts of redemption (cf. Jer 31:1ff.). This is no less true of the new covenant than it was of the Sinai covenant before it (cf. Deut 6:20–25). Rather than suggesting that the law is somehow negated in the new covenant, Jer 31:31–33 emphasizes that it is the *ability* to *keep* the law as a result of having a transformed nature, not its removal, that distinguishes the new covenant from the covenant at Sinai. Nor is there any indication in this text, or in Jeremiah as a whole, that the future eschatological restoration will entail the giving of a new law, or that the "law" of the new covenant will be merely an abstract revelation of the general will of God quite apart from the specifics of the Mosaic code. The LXX manuscript tradition that reads the plural "laws" for the singular "torah" in Jer 38:33LXX [MT 31:33] underscores this latter point. For Jeremiah, the "law written on the heart" is the Sinai law itself as the embodiment of God's will. The contrast between the two covenants remains a contrast between the two *different conditions of the people* who are brought into these covenants and their correspondingly different responses to the *same law*. The former broke the Sinai covenant, being unable to keep it due to their stubborn, evil hearts; the latter will keep the new covenant as a result of their transformed nature.

Fourth, verse 34 depicts the result of this new covenant transformation of God's people and its ultimate ground. With God's law written on their hearts, the people of the new covenant will not need to be taught to "know" the Lord, since they will *all* know him directly. The new heart that is promised as essential to the new covenant thus provides the conceptual transition from verse 33 to verse 34, since in OT anthropology the "heart" is not only the seat of volition and desire, but also the organ most often associated with the function of understanding and intellectual knowledge (cf. e.g., Deut 29:3; Ps 90:12). To have the law "within one's heart" is to "know" the law as the expression of the One who gave it. Against the backdrop of the Sinai covenant, which we have seen forms the point of comparison, verse 34 points to a time when the role of Moses as the mediator of the will, knowledge, and presence of God is no longer necessary. In the new covenant, God will renew the people's ability to know God directly, whereas under the Sinai covenant, beginning with the sin of the golden calf, the presence of God had to be kept veiled and separated from the people in order to protect them from destruction due to their sinful, "stiff-necked" state (cf. Jer 7:26; 19:15 with Exod 32–34, especially 33:3, 5; Deut 9:6, 13, on the one hand, and the many parallels between Deut 32 and Jeremiah, on the other). It also indicates that under the new covenant there will no longer be any distinction between those within the community who have a transformed heart and those who do not. *By definition*, all those who belong to the new covenant community do so *by virtue* of their transformed nature. Unlike the role played by the prophets and remnant within Israel, the new covenant community will not need to admonish others within the community to "know the Lord." This is why the foundation of the new covenant is the fact that, despite Israel's past rebellion, God will "remember their sin no more" (v. 34). Both the changed condition of God's people and their resultant obedience to the covenant, together with their renewed access to the knowledge of God, are based upon the divine forgiveness that makes the new covenant possible.

In short, Jer 31:31–34 looks forward to what we now call a "believer's church." The people of the new covenant are an extension of the faithful remnant within Israel who knew the Lord, not a continuation of the "mixed multitude" that constituted Israel's life as a nation and ethnic people under the old covenant (cf. Rom 11:1–24). As a consequence, this transformation under the new covenant will mean the overturning of the lack of trust and deceit that characterized Israel's past relationships, in which they did not teach the truth but spoke lies to one another, and through their deceit "refused to know" the Lord (Jer 9:4–6). In Paul's words, under the new covenant "to each one is given the manifestation of the Spirit for the common good" (1 Cor 12:7). This may be why in 1 Cor 6:1–8 Paul condemns lawsuits and fraud between believers and calls for the necessity of judging those within the church, whereas God judges outsiders (1 Cor 5:12–13). Furthermore,

Paul's reference to the manifestation of the grace of God in the spiritual gift of knowledge, with which *all* the Corinthians have been enriched by God (cf. 1 Cor 1:4–7), and his corresponding emphasis on the Spirit as the one who reveals to believers the things and thoughts of God (1 Cor 2:9–11), take on particular significance as fulfillments of this new covenant promise and as evidence of its reality. For as William Lane observed, "Paul's pastoral response to the disruptive situation at Corinth" entailed "an appeal to the new covenant and the administration of its provisions," so that, like the OT prophet who was called to be a "messenger of the covenant lawsuit of God," Paul was called to proclaim the "divine complaint against the rebellious Corinthians and to call them back to the stipulations of the covenant."[7] Lane points out that this is confirmed by Paul's portrayal of his ministry in 2 Cor 10:8 and 13:10 (cf. Gal 2:18) in terms of the covenantal tasks of "building up" and "tearing down" that derive from Jer 1:10 and recur in the preamble to the new covenant in Jer 31:28.

THE NEW COVENANT CONTEXT OF 1 AND 2 CORINTHIANS

In 1 Cor 11:25 and 2 Cor 3:6 Paul refers to the "new covenant" in relationship to the two fundamental aspects of his theology: the death of Christ as the salvific foundation of the church, expressed in the tradition of the Lord's Supper, and the relationship between Israel and the church (or within the Reformation tradition, between the law and the gospel), expressed in the letter/Spirit contrast. As is well known, Jer 31:31 is the only explicit reference to the terminology "new covenant" in the OT. The obvious suggestion that Paul is therefore alluding to this passage in 1 Cor 11:23 and 2 Cor 3:6 is certainly not new and, though disputed by some, is accepted by most. But few interpreters of Paul have attempted to take this covenant framework seriously as the key to understanding the structure of Paul's thought, especially his view of the Spirit.[8] However, the framework for understanding Paul's admonitions to the Corinthians concerning their life as members of

---

7. Lane, "Covenant," 6, 10. The covenant lawsuit against the Corinthians therefore provides a necessary key for understanding the character, content, and unity of 2 Corinthians, especially in view of the link between the new covenant and second exodus motifs in 2 Cor 2:14—7:1, now established by Webb, *Returning Home*.

8. For a very insightful exception to this rule, see the programmatic work of Dumbrell, *End of the Beginning*, 79–96, on the meaning of the new covenant in Jer 31:31–34 (including its relationship to Ezek 36:25–26), and 107–12 on its application to 2 Cor 3. Although arrived at independently of Dumbrell, many of the following conclusions concerning Jer 31:31–34 are corroborated by his work.

the church of Jesus Christ is precisely his conviction that they constitute the community of the new covenant (cf. 1 Cor 11:25). Likewise, Paul's apologetic for his own legitimacy as an apostle is based on his persuasion that to be an apostle of the gospel is to be a "servant" of that same new covenant (cf. 2 Cor 3:6). Although there are only two explicit references to the "new covenant" in the Corinthian correspondence, they are therefore not ornamental, but fundamental to Paul's thinking; nor are they merely the unreflected adaptation of an early church tradition in the first case or the product of polemics in the second. Rather, they indicate that the church's identity as celebrated in the Lord's Supper and Paul's identity as focused on his call to be an apostle both derive from the establishment of the new covenant through the substitutionary atonement of Christ's death on the cross for both Jews and Gentiles. This corresponds to the point made in Jer 31:31-34 itself, in which the basis of the promised knowledge of God is the anticipated forgiveness of sins.

In addition, two texts show clearly that Paul understood the dawning of the new covenant as deriving from Jesus himself. The mention of the "new covenant" in 1 Cor 11:25 is part of the Jesus-tradition inherited from the early, Jerusalem church that Paul faithfully handed down to the Corinthians. In 2 Cor 3:4-6 he refers to his own call to be an apostle, which came from Christ himself, as the means by which God made him sufficient to be a servant of this new covenant. In turn, Paul's reference to the tradition of the church in 1 Cor 11:23; 15:1-3, together with the fact that he can refer to the "new covenant" in 2 Cor 3:6 without explanation, demonstrate that through their own celebrations of the Lord's Supper and catechesis the Corinthians were well aware of the significance of the "new covenant." They knew Jesus's death had brought about this "new covenant" and that they had their own identity as members of it (cf. 1 Cor 1:2, 17f., 23f., 26-31; 2:2; 3:16; 6:19; 7:23; 12:13, 27; 2 Cor 6:14—7:1, etc.).

In focusing on the role of the "new covenant" as the substratum of Paul's theology, it is important to keep in mind that the use of the English word "covenant" (διαθήκη) to translate 1 Cor 11:25 and 2 Cor 3:6 does not imply any sort of "agreement," "contract," or "treaty" (συνθήκη) that is mutually initiated, arranged, or disposed. Nor does the covenant relationship begin with its stipulations. Paul's emphasis on the priority and centrality of the cross in salvation and on the work of the Spirit in sanctification makes it evident that the initiative, inauguration, realization, and sustaining power of the new covenant, like God's covenant with Israel at Sinai, is due solely to the unilateral and gracious work of God on behalf of his people (cf. again 1 Cor 1:17-31; 2:1-5; 15:3-4; 2 Cor 1:19-20; 3:5-6; 4:1-3; 5:18-19, etc.).

Nevertheless, in *response* to God's gracious act of redemption, both parties are obligated within the new covenant to remain faithful to their covenant partner. For his part, God will remain faithful to the covenant by meeting the needs of his people according to his wisdom so that they might be able to endure in the midst of adversity and persevere in faith (1 Cor 1:8-9; 10:13; 2 Cor 1:7; cf. 1 Thess 5:9; Phil 1:6). For their part, the Corinthians must keep the covenant stipulations as the organic expression of their genuine dependence upon God (cf. e.g., 1 Cor 3:1-3; 6:9-11; 2 Cor 5:10; 13:5). In the new covenant, like the old, what "counts" is not ethnic identity (physical circumcision), but "keeping the commandments of God" as a result of knowing him (i.e., "spiritual circumcision of the heart"; 1 Cor 7:19; cf. Jer 9:23-26; Lev 26:41). And at the heart of this covenant reality of obedience stands the Spirit. For, from Paul's perspective, given God's justifying and sanctifying work in the lives of his people *as brought about and guaranteed by the presence and power of the Spirit*, there is no excuse for the continuing, habitual disobedience that results from failing to trust God's gracious provisions and promises in Christ (cf. 1 Cor 1:20; 5:7; 6:11, 19-20; 10:13; 13:1-3 [love as the work of the Spirit]; 2 Cor 1:22). It is the Spirit who brings one to Christ for the forgiveness of sins that makes the new life of the "new creation" possible (cf. 1 Cor 2:6-16 in light of the wisdom of God in the cross; 1 Cor 12:3 for the confession of Jesus as "Lord" and 12:13 for the concomitant baptism into the body of Christ, both by the Spirit; and 1 Cor 15:17 in light of the Spirit's testimony to the lordship of Christ). One can swear allegiance to Christ and remain faithful to him only by the power of the Spirit (cf. 1 Cor 2:9-13; 6:11; 2 Cor 3:3, 17-18; 4:13-14).

In the new covenant, as in the Sinai covenant before it, obedience to God's will is the inextricable manifestation of trusting in God's promises.[9] Conversely, Paul's warnings make it clear that if the Corinthians are not faithful, God's discipline will be poured out on them, with a corresponding threat of ultimate judgment for those who, together with the rest of the unrighteous, habitually dishonor God by failing to trust in his promises as this comes to expression in disobedience to his commandments (besides 1 Cor 11:32, cf. 1 Cor 4:19-21; 5:9-13; 6:9-11; 11:27, 30; 15:1-2; 16:22; 2 Cor 5:10-11; 6:1-3; 12:19-21; 13:2-10). Thus, as a delineation of the threefold

---

9. For the crucial theological and anthropological link between faith, hope, and obedience, see Fuller, *Gospel and Law*, 105-17. As Fuller insightfully argues, for Paul "sanctification, like justification, is by faith alone," since, "according to Paul, a faith which banks its hope on the promises of God can never be devoid of the works of love, and therefore faith is all that is needed for carrying on the Christian life" (cf. Gal 5:6) (115). Conversely, "any teaching that implies that good works are done alongside of and coordinately with faith, instead of as the result of faith, is Galatianism" (115). This perspective has now been fleshed out in Fuller's important work, *Unity*, 269-323.

covenant structure, Paul's ethical admonitions (the "covenant stipulations") are grounded *both* in the past indicative of justification (the "covenant prologue") *and* in the future indicative of eschatological judgment (the "covenant promises" of blessing or curse), which, rather than being in conflict, flow inextricably from one another. Note, for example, how both of these indicatives can be brought together to support Paul's imperatives in 1 Cor 6:9–11 and 2 Cor 5:11–16. *And the evidential basis of both justification and judgment is the Spirit:* "Do you not know that you (plural) are God's temple and that God's Spirit dwells in you? If any one destroys God's temple, God will destroy him. For God's temple is holy, and that temple you are" (1 Cor 3:16–17).

The Corinthian correspondence thereby makes it clear that even Paul's warnings of judgment are part of God's gracious "new covenant" provision, since among God's people they bring about either the fear of judgment that keeps one from sinning (1 Cor 10:6–13), or the "godly grief" that brings one to repentance (1 Cor 6:9–20; 2 Cor 7:9–13; 13:5). Here too, Paul's confidence in the transforming impact of the prophetic call to repentance under the new covenant *derives from the Spirit*. The church in Corinth was well aware that the inextricable link in Paul's thinking between the redemptive work of Christ on the cross and the corresponding ethical admonitions of the gospel is based on the conviction that those who possess the Spirit of God as their "seal" and "guarantee" of salvation (2 Cor 1:22; 5:5; cf. Rom 8:23) will grow from being "babes in Christ" to mature "spiritual people" (πνευματικοί; 1 Cor 3:1; cf. 6:20; 9:24; 10:7–10, 14; 15:58; 16:13–14; 2 Cor 7:1; 8:7–8; 9:13, etc.). In Paul's words: "We all, with unveiled face, beholding the glory of the Lord, are being changed into his likeness from one degree of glory to another; for this comes from the Lord *who is the Spirit*" (2 Cor 3:18). For Paul, to speak about the saving power of the new covenant is to speak about the Spirit. The new covenant context of the Corinthian correspondence is the context of the Spirit.

THE NEW COVENANT AND THE SPIRIT: 2 CORINTHIANS 3:3, 6

As soon as such a conclusion is reached the objection is immediately raised that Jeremiah 31 makes no mention of the Spirit. Surely, then, it is argued, Paul's theology, with its focus on the presence of the Spirit, cannot derive from an understanding of the new covenant as now fulfilled "in Christ." But in describing the nature of his apostolic ministry in 2 Cor 3:3b, Paul establishes a contrast between God's work in the past, in which he engraved his covenant document on stone tablets (cf. the LXX of Exod 24:12; 31:18; 32:15; 34:1; Deut 9:10), and his present work, in which he "engraves" his "letter of Christ" on the "tablets of human hearts" by means of the Spirit. The motif of the new "fleshly heart" and the reference to the Spirit in 2 Cor 3:3b both derive from Ezek 11:19 and 36:26–27.

Against this backdrop, and in view of the development of the motif of the stone tablets in postbiblical Judaism (see below), the significance of the contrast between the tablets of stone and the tablets of fleshly hearts in 3:3b is twofold. First, read as a fulfillment of the promises from Ezekiel concerning the future restoration of God's people, the contrast between the stone tablets of the law and the heart of flesh is not a contrast between the nature of the law and of the heart themselves. Nor is it a contrast between the law and the Spirit, which in turn creates a contrast between two conflicting qualities or ways of salvation. Paul's concern in 3:3 was not with two distinct messages, but with the two "materials" used by God as a "writer."[10] As such, 2 Cor 3:3b establishes a

> contrast between the two spheres of God's revelatory-salvific activity—that is, the "law" and the "heart" . . . as a contrast between the two basic ages in the history of salvation. . . . While in the "old age" the locus of God's activity and revelation was the law, in the "new age," according to Ezekiel, God will be at work in the heart.[11]

Second, the contrasts in 3:3 do not introduce a negative assessment of the nature or content of the law itself. Rather, the reference in 3:3 to the law under the rubric of the "tablets of stone" is part of a long tradition in which this designation is, at the least, a normal, neutral way of referring to the law, and more probably functions to emphasize its permanence, divine authority, honor, and glory (cf. 2 Cor 3:7, 9, 11).[12] Read against the backdrop of

---

10. For these and the following points, together with their support and a critique of opposing positions, see my earlier work, *Suffering and the Spirit*, 199–218.

11. Ibid., 214.

12. Besides the references from the OT that support the point argued here (cf. Exod 24:12 with 31:18 and the reference to the tablets as the "work of God" in Exod 32:16LXX, written with the finger of God [Exod 31:18; Deut 9:10]), see the development of the stone tablet motif in *Jub.* 1:1, 26f.; 2:1; 3:10, 31; 6:22; 16:30; 32:10f., etc.; *1 En.* 81:1f.; 103:2–4; *T. Levi* 5:4; 7:5; *2 Bar.* 6:7–9; *Liv. Pro.*, 2:14; 4Q180; *Tg. Ps.-J.* on Exod 31:18; *Exod. Rab.* 41:6; 46:2; *Lev. Rab.* 32:2; 35:5; *Num. Rab.* 9:48; *b. Ned.* 38a; *Pirqe R. El.* 45; Eupolemus, fragment 4 (= Eusebius, *Praep. ev.* 9.39.5); and 2 Macc 2:1–10, where we read of Jeremiah preserving the tablets after the destruction of Jerusalem, which in view of Paul's reference to Jer 31 may be of special significance as underscoring the abiding validity of the law in the new covenant. Finally, see Philo, *QE*, where Philo gives his answer to why the commandments were written on tablets of stone—i.e., to signify

Ezek 11:19 and 36:26-27, and in anticipation of the reference to the new covenant from Jer 31 referred to in 3:6, there is no indication in the context of 3:3 that Paul is intending to qualify this common ground assumption negatively. Instead, "if anything is to be assumed as implicit in Paul's contrast in regard to the law, it is that the law is now being kept by those who have received the Spirit, as Ezekiel prophesied!"[13] In 2 Cor 3:3,

> Paul affirms that the age characterized by the law as the locus of God's revelatory activity is over. Thus, the Corinthians owe their relationship to Christ not to the revelation of God in the law, but to God's work in changing their hearts through his Spirit. Conversely, the conversion and new life of the Corinthians are evidence that the new age has arrived; that is, the age of the "fleshly heart" prophesied by Ezekiel.[14]

Furthermore, the flow of Paul's argument from 2 Cor 3:3 to 3:6 demonstrates that Paul understood the coming of the Spirit as promised by Ezekiel 36:27 (3:3) to be of one piece with the promise of the new covenant from Jeremiah 31:31-34 (3:6).[15] In 3:6a Paul thus makes it explicit that his *apostolic ministry of the Spirit* in fulfillment of Ezek 11:19; 36:26-27 is conceptually equivalent with his role as a *servant of the new covenant* in fulfillment of Jer 31:31-34. Paul's new covenant ministry is a ministry of the Spirit and vice versa. This means that the main point of Ezek 36:27 regarding the eschatological restoration of God's people—that God will pour out the Spirit on those whose hearts were previously made of stone *so that he might cause them to observe his statutes and ordinances*—corresponds to the emphasis on *the law being written on the heart* from Jer 31:33. The passages from Ezekiel supply Paul's references to the work of the Spirit in 3:3b, while Jer 31:31-34 provides the focus on the new obedience to the law in 3:6. Moreover, as was true for Jeremiah, for Ezekiel too, this eschatological promise of a new heart and a Spirit-caused obedience to the law is a reversal of the hard-heartedness that has characterized Israel since the exodus (cf. the "stone heart" imagery in Ezek 11:19b; 36:26b with Ezek 2:1-8; 20:1-31). Ezekiel also parallels Jeremiah in emphasizing that this new, heart-sourced

---

their permanence and to ensure their fixed nature by providing a material that would make it possible for them to be spread abroad without corruption.

13. Hafemann, *Suffering and the Spirit*, 214.

14. Ibid., 215.

15. For the conceptual relationship between Ezek 36:27-28 and Jer 31:33 within the OT texts themselves, see Daniel I. Block's very helpful survey, "Prophet of the Spirit," 38f. Block argues convincingly for taking the reference to the "spirit" in 36:26f. in both cases to be the divine Spirit.

obedience to God's law will be made possible only by a divine act of redemption and forgiveness, which for Ezekiel is pictured in the priestly terms of God's cleansing his people from their uncleanness and idolatry (Ezek 36:25, 29).

In bringing these two texts together, the framework that emerges for understanding Paul's ministry as a "servant of the new covenant" is that his role involves mediating the work of the Spirit, which in turn brings about the transformation of the heart that makes obedience to the law possible. In his role as an intermediary agent of the Spirit (3:3b), Paul "serves" or "delivers" the "letter of Christ" (i.e., the conversion of the Corinthians) as a "servant" of the new covenant (3:6). The validity of Paul's ministry of the Spirit is therefore testified to by the transformed existence of the Corinthians as Christians. In turn, Paul's "confidence" and "sufficiency" are both defined by and based upon this work of the Spirit in and through his ministry (3:4–5). Hence, in typical Pauline style, the relative pronoun clause that begins 3:6 ("who made us sufficient as servants of the new covenant") functions to *ground* Paul's prior assertion in 3:5b that his sufficiency is from God. It does so by pointing to the reality of what is being fulfilled through his apostleship in the lives of the Corinthians, since it is *God's* work of *pouring out his Spirit* that is the basis of Paul's sufficiency as an apostle of the new covenant.

Moreover, if Ezek 36:26–27 and Jer 31:31–34 are taken as the keys to Paul's conceptuality in 3:6bc, then the enigmatic meaning of the letter/Spirit contrast becomes more readily apparent. In accordance with these OT passages, Paul is careful in 3:6 *not* to establish a contrast between the law and the Spirit. This is reflected in the fact that Paul does not refer to the law *as such* in introducing this contrast, a fact that must be taken seriously. Nor is the Spirit to be read as a codeword for the gospel, so that the letter/Spirit contrast is transformed into a law/gospel contrast. For Ezekiel and Jeremiah testify that the problem with the Sinai covenant was not with the law itself, but with the people whose hearts remained hardened under it. The law remains for Paul, as it did for the Jewish traditions of his day, the holy, just, and good expression of God's covenantal will (Rom 7:12). The law itself is characterized as "spiritual" (Rom 7:14). It is as permanent as stone (2 Cor 3:7). Viewed from this perspective, the letter/Spirit contrast is not a contrast between the law and the gospel as two distinct ways of relating to God. Nor is it a contrast between two distinct ways of God relating to his people (i.e., externally in the old covenant and internally in the new), since what distinguishes the new covenant in Jer 31:31–34 is that the law *itself* is to be kept as a result of a transformed heart. So it is not the law *per se* that kills, but the law *without the Spirit*—that is, the law as "letter."

Paul's choice of the "letter" (γράμμα) terminology in 3:6 (cf. Rom 2:27-29; 7:6) encapsulates in a word the distinction between the *roles* of the law under the old and new covenants. By choosing this designation Paul highlights the function of the law under the old covenant (cf. 3:14) as that which remained *merely* expressed in writing, rather than being written on one's heart by the Spirit. The pouring out of the Spirit concomitant with the establishment of the new covenant becomes the reversal of this state of affairs. The letter/Spirit contrast is therefore a contrast between the law *without the Spirit*, as it was and still is experienced by the majority of Israelites under the Sinai covenant (cf. 3:14-15), and the law *with the Spirit*, as now experienced by those under the new covenant brought about by (the) Christ. *At the center of this contrast is once again the determinative role played by the Spirit as the mark of the new covenant.* Accordingly, Paul's assertion in 3:6b that God has made him sufficient to be a servant of the Spirit, in contrast to serving the "letter," points to his underlying assumption that just as Moses was called to be the mediator between God and Israel, Paul has been called to be an apostle of Christ to the church. But the *function* of their ministries is radically different. Moses was called to mediate the law to a stiff-necked people who could not obey it. As a result of the cross of Christ, Paul is called to mediate the Spirit in order to create a people who obey the law as appropriated under the new covenant.

All of this indicates that fundamental to Paul's self-understanding is his conviction that he is participating with those "upon whom the end of the ages has come" (1 Cor 10:11). As the context of 1 Corinthians 10 demonstrates, this conviction determines Paul's understanding of the ethical applicability of the Scriptures to the church, which now finds her identity in Christ as the eschatological people of God gathered from among both Jews and Gentiles (1 Cor 10:32; cf. Gal 6:15-16). For those who have been justified "in the name of the Lord Jesus Christ and *in the Spirit of God*," and are consequently living *in the Spirit*, are *already* participating in the reality of the kingdom of God, while the unrighteous will not inherit the kingdom when it is established in all its fullness (1 Cor 6:9-11; cf. Gal 1:4; 5:21). For Paul, the Spirit is the present guarantee of our future redemption (2 Cor 1:22; 5:5). It is this eschatological expectation that fuels Paul's immediacy and indignation concerning the lack of spiritual growth and flagrant, habitual disobedience within the Christian community (cf. e.g., 1 Cor 3:1-4, 16-17; 5:1-13; 6:1-8, 15-20; 10:14-22; 11:17-22; 2 Cor 2:4; 6:14—7:1; 12:19—13:10). Since such a lifestyle of sin is a fundamental rejection of the Spirit's presence, Paul insists that those who refuse to repent be cast out from the people of God, for by definition they cannot be considered part of them (1 Cor 5:2, 9-13; 6:9-10; 2 Cor 12:21; 13:2, 10). As a result, inasmuch as the people of the new covenant are *defined* by their reception of the Spirit who transforms, Paul could not in good conscience address the Corinthians as "spiritual people" (πνευματικοί) in 1 Cor 3:1–3 because they still exhibited so much jealousy and strife. Instead, they remained "fleshly" (σαρκικοί).

THE PEOPLE OF THE NEW COVENANT AS THE TEMPLE OF GOD'S PRESENCE IN THE SPIRIT

The presence of the Spirit within and among the Corinthians as a fulfillment of the promises of the new covenant led Paul to the conclusion that those truly in Christ will be able to know God directly and respond to him positively with both the desire and ability to keep his covenant stipulations. That is to say, in the words once again of 1 Cor 3:16–17 and 6:19, those in Christ are "the temple of God." As such, they are not "their own," but are "holy." Here too, Paul's move from the idea of the presence of the Spirit under the new covenant to the concept of the church as the temple of God corresponds to the expectations of the "new covenant" outlined in Jer 31:31–34. As we have seen, because the new covenant pictured in Jer 31:31–34 will not be broken by a people who now belong to the Lord from the heart, it is described as an "everlasting covenant" in Jer 32:40. In turn, Jer 32:40 is conceptually related to the statement concerning the "everlasting covenant" in Ezek 37:24b–28, where as a summary of the prior passage of restoration in Ezek 36:25–27 we read:

> And they will walk in my ordinances, and keep my statutes, and observe them ... I will make a covenant of peace with them; it will be an everlasting covenant with them. And I will place them and multiply them, and will set my sanctuary in their midst forever. My dwelling place also will be with them; and I will be their God, and they shall be my people. And the nations will know that I am the Lord who sanctifies Israel, when my sanctuary is in their midst forever. (NASB)

Hence, both Jeremiah and Ezekiel have at the center of their expectations concerning the future "everlasting covenant" the establishment of a relationship between God and his people that is expressed in the covenant formula, "I will be their God and they shall be my people" (Jer 31:33; cf. 31:1; 32:38; Ezek 37:27). For both prophets this entails God's dwelling in the midst of his people (Jer 31:34; Ezek 37:26–27). Moreover, as Block has emphasized, Ezek 39:29 makes it clear that the promise of the Spirit in Ezek 36:27, "poured out upon his people, served as the permanent witness and seal of the *bryt šlwm* ["covenant of peace"] and the *bryt 'wlm* ["eternal covenant"].... When we think in terms of the OT understanding of the *rwḥ* of Yahweh, of which *to pneuma to hagion* is the counterpart, we should think first and foremost of the divine presence on earth."[16] In this light, Paul's reference in 2 Cor 1:22 and 5:5 to the Corinthians' being sealed in the Holy Spirit can be seen to be a divine confirmation of the covenant relationship in which they now stand.[17]

It is this eschatological perspective, in which the inaugural fulfillment of the age to come is understood to be taking place already in the present experience of the Spirit, that provides the primary presupposition for the structure of Paul's thought. In Christ, the people of the new covenant have already become the eschatological temple of God's presence via his Spirit. For in Paul's understanding, the glory experienced by believers as the result of the transforming work of the Spirit in 2 Cor 3:18 is in 2 Cor 4:6 the revelation of the glory of God himself, now seen on the face of Christ. The wonder of the gospel is that all those in Christ, like Moses before them in the tent of meeting, may enter into the very presence of God "with unveiled faces" without the fear of destruction. This is the "freedom" that exists wherever the Spirit resides (2 Cor 3:17). As the gift of the new covenant, the Spirit liberates the followers of Christ from the hard-heartedness that necessitated the veiling of God's glory in the past. Thus, Paul's "message and [his] preaching were not in persuasive words of wisdom, but in demonstration of the Spirit and of power, that your faith should not rest on the wisdom of men, but on the power of God" (1 Cor 2:4–5). In other words, as an apostle of Christ, Paul was called to exercise the new covenant "ministry of the Spirit" that abounded in glory for the people of God (2 Cor 3:8–11).

---

16. Ibid., 48. Block points to Joel 3:1; Zech 12:10; Isa 32:15; 44:1–4 in addition to Ezek 39:29 as texts that indicate that the pouring out of the Spirit "signified the ratification and sealing of the covenant relationship" (47). Block notes the implications of this for Acts 2 and for the subsequent pouring out of the Spirit in Acts 8:14–17; 10:44–48; and 19:6.

17. Following Block, "Prophet of the Spirit," 48, who also refers to Eph 1:13 and 4:30 for this same concept.

11

Paul's Concern for the Unity of the Church
An Embodiment of His New Covenant Theology[1]

The task now before us is to examine the way in which Paul applied his understanding of the church as the people of the new covenant to the issue of the unity of the church itself. The purpose is to show that both Paul's ecclesiology and his concern for unity among God's people derive ultimately not from pragmatic concerns but from biblical-theological ones. The reality of the church as the outpost of the kingdom of God in the midst of this evil age demands intrinsically and as a matter of witness that she reflect the unity of the triune God in her life together. For Paul, the reality of the invisible God is made visible in the life of his people. The dawning of the new creation (2 Cor 5:17) of the new covenant (2 Cor 3:6), of which Paul was a minister (2 Cor 3:4–6), rises to visibility in the transformed relationships that exist among those made new by the Messiah (cf. Rom 15:1–7 and Eph 2:10 as unpacked in 2:11–22!).

The approach of this paper is therefore exegetical, with a special eye on Paul's use of the OT in his arguments. In following this approach, I am

---

1. This paper was read and discussed at the Faculty Seminar, July 16, 2007, at Luther W. New Jr. Theological College, Dehradun, India. I am thankful for the occasion this seminar provided to be able to draw out the implications of my previous work for the issue of church unity in Paul's letters, and for the helpful responses, which have sharpened my thinking. Though this issue and their underlying passages are often discussed, to my knowledge the formative influence of Paul's new covenant theology has not been brought to bear on the topic. Now from Scott J. Hafemann, "Paul's Concern for the Unity of the Church: An Embodiment of His New Covenant Theology." *DTJ* 4/2 (2007) 117–37.

drawing heavily from my work in the preceding chapters on Paul's understanding of the church as the fulfillment of the OT hope for a new covenant people of God. The goal here is to see how this understanding impinges on Paul's concern for the unity of the church as a fulfillment of that same hope. For one cannot read Paul's letters for very long before being struck by how troubled he was that believers were divided over doctrinal, moral, and personal issues. The reason is clear. A central feature of Paul's job description as an apostle was to establish local churches that in their internal life together (Rom 14:1–23; Phil 2:1–4; Col 3:15) and in their fellowship with other churches (e.g., Rom 16:16; 1 Cor 11:16; 14:33; 16:19; 2 Cor 8:14–19; 9:2) would make up the one, unified, eschatological people of God (Eph 2:11–22; 4:1– 16). Indeed, Paul would conclude toward the end of his ministry that those gathered in Christ's name are now nothing less than "the house of God, which is the church of the living God, the pillar and bulwark of the truth" (1 Tim 3:15).[2]

As the sum total of the individual churches throughout the world, the church universal was to be one in her belief and practice, since the particular church to which one belonged was to be unified internally and with other believers as Christ's "body" (Rom 12:4–5; 1 Cor 12:13, 27; Eph 4:4–6, 12; Col 3:15). Thus, the main section of Romans, Paul's *magnum opus*, is not the delineation of Paul's gospel (chs. 1–8), or its significance within redemptive history (chs. 9–11), but its demand for the unity of the church (chs. 12–15).[3]

---

2. The designation "house of God" (οἶκος θεοῦ) in 1 Tim 3:15 recalls Jacob's dream-encounter with God, through which the covenant promises to Abraham were passed on to him (Gen 28:13–15), leading to Jacob's designation of that place as "the house of God" (בֵּית אֱלֹהִים) (Gen 28:17, 22). He consequently renames it "Bethel" (בֵּית־אֵל [Greek = Βαιθηλ]; Gen 28:19). In addition to the place name for the city of Bethel (Gen 12:8; 13:3; Exod 22:7; Josh 7:2; Jer 48:13, etc.), the "house of God" can thus also be used in the OT to refer to the place of God's presence in the temple (Isa 2:3; Hos 9:8; Joel 1:13, 16; Ps 134/133:1 LXX, etc.). Already here, therefore, we see an indication of the biblical backdrop for the significance of the church as the place and location of divine encounter. This is confirmed by Gal 2:9, where the temple "pillars" of the church are the Jerusalem apostles as authoritative tradents of the revelation in Christ (cf. Rev 3:12, for those who conquer in Christ as "pillars" in the temple of God!).

3. This point represents a growing consensus. Cf. the transitional conjunction, "therefore" (οὖν), in 12:1, linking what follows to what precedes as its inference. Though Rom 1–8 may be the theological heart and emphasis of the letter, the rhetorical main point is the expression of this theology in the life of the church, revolving around the call for unity between those who are weak and strong in faith. See, e.g., Stuhlmacher, *Romans*, 185: "12:1—15:13 is anything but a mere appendix to the theological expositions of chapters 1–11. Rather, it deals with the verification of justification in the life of the church"; Dunn, *Romans 9–16*, 705: "Chs. 12–15 follow naturally from and constitute a necessary corollary to the overall argument of chs. 1–11"; and Wright, *Romans*, 700: "The unveiling of God's righteousness . . . is not complete until Paul has shown

And the main point of Romans "is precisely the relationship between Jews and Gentiles, both in history and within the church, [which] forms 'the climax of the entire epistle' in Romans 15:7–13."[4] The theological doxology in Rom 11:33–36 thus leads to the ecclesiological doxology in 15:33, with its prayer that the God of peace be with *all* the Romans in their life together as those who are weak and strong in the faith.

We therefore misunderstand Paul's concern for the unity of the church if we think that it derived merely from a concern for the church herself. Paul's ultimate goal was not to keep people from getting upset or having their feelings hurt *per se*. The apostle Paul was theologically, not therapeutically, driven. Paul's ethics were an embodiment of his knowledge of what God has done and is doing in Christ to create a people for himself in this last stage of the history of redemption. Paul's concern for the unity of the church was therefore *based* in his eschatology (the new covenant has dawned in Christ, so that God's salvation and judgment are now being revealed among the nations!), *tempered* by his eschatology (the spiritual battle for the kingdom of God is still being waged until Christ returns!), and *inspired* by his eschatology (the future unity of God's people is a new covenant reality that cannot be thwarted!).

THE NEW COVENANT FOUNDATION OF CHURCH UNITY

It is revealing that in his consternation over the divisions between rich and poor at the Lord's Supper Paul turns in 1 Cor 11:23–26 to the tradition concerning the new covenant already embedded in the practice of the Lord's Supper that he inherited from the early Jerusalem church. Within the structure of Paul's argument, the reality of the new covenant becomes the basis for both his dismay over their disunity (1 Cor 11:17–22) and his declaration of warning for anyone who eats and drinks the cup "in an unworthy manner" (1 Cor 11:27). Just as Adam and Eve suffered death for breaking the Sabbath, which characterized their covenant relationship with God in the garden of Eden (Gen 2:17), and Israel was given the death penalty for breaking the Sabbath under the Sinai covenant (Exod 31:14), so too the church suffers death for breaking her new covenant relationship under Christ as "Lord of the Sabbath" (Mark 2:28; 1 Cor 11:30).

---

how the 'justified' community lives its life on the basis of its shared belief in Jesus as Lord.... Romans 12–16 is the ultimate answer to those who suggest that Paul's 'ethics' are not really related to his 'theology.'"

4. From my article, "Eschatology and Ethics," 161–62, quoting J. R. Wagner.

In turning our attention to the realities of the new covenant undergirding this severe warning, and for the sake of reference regarding the argument to follow, it will be helpful to be reminded again of the argument of Jer 31:31–34:

31:31	"Behold, the days are coming," declares the Lord, "when I will make a new covenant with the house of Israel and with the house of Judah.
32a	*Specifically*, I will not make it like the covenant that I made with their fathers . . .
32b	*since* they broke this covenant of mine
32c	*even though* I was a husband to them," declares the Lord.
33a	"*The reason the new covenant will be different in this regard* (כִּי) *is that* this is the covenant that I will make with the house of Israel after those days," declares the Lord, "I will put my law within them, and I will write it on their heart.
33b	*The result of this new covenant will be that* I will be their God, and they shall be my people.
34a	*The ultimate consequence of this new covenant relationship in which I am their God and they are my people is that* they shall not teach again each man his neighbor and each man his brother saying, 'Know the Lord,'
34b	*because* (כִּי) they shall all know me, from the least of them to the greatest of them," declares the Lord.
34c	"*The basis for all of this* (כִּי) *is that* I will forgive their iniquity, and I will remember their sin no more."

Within the argument of Jer 31:31–34, verse 34c makes clear that the foundation of the new covenant is the fact that, despite Israel's past history of rebellion (v. 32), God will "remember their sin no more." Verses 33a–34b affirm that the promised changed condition of God's people (v. 33a) and the resultant unbroken nature of the new covenant (vv. 33b–34b) are both to be based upon the bestowal of this divine forgiveness. As the history-of-redemption unfolded, this "new covenant" bestowal of forgiveness was eventually made possible by the life, death, resurrection, and ascension of the Messiah, whose death provided atonement for the sins of his people (cf. 1 Cor 8:11; 15:3; Rom 3:21–26; 4:25; 5:6, 8; Gal 3:10). The realization of the new covenant relationship between God and his people is consequently derived from the reality of the cross.

This is why those who humiliated others at the Lord's Supper, which commemorates the death of Christ for the sins of his people, were in reality "sinning against the body and blood of the Lord" (1 Cor 11:27; cf. Rom

14:15).[5] Since love is the fulfillment of the Sinai law, which is now written on the heart under the new covenant (cf. 1 Cor 7:19; Rom 13:8; Gal 5:14), not to love one another is to deny the reality and power of the cross in one's life. For Jer 31:34 indicates that the result of this new covenant transformation of God's people brought about by Christ's death is that the people of the new covenant will not need to be taught to "know" the Lord, since they will *all* know him (cf. 1 Thess 4:9). The need for the continual teaching spoken of in Deut 6:6–9 and 11:18–21, so that the law might be on one's heart, should no longer be necessary (hence Paul's condemnation of the Corinthians in 1 Cor 11:17–22). For to have the "law written on the heart" (Jer 31:33) is a metaphor for the reversal of the hard-heartedness that is characterized by having sin engraved on the heart (Jer 17:1).

The argument of Jer 31:31–34 makes clear that the result of this change of heart is that the new covenant, unlike the old, will not be broken (Jer 31:31–32 and 34 are both supported by v. 33). And the unity of the church is an essential expression of this heart-transformed obedience to the law that characterizes the new covenant. The new covenant transformation of God's people entails the overturning of the lack of trust that characterized relationships between neighbors under the old covenant, in which they did not teach the truth but spoke lies to one another and through their deceit "refuse(d) to know" the Lord (Jer 9:4–6). Hence, it is not as if the knowledge of God has been altered or intensified or made easier to comprehend under the new covenant. It is not that pastor-teachers are no longer needed in the church, as Paul's own ministry testifies! Instead, under the new covenant God will simply do for the people of God *as a whole* what he had done for the remnant alone under the old covenant.[6] There is therefore no excuse for such a breaking of the law within the new covenant community.

---

5. For an insightful treatment of the covenant context for understanding the nature, unity, and calling of the church, see now Martens, "People of God." Martens (231) argues persuasively that the covenant formula, "I will be your God and you shall be my people," has "a definite sociological dimension." Thus, against its covenant backdrop in the Passover, which, like all of Israel's festivals, functioned to express the "sociological bondedness" of Israel as God's people, Martens argues that "the communion commemoration is, among other things, a communal event of solidarity. All believers partake of the bread; all believers partake of the cup. One message from this symbolic action is that members of the community belong together. Just as the Passover emphasized 'the unity and the common identity of those who share it,' so also in the Last Supper 'the unity and fellowship of the participants [was] a significant part of the ongoing celebration of the Lord's Supper'" (239, quoting Routledge).

6. This renewal is accomplished by God's dwelling in the midst of his people, a reality now made possible under the new covenant. For under the Sinai covenant, beginning with the sin of the golden calf, the glory of God had to be kept veiled due to Israel's sinful, "stiff-necked" state (cf. Jer 7:26; 19:15 with Exod 33:3, 5; 34:29–35 and Deut 9:6,

The new covenant promise of writing the law on the heart for *all* those within the covenant community (Jer 31:33), as the consequence of the forgiveness of sins (Jer 31:34) and the presence of the Spirit (Ezek 36:26-27), is thus the source of Paul's serious concern for the unity of the church.[7] In response to the inauguration of this promise now taking place in the church, Paul declares that since *all* those who belong to Christ are "sons of God through faith in Christ," "there is neither Jew nor Greek, there is neither slave nor free, there is neither male nor female; for you are all *one* in Christ Jesus" (Gal 3:26-28). No human distinctives or achievements are required as prerequisites for being full-fledged members of God's people. As a consequence of the *one* gospel, all of God's people, regardless of their ethnic identity or previous moral track record, become covenant keepers (Rom 1:16; 3:29-30). There is one basis of justification for all (Christ), one means of justification for all (faith), and one justified life for all (living in accordance with the "law written on the heart" by the power of the Spirit). Whether one is Jew or Gentile, slave or free, male or female, all know the Lord together as a result of the coming of the Christ to inaugurate the new covenant.

For Paul, though the new covenant is the means by which the unity of the church is established, the oneness of the church is grounded ultimately in the oneness of God, who reveals himself in Christ (cf. the Christological adaptation of the "Shema" from Deut 6:4 in 1 Cor 8:5-6).[8] Because God is one, the *one* gospel is the saving power of the *same* God to *all* who know him in the *same* way (Rom 1:16; Phil 1:27; 1 Tim 2:3-6). So too, God judges all people *equally* and by the *same* standard, regardless of whether they are

---

13). At the cross this veil separating God from his people is rent in two (Mark 15:38). As a result, the renewed access to God's presence, now experienced in the down payment of the Spirit (2 Cor 1:22; 5:5; Rom 8:23; Eph 1:13-14), brings with it the progressive transformation of all God's people into God's own character (Jer 31:33; 2 Cor 3:6, 18).

7. I owe this emphasis to the insightful response to my paper by Roji T. George of New Theological College, Dehradun, India, who helped to clarify this aspect of my argument.

8. This point was made already by Ridderbos, *Paul*, 372, who argued that although the Spirit is instrumental in understanding the church as the body of Christ, the church does not rest "on the pneumatic indwelling of Christ in his Church," but is "in the first instance ... a redemptive-historical, 'objective' unity" (pointing to Rom 12:5; 1 Cor 6:15-16; 12:13, 27; Gal 3:27-29, etc.). Thus, the sequence of Paul's thought is not from Christ to the Spirit to the body of Christ, but from Christ to "the body-in-Christ" to the Spirit (372). We have seen that this redemptive-historical unity derives from the promise of the new covenant itself, in which in both Jeremiah and Ezekiel forgiveness precedes the Spirit and makes his coming possible. Therefore, in 1 Cor 12, the first work of the Spirit is the confession of Jesus as Lord (v. 3), followed by the Spirit's gifting of the body of Christ (vv. 4-11).

Jew or Gentile, since "there is no partiality with God" (Rom 2:11; cf. 2:6–16; 2 Cor 5:10; 1 Thess 5:1–10). In turn, the unity of God's people is the public demonstration par excellence of the gospel (note how Eph 2:1–10 leads to the inference of 2:11–22), since such unity is not based on our cultural, racial or socio-economic similarities, but in the grace of God manifested in the humility and mutual acceptance of his people (Rom 14:1–23). The unmerited grace of God, demonstrated in God's unconditional election (Rom 9:11), levels the playing field in his presence (1 Cor 1:16–31). In contrast, the world's envy and strife reveal God's wrath and the absence of his presence (cf. Rom 1:29; cf. 1 Cor 3:3; Gal 5:20).

THE NEW COVENANT CALL TO MAINTAIN CHURCH UNITY

Paul is clear that the unity of the church is derived solely from our common confession of Christ as Lord, from our kindness and forgiveness toward one another in light of God's grace toward us, and from our life together of mutual dependence on one another's gifts, all of which are brought about by the Spirit, whose presence among us is made possible by the cross (1 Cor 12:1–31; Eph 4:30–31). "For by one Spirit we were all baptized into one body—Jews or Greeks, slaves or free—and all were made to drink of one Spirit" (1 Cor 12:13). In Trinitarian terms, this unity with God made possible by the cross of Christ expresses itself in a bond of unity with one another created by the fruit of the Spirit (Gal 5:22–23). And since this fruit of the Spirit is what God's law requires, there is no judgment from the law against those who evidence such fruit; that is, "there is no law against" such a life (Gal 5:23b).[9] Love is the fulfillment of the law (Gal 5:14).

God ensured this unity by not endowing his people equally with the gifts of his Spirit (Rom 12:4). Every one who confesses Jesus as Lord receives at least one gift of the Spirit, but nobody has them all (1 Cor 12:4–11). As a result, those who belong to Christ, though all filled with the Spirit, are nevertheless inextricably intertwined with each other and need each other to be

---

9. For this point and its development in Galatians, see now Wilson, *Curse of the Law*, esp. 122–25, where he shows that the phrase in 5:23, "against such things there is no law," is a reference to the curse of the law. Hence, those who evidence the fruit of the Spirit are not judged by the law, since "those who are led by the Spirit actually satisfy the law's demands" (123). Thus, 5:23 is to be understood as a parallel expression to being "under the curse of the law" in Gal 3:10, 13, which is also given in shorthand by Paul with the phrase "under law" in 3:23; 4:4–5, 21 and 5:18. To maintain the unity of the church in love is thus part of what it means to keep the law as made possible under the new covenant.

whole (Rom 12:5; 1 Cor 12:12-26). This is one reason why Paul likens the church to a body: "If one part suffers, every part suffers with it; if one part is honored, every part rejoices with it" (1 Cor 12:26; cf. 2 Cor 11:29 for another outworking of this same principle). Love, which is the active sharing of our strengths with others, together with the mutual acceptance of each other's weaknesses, is therefore the ligament that holds the church as "the body of Christ" together (Rom 12:10, 16; 13:8; 14:2-20; 15:1-6; Gal 5:13-15; 6:2-3; Eph 4:31). Paul "pictures the Church not as a body of Christians but as the body of Christ. There is unity in plurality, but not uniformity. . . . Soards . . . observes that Paul's point is not unity in diversity and diversity in unity, as many have it, but rather 'unity dominates diversity and makes diversity genuinely meaningful and constructive.'"[10]

For this reason, when Paul encounters disunity in the Corinthian church, he reminds them that the cross of Christ, as the power and wisdom of God, is the sole basis of their salvation (1 Cor 1:18-31), since the cross makes it possible for God to dwell among his people without destroying them, but instead transforming them into his own image (1 Cor 2:6-16; 2 Cor 3:18). Paul therefore queries them in amazement, "Do you not know that you are God's temple and that God's Spirit dwells in you?" (1 Cor 3:16), and wonders how any one part of the body can say that it does not need the others (1 Cor 12:21). By its pride, disunity in the church denies the cross, quenches the Spirit, and destroys the love that is at the heart of the church's testimony to the world of the reality of the new covenant. Again, therefore, Paul warns that "if any man destroys the temple of God, God will destroy him, for the temple of God is holy, and that is what you are" (1 Cor 3:17).[11]

Since so much is at stake in the unity of the church, Paul again returns to the theme of the church as the temple of God's presence in 2 Cor 6:14-16a in order to call the recently repentant Corinthians to separate from those in their midst who are trying to destroy the church with their false teaching and practice:

> Do not be mismated with unbelievers. For what partnership have righteousness and iniquity? Or what fellowship has light with darkness? What accord has Christ with Be'lial? Or what has a believer in common with an unbeliever? What agreement has the temple of God with idols? For we are the temple of the living God.[12]

---

10. Garland, *1 Corinthians*, 590.

11. In support of the above summary, see chapter 10.

12. Many scholars argue that 6:14—7:1 is an interpolation into this context, either written by Paul for another setting or from a non-Pauline origin, that disrupts the flow

The reference in verse 16a to the Corinthians as "the temple of the living God" is the climax to Paul's string of contrasts in 2 Cor 6:14–16a, by which he describes the incompatibility between the church and the world. To be the people of God's presence is not only to be unified with one another but also to be radically distinct from unbelievers and their idols.

Not surprisingly, in 6:16b–18 Paul then bases this call to purify the church on the reality of God's Spirit in their lives as believers:

16b	*just as God said that,* "I will dwell among them and I will move among [them],
16c	*so that* I will be their God
16d	*and* they will be my people [Lev 26:11–12 + Ezek 37:27].
17a	*Therefore,* go out from their midst,
17b	*and* be separate, *says the Lord,*
17c	*and* do not touch uncleanness [Isa 52:11]
17d	*so that* I will receive you [Ezek 20:34 + 2 Sam 7:14]
18a	*so that* I will be to you a father
18b	*and* you will be to me sons and daughters [2 Sam 7:14 + Isa 43:6], *says the Lord Almighty.*

The identification of the church as the temple of God is the only one of Paul's descriptions in 6:14–16a that has its own support in what follows, thereby further highlighting its significance as a designation of the people of the new covenant. Indeed, nowhere in the Old Testament is Israel ever identified with the temple. But the parallel between the phrase in 6:16b, "the *temple* of the living God," and Paul's earlier reference in 2 Cor 3:3 to "the *Spirit* of the living God" indicates that Paul can equate the *church* with the temple because, under the new covenant, believers are now the revelatory "location" of God's presence on earth (cf. again 1 Tim 3:15 and the pouring out of the Spirit as the fulfillment of Ezek 36:26–27 in 2 Cor 1:22; 3:3–6, 8, 17–18; 4:13; 5:5). Since the church, both in regard to its individual members (1 Cor 6:19) and in its life together corporately (1 Cor 3:16), is the place of God's unique presence in the world, there can be no idols in her midst.

Here, as in 1 Cor 3:16–17, the identification of the church with the temple consequently contains the same uncompromising call to maintain the purity of the church that was associated with the Jerusalem temple under

---

of thought from 6:13 to 7:2. For my own arguments in favor of its Pauline authorship and important contribution to this context (i.e., the way by which the Corinthians will open their hearts to Paul [6:13] is by separating from the unbelievers in their midst who are continuing to bring disunity to the church), see my *2 Corinthians,* 277–78.

the old covenant, albeit not kept (cf., e.g., Amos 5:21–24; Isa 1:10–17; Jer 7:1–20; 19:1–15; Ezek 8:1–18). Verses 16b-18 underscore that Paul's command to separate from unbelievers within the church (not from the world! cf. 1 Cor 5:9–10[13]) is therefore not an expression of hubris or self-defensive

13. There are three basic views of the identity of the "unbelievers" in 2 Cor 6:14. Some argue that "unbelievers" and "idols" in this passage are general terms that refer to all those who do not follow Christ; see for example, Furnish, *II Corinthians*, 372. Interpreted in this way, the passage is applied to all areas of life, from worship and work to marriage and education, in order to maintain purity in the world from all idolatrous defilement. When taken in this way, 2 Cor 6:14 creates an irresolvable tension with 1 Cor 5:9–10, where Paul recognizes the necessity of participating in the affairs of this world. Elsewhere, Paul never calls Christians to separate from "unbelievers" in the common affairs of society. Moreover, in our present context Paul is not concerned with relationships in the world but with relationships *within the church* (cf. 1 Cor 5:11–13).

On the other extreme, some take the terms "unbelievers" and "idols" to be very specific references back to the particular problem of eating meat offered to idols addressed in 1 Cor 8–10; see, for example, the programmatic work of Fee, "II Corinthians vi.14—vii.1," 140–67. From this perspective, Paul is once again calling the Corinthians to abstain from food that has knowingly been offered to idols and from participating in the worship of idols. Read in this way, the passage remains a concrete warning against participating in non-Christian worship. But although there are parallels in terminology between 2 Cor 6:14—7:1 and 1 Cor 8–10, this interpretation does not do justice to the distinct context of 2 Corinthians. There is no indication in 2 Corinthians that Paul is still concerned with the question of sharing in food offered to idols. In our present context, Paul is concerned with those who are in rebellion against his authority and gospel.

In contrast to these alternatives, Paul's concern is best seen as a call to the Corinthians to align with his ministry by separating themselves from those within the Corinthian church who continue to side with his opponents. Paul drives home the seriousness of this point by identifying those still in rebellion against him as "unbelievers," despite their own claims to the contrary, and by framing the issue in terms of idolatry and the temple of God! Paul calls the Corinthians of genuine faith to separate from those "unbelievers" whose lives, under the deceptive influence of "Belial," are characterized by the wickedness and darkness of unbelief (cf. 11:3–4, 13–15). The call in 6:14—7:1 for "the temple of God" to separate from "unbelievers" and "idolatry" parallels Paul's earlier warning in 1 Cor 3:16–17 concerning destroying the temple of God and his call in 1 Cor 5:11 to disassociate with any one who bears the name of "brother" if he is guilty of immorality or idolatry.

Given the polemical situation in which Paul finds himself, "opening up" to Paul (2 Cor 6:13) will necessarily mean closing oneself off from those who oppose him (6:14–16a; 7:1), whom Paul now shockingly labels "unbelievers." Paul's statement is shocking because, for Paul, "unbelievers" is not a term used to refer to erring, but still genuine Christians (as described, for example, in 1 Cor 3:10–15). Paul's use of this designation elsewhere shows that it refers only to those who are manifestly outside the sphere of God's people, even if they profess otherwise (cf. 1 Cor 6:6; 7:12–15; 10:27; 14:22–24; 2 Cor 4:4; 1 Tim 5:8; Titus 1:15–16). "Unbelievers" are non-Christians, not temporarily "misled Christians." Thus, to make clear precisely what is at stake in supporting his opponents, Paul employs much of the same terminology in 6:14–16 and 7:1 that he used earlier to describe the absolute necessity of breaking free from demon-dominated idolatry (cf. too 1 Cor 10:16–21 with 6:14 and 1 Cor 8:7 with 7:1).

fear, but the immediate application of the Scripture's expectation regarding the reality of the new covenant. Note that the chain of OT passages quoted in verses 16b–18 is introduced in verse 16b with a single citation formula, "just as God said," and closed off in verse 18c with the corresponding formula, "says the Lord Almighty." Thus, as James Scott observes, the intermediate "says the Lord" in verse 17 serves to divide the quotations into two halves, with three lines each.[14] Structured in this way, the chain of quotes is presented as a *single citation*, composed of six OT passages, which, *when read as a whole*, is designed to support the command of verse 14 ("Do not be mismated with unbelievers") and its restatement in 7:1 ("Let us cleanse ourselves from every defilement of body and spirit, and make holiness perfect in the fear of God").

The first Old Testament reference in Paul's chain of quotes is taken primarily from the promise of God's covenant presence in Lev 26:11–12. However, the promise was originally stated in the second person ("I will put my dwelling place *among you*," etc.), not the third, as it is in 2 Cor 6:16 ("I will live *with them*," etc.). Scott demonstrates that this alteration comes about because Paul conflated Lev 26:11–12 with the *new covenant* promise of Ezek 37:27 ("My dwelling place will be *with them*").[15] By interpreting Lev 26:11–12 in terms of Ezek 37:27 and applying it to his readers, Paul is reflecting his conviction that the original covenant promises are *now* beginning to be fulfilled in the Corinthian church as God's temple!

In 6:17 Paul draws the scriptural conclusion (note the "therefore" of 17a) that flows from the establishment of this new covenant relationship with the Corinthians: three commands from Isa 52:11 ("come out . . . be separate . . . touch no unclean thing") and three ensuing promises from Ezek 20:34; 2 Sam 7:14, and Isa 43:6 ("and I will receive you, I will be a Father to you, and you will be my sons and daughters"). In its original context, Isa 52:11 is directed to Israel, calling her as a priestly people to separate from her former oppressors in conjunction with her anticipated "second exodus" redemption from captivity. Paul's application of these commands to the Corinthians again reflects his conviction that the promised restoration of God's people, though not yet fully consummated, is beginning to take place

---

Now, however, it describes the absolute incompatibility between those who believe (and hence support Paul's ministry!) and those who are calling Paul's apostleship into question. Paul's point is stark. In the final analysis, the believers in Corinth must recognize Paul's opponents to be "unbelievers" and separate from them. Conversely, if they refuse to obey Paul's command, they too will be considered unbelievers (cf. 13:5).

14. Scott, "Use of Scripture," 76, 83. The following discussion of the OT background to 2 Cor 6:16–18 is a based on Scott's insightful work.

15. Ibid., 78–79, 97.

in the establishment of the Corinthian church. If the Corinthians are part of God's new covenant people, they too must separate from the unbelievers around them in order to maintain the purity of God's "temple."

In fulfillment of Isa 52:11, Paul therefore views the Corinthians as priests fulfilling the role of mediating God's glory to the world originally proclaimed for Israel in Exod 19:6, so that, like Isaiah, Paul calls them to separate from what is unclean. Given the reality of the new covenant, the church, unlike the Israel of old, cannot be allowed to remain a mixed multitude of believers and unbelievers. Paul's argument in 6:14–17 illustrates that it is simply impossible to identify the Corinthians as a *priestly* people who are *themselves* the *temple* of God without drawing the theological and moral implications that are inextricably a part of this identity.

That the stakes are high in the call to purify the church is again evident in the next step in Paul's argument. The threefold scriptural command of verse 17abc leads directly to the threefold promises of 17d–18, which, like the commands, are also a conflation of Old Testament texts, this time Ezek 20:34bLXX, 2 Sam 7:14 and Isa 43:6. In its original context, Ezek 20:34 is God's promise of welcome to those who will return home from the exile.[16] Just as Isa 52:11 calls God's people to "come out" from the world as a result of the "second exodus," Ezek 20:34 promises that God will "receive" them back when they do so. Its combination with the promise of a Davidic messiah from 2 Sam 7:14 reflects the expectation that the redemption from exile would take place through the reign of David's long-promised "son," who is also identified as *God's* "son."

In accordance with this expectation, in verse 18 Paul quotes the adoption formula from 2 Sam 7:14, but now makes it plural ("sons") to refer once again to the Corinthians, just he applied the previous texts to them as well. Paul then combines it with the reference to "daughters" from Isa 43:6, where the "second exodus" restoration of Israel is expressed in terms of sons *and daughters* (cf. Isa 49:22; 60:4). Here too the new covenant context of Paul's argument comes to the fore, since "I will be a father to you, and you will be my sons and daughters" is the "adoption" formula used in Scripture to indicate the *covenant* relationship between God and his people. In using this formula, Paul is reflecting the Jewish expectation that God's people would one day be "adopted" as God's children by virtue of their allegiance to and incorporation into God's "adopted son," the Messiah.[17] In fulfillment of this

---

16. For the use of the verb, "to receive" (εἰσδέχομαι), in 6:17 as a promise of deliverance from exile, see Hos 8:10; Mic 4:6; Zeph 3:19, 20; Zech 10:8, 10; Jer 23:3; Ezek 11:17; 20:34 and 22:19, as adduced by Scott, "Use of Scripture," 85n51.

17. See Scott, "Use of Scripture," 87–88. In the same way, the *adoption* formula in 2 Sam 7:14 corresponds to the *covenant* formula used in 2 Sam 7:24 and Jer 31:1. In the

expectation, the Corinthians are promised that, if they "come out" and separate from uncleanness, they too, as God's "sons and daughters," will one day participate with God's Son in the consummation of his salvation (for the corresponding use of the concept of "adoption," cf. Rom 8:15, 23; 9:4; Gal 4:4–5; Eph 1:5).

Paul's point is as uncompromising as it is clear. Since the Corinthians are *already* part of God's new covenant people in fulfillment of the prophets' hopes (the "covenant prologue" in vv. 16b–16e), they must separate from the unbelievers among them (the "covenant stipulations" in vv. 17a–c) in anticipation of God's final deliverance (the "covenant promise" in v. 18). The promise of a continuing covenant relationship and final redemption (v. 18) is given only to those who keep the covenant stipulations (v. 17). In this case, such covenant keeping entails living out their covenant identity by separating from impurity for the sake of the unity of the church (vv. 14–16a). As members of the same covenant, God, as Father, and the Corinthians, as his sons and daughters, belong to one another in the same "family," each with their own roles and responsibilities.[18] In this context, the emphasis falls on the responsibility of God's "children" to separate from those within the covenant who, in reality, do not belong and hence are rendering it unclean.

The gravity of Paul's words makes sense once we come to grips with the implications of the fact that Paul interprets the church as "the temple of the living God" (v. 16a) in terms of her being "adopted" as God's sons and daughters (v. 18).[19] This identification is the key to Paul's passion for the purity of God's people. The church is not simply one among many social institutions playing an essential role within the fabric of society. Nor is the church merely a service organization meeting the immediate needs of her neighbors. Such a domestication of the church could not be more foreign to Paul's view of God's people as the continuation of the remnant of Israel, or to her status as a disenfranchised minority within the Roman world in which Paul lived. Instead, as the community of the new covenant, the church is

---

NT, compare Rev 21:3 (covenant formula) with Rev 21:7 (adoption formula).

18. For the inextricable link within the covenant conception between God as King and Father, see the programmatic essay of Cross, "Kinship and Covenant."

19. For a biblical-theological development of the theme of the temple in relationship to the church, see Beale, *Temple*, esp. 253–56, where he explicates 2 Cor 6:16–18 as "Paul's most explicit reference to believers forming an end-time temple ... which Paul identifies as part of the dawning restoration promises" (253; he sees the church, therefore, as a beginning fulfillment of the promise of a new temple as part of Israel's restoration according to Ezek 37:26–28; 40–48; see 275–76, 316–17).

the "family of God" united by her common identity in Christ and gathered around her common worship and fear of "the Lord Almighty" (v. 18b).[20]

THE REALITY OF DISUNITY IN A FALLEN WORLD

We have seen that Paul's concern for the unity of the church is based on the history-of-redemption fact that the kingdom of God has dawned, thereby establishing the eschatological people of the new covenant. At the same time, part of the mystery of the kingdom is that it is being inaugurated short of its consummation. The kingdom of God is here but it is not yet here in all of its fullness. The new age of the new creation under the new covenant is dawning but the old age continues on. Only when Christ returns will this age come to an end. Consequently, the church lives between the first and second comings of the Christ in the "overlapping of the ages," during which she is to be salt and light in the midst of this evil age.

This means that the church will remain engaged in a spiritual battle against sin until the Lord returns.[21] Part of this battle is within the church herself, since her present place in the history of redemption means that disunity and conflict within the people of God will sometimes be necessary for the sake of the truth (1 Tim 4:1-3; 2 Tim 4:1-4; Titus 1:7-16). As Paul put it to the divided Corinthians in 1 Cor 11:19, "*there must be factions among you in order that those who are genuine among you may be recognized.*" Nevertheless, despite living in a fallen world, Paul is not content with this disunity, as if a divided church were to be accepted as the norm (see 1 Cor 1:10-17)! When faced with unbelievers within the church, Paul's response was to call for purity (2 Cor 6:14-7:1) and to exercise church discipline (cf. also 1 Cor 5:1-8; Phil 3:2; 1 Tim 1:19-20; 2 Tim 3:1-9). At the same time, Paul's stern response to the kind of unbelief within the church that denies the gospel in word and deed is matched by a call to persevere in patience with the newly

---

20. See again Martens, "People of God," 232, who points out that, unlike in the ancient Near East, where "gods were usually associated not first with people but with a given territory . . . Yahweh is connected to a community" (see Exod 12:12; 2 Kgs 18:35). So too, whereas the imperial cults of the NT era "extolled Caesar as a 'god'" over the Roman empire, the church under Jesus as Lord "was an alternative community, and in some ways even an alternative political entity" (232). This is in stark contrast to Gnosticism and the mystery religions, early Christianity's religious competitors, which stressed the private experiences of the individual and "were not marked by a high consciousness of community" (232). But to be bonded to God as his covenant people "in Christ" meant that "as a 'people' each constituent belongs to the other" (237; relying on Paul's arguments in Eph 1-2 and 1 Cor 12).

21. For a classic presentation of this basic NT conception of inaugurated eschatology, see still the summary by Ladd, *Gospel of the Kingdom.*

converted and with those who are struggling as believers. The "overlapping of the ages" demands that for the sake of the unity of the church an essential aspect of our spiritual battle will be to forgive, accept, and suffer on behalf of those who are "weaker" in the faith (1 Cor 8–10; 2 Cor 11:28[!]; Rom 14:1—15:13; Gal 6:1–10; 1 Thess 5:14; 2 Tim 2:10, 24–26; 4:2, etc.).

Paul exemplified this himself, even when it cost him his own reputation. When he first went to Corinth, Paul readily gave up his right as an apostle to be supported financially by the Corinthians in order not to put any obstacle in the way of the gospel (1 Cor 9:1–19). He did so even though it meant deprivation and disgrace (1 Cor 4:10–13). Later, he could point to his own practice in this regard as an example of how the strong in Corinth ought to give up their rights for the sake of their weaker brethren (cf. 1 Cor 8:10–13). So too, Paul discloses that his second change of travel plans regarding his return to Corinth was likewise motivated by his desire to be merciful to the Corinthians (2 Cor 1:23—2:4).[22] Earlier, when the Corinthians had rebelled against Paul and his gospel during his previous visit, he had left town rather than bringing the conflict to an end immediately. To do so would have maintained his own status as an apostle, but it would have meant pouring out the judgment of God upon the congregation and splitting the church. Thus, rather than maintaining his own rights and reputation, Paul again suffered personal rejection in order to give the Corinthians an opportunity for repentance (his opponents no doubt labeled Paul a coward for leaving; see 2 Cor 10:1, 10). Then, rather than returning as planned, he sent Titus in his place with a "letter of tears" to warn the Corinthians of the peril they faced for rejecting the gospel, giving them yet another chance to come back to their spiritual senses (2 Cor 2:4; 7:8–10). For Paul knew that when he did return for his third visit he would have to excommunicate those who had not repented of their rebellion against the gospel as expressed in their repudiation of his own apostolic life and ministry. Hence, when the majority of the church did repent in response to his tearful letter (2 Cor 2:5–11; 7:5–16), Paul postponed his visit yet again rather than returning in triumph to vindicate himself! Instead, he wrote still one more letter, now our canonical "2 Corinthians," in order to strengthen the newly repentant in their faith and to call the rebellious back to the Lord one more time.

Again and again Paul was willing to give up his own rights for the sake of others. He was quick to give the Corinthians the benefit of the doubt that the opponents were temporarily misleading them, rather than concluding

---

22. Paul's first change of plans regarding coming to Corinth was motivated by his desire for the Corinthians to have an even greater opportunity to be merciful *to others* by giving them a second possibility to give money to the suffering Christians in Jerusalem (2 Cor 1:15–16; cf. 1 Cor 16:1–9).

that they were definitively rejecting Christ as unbelievers. If Paul were to err in this regard, he would do so on the side of patience and self-denial rather than being too quick to judge. The theological principle guiding Paul's actions at this point was his understanding of how God had revealed himself in Christ (see 2 Cor 1:15-22). For to Paul, the gap between the coming of Christ to die on the cross and his coming again to judge the world demonstrates that an essential aspect of God's purpose is to create a patient and prolonged opportunity for God's people to repent in order that they might be spared the eventual judgment of God (cf. 2 Cor 1:23—2:1 with 13:1-10).[23] Paul changed his plans in order to act toward the Corinthians in the same way that God is now acting toward his people between the first and second comings of Christ—that is, between the inauguration and consummation of the new creation of the new covenant established under the kingdom of God. And here too, Paul's actions were guided by his commitment to the unity of the church as the new covenant people of God. For just as Paul had extended mercy to the Corinthians, he expected them to do the same by welcoming the repentant offender back into their midst in order to thwart Satan's desire to maintain disharmony in the church (2 Cor 2:6-11; cf. Col 3:13).

CONCLUSION: THE HOPE OF CHURCH UNITY IN THE AGE TO COME

Despite the problems of church unity in the present, Paul confidently looked forward to the purification of God's people, Jew and Gentile, as *one* people in Christ, for he knew that this was God's future for his church (cf. 1 Thess 3:12-13; 5:23; Eph 1:3-4; 2:7; 5:27; Phil 1:9-11; Col 1:22). It was this hope, based on the coming of Christ in the past and focused on God's promises regarding the redemption of Israel and the nations still to come (see esp. Rom 15:1-13),[24] that led Paul to pray for and call the church already now to the kind of harmony created by love that glorifies God:

---

23. Note how 2 Pet 3:15-16 understands this to be the point of Paul's teaching concerning the apparent delay in Christ's return: Peter points to Paul's teaching in support of his own conclusion that we are to "count the forbearance of our Lord as salvation" (2 Pet 3:15), since "the Lord is not slow about his promise as some count slowness, but is forbearing toward you, not wishing that any should perish, but that all should reach repentance" (2 Pet 3:9).

24. The following argument is taken from and supported by my article, "Eschatology and Ethics."

> May the God of steadfastness and encouragement grant you to live in such harmony with one another, in accord with Christ Jesus, that together you may with one voice glorify the God and Father of our Lord Jesus Christ. Welcome one another, therefore, as Christ has welcomed you, for the glory of God (Rom 15:5-7).

This hope, prayer, and command are the climax of Paul's letter to the Romans. In view of the history of redemption outlined in this magisterial letter, Paul calls the "strong" and the "weak" to accept one another for two reasons: (1) because of the unity that Christ has created in the church through his own accepting of us all (Rom 15:1-6); and (2) in view of the salvation of Jew and Gentile still to come at the end of the age, in which the nations will one day join Israel in worshipping the one, true God (Rom 15:9b-12). The Messiah has come and a remnant of Jews and Gentiles is now being saved to the glory of God (this is the point of Ps 18:49; Deut 32:43; and Ps 117:1 as quoted in Rom 15:9-11). But in accordance with the promises to the fathers (Rom 15:8), Christ must return again to vindicate his people, judge the nations for their rebellion, restore Israel, and save the Gentiles (Isa 11:10 in Rom 15:12). Between the two comings of Christ, the unity of the church in worship and love is therefore an essential demonstration of the saving power of the cross behind us and a signpost of the reality to come that glorifies God in advance of the full manifestation of God's glory at the return of Christ (Rom 15:1-2, 7).[25] Paul's eschatology drove his ethics.

The hope-driven life of mutual acceptance within the body of Christ is thus an anticipation of the fulfillment to come, the dawning of the new creation in the midst of the old. Such a hope in the promises of God is sure. It is confirmed by what Christ has already done (Rom 15:8) and secured by the presence and power of the Spirit as a down payment of the age to come (Rom 15:13). Since all of this comes from God, it returns to him in praise for his grace and glory (cf. again Rom 11:33-36 with 15:33). As a result, the way to praise God for what he has done, is doing, and will do for his people is to

---

25. We thus end where we began, with the relationship between 2 Cor 5:17; Rom 15:1-7; and Eph 2:10-22. See, e.g., Stuhlmacher, "He is our Peace," 191, commenting on 2 Cor 5:17; Eph 2:15; 4:24; and Gal 3:28: "The meaning of the cross is the establishment of a new communion between God and humanity and the new creation . . . of the one new humanity out of Gentiles and Jews which serves God in freedom and gratitude. . . . Reconciliation reaches its goal in the creation of the new humanity that overcomes the ancient separation of Gentiles and Jews through life together in the community." Stuhlmacher (191) points out that Eph 2:17-18 makes it clear that this new creation of a new humanity comes about through the fulfillment of the prophetic hope of redemption: "This mission of Jesus, as the realization of the reconciliation of Jews and Gentiles, is the fulfillment of the promise of coming salvation expressed in Isa 57:19."

"please [one's] neighbor for his good" through extending to one's brothers and sisters in Christ the same acceptance he or she has experienced from Christ (Rom 15:2).

From Paul's perspective, denying oneself for the sake of the unity of the church is not something *added* to the gospel for those who are mature; it is the expression of the very gospel *itself* in the lives of God's people (Phil 1:27; 2:2). Paul's concern for the unity of the church is based on his awareness that the church is the people of God, created by the presence of God, living in relationship to God, and existing for the purpose of glorifying God. In the midst of this evil age, God is establishing outposts of the kingdom in anticipation of the return of Christ. The people of the new covenant have *cosmic* significance as the people of the "last days," who in their life together embody God's unfolding plan for the world.

12

Divine Judgment and the Completion of the Missionary Task

Paul's Motivation for Ministry in 1–2 Thessalonians[1]

Professor Dr. Peter Kuzmič, to whom this essay is dedicated, has encountered the evil of our world in the tangled web of ecclesial and political realities more than most Christian leaders of our generation. Rather than shrinking back in understandable horror or giving in to debilitating discouragement, he has worked tirelessly to match these realities with the reality of the Christian gospel, serving both church and state to bring about reconciliation with justice, to strengthen hope in the midst of suffering, and to pass on a vision for God's righteousness to his students. As a former colleague, it is an honor to honor him for his relentless mission work, in the very best sense of that calling, with some reflections on another missionary-theologian, the apostle Paul. For Paul too faced head-on the relentless evil of his day. In stepping back from Paul's later interactions with the Corinthians treated in the previous chapters, this essay looks at Paul's early, programmatic letters to the Thessalonians in order to ask what motivated Paul in his mission-ministry in the midst of adversity, and in so doing to place Peter's own life of faithful perseverance in its biblical context. To that end, this es-

---

1. From Scott J. Hafemann, "Divine Judgment and the Completion of the Missionary Task: Paul's Motivation for Ministry in 1–2 Thessalonians—A Response to Thor Strandenæs." In *First the Kingdom of God: Global Voices on Global Missions*, edited by Daniel Darko and Beth Snodderly, 225–34. Pasadena, CA: William Carey International University Press, 2014.

say offers a modest response to the insightful work on Paul's missionary motivation by the Norwegian missiologist, Thor Strandenæs's.[2]

THOR STRANDENÆS'S THESIS

Strandenæs's thesis takes its starting point from the question first posed by Nils Dahl in response to Paul's use of the verb ἐνορκίζω ("to cause a person to say under oath") in 1 Thess 5:27: "Why is it . . . that Paul, in a letter so full of praise and commendations to the Thessalonian Christians, urged them to swear by oath [in the name of the Lord!] that they would read the letter to 'all the brethren'?" (69). In other words, why would Paul make such a binding, divinely sanctioned demand?

The answer: Paul compels his readers to share his letter with all the believers in Thessalonica because of the (1) *function* and (2) *purpose* of Paul's letters themselves. As to their *function*, reading the letter to the churches "was a necessary ingredient in Paul's enterprise of completing his mission to the inhabitants of Thessalonike in that both 1 and 2 Thessalonians were needed to further confirm and develop Christian belief and behavior among all the Thessalonian Christians" (69). As to their *purpose*, the goal of the letters was to move their recipients "toward a modified or transformed worldview" (70, restated on 77). All Thessalonian Christians must hear these letters because of the "*role* of [Paul's] message in preparing common standards for Christian belief and behavior when negotiating new core values in the Christian community in Thessalonike" (70, emphasis mine). Hence, "the likely reason for Paul's demand . . . is that he wanted all the converts to be reminded and informed about common standards for belief and behavior, and to abide by these." In other words, "all this is done with a view to confirm and further develop Christian faith and practices in harmony with the gospel and ethos that Paul serves as a missionary" (77). Paul's letters were therefore part of his missionary enterprise of sharing his life and gospel with them (cf. 2:8), and in so doing of "contributing to their *continuous* conversion, by developing their Christian knowledge (1 Thess 4:13–18) and behavior (1 Thess 4:1ff., 9ff.; 5:6–11, 12–22; cf. 2 Thess 1:11; 3:5). This he did in order that the Thessalonians might *remain* sanctified (1 Thess 3:13; 5:23–24; cf. 2 Thess 2:13) and with the Lord until his Parousia (1 Thess 4:17; 5:10; 2 Thess 2:14)" (86, emphasis mine). Paul's writing to the Thessalonians, like his visiting

---

2. This essay is based on my response to Thor Strandenæs's paper at the August 2009 congress of the Societas Novi Testamenti Studiorum in Vienna, now published as "Completing the Mission." Citations to his article will be given within the body of the paper. When not otherwise noted, all biblical references are to 1 Thessalonians.

the newly converted, is part of the *process* of transforming their worldview begun at their conversion (70, emphasis mine).

Strandenæs's main point is well taken. To recognize the role of Paul's letters in confirming and developing the Christian worldview in order to further the believers' life of faith is an important missiological insight. It reminds us that the use of the epistle-genre as an extension of the apostolic mission and ministry was a crucial Christian "invention."[3] The equation in 2 Thess 2:14–15 and 3:14 of the apostolic preaching of the "gospel" (εὐαγγέλιον) or "word" (λόγος) with the apostolic epistle (ἐπιστολή) reflected the authority of the apostolic ministry embodied in the letter as well as providing the beginning of the canon consciousness that led to the eventual use of the epistles as Scripture in the life of the church.

ETHICS AND ESCHATOLOGY IN THE ONGOING CONVERSION OF THE THESSALONIANS

For the majority of the Thessalonians, who came from a background of pagan polytheism, coming to trust in the gospel of the "God of history" entailed a radical conversion of worldview that led to a cultural dislocation (74). In contrast to the remote, arbitrary, unpredictable, and mixed moral character of the pagan deities, Paul's writings detail what it means that God is the faithful, "living and true God," to whom they had turned from "idols" (1:9). Paul unpacks this reality "by focusing on the saving and sanctifying activities of God, Jesus Christ, and the Holy Spirit in the recent *historical events of salvation—including also the lives of the Thessalonians, and the expected Parousia*" (72, emphasis mine; cf. 92).

Strandenæs rightfully stresses from the content of the letters to the Thessalonians themselves that for Paul their "conversion" is something that has taken place in the past (1:9–10), while at the same time remaining an ongoing process that is not yet complete (2 Thess 1:11–12; 2:2–3, 15–17) (75). He points to the fact that the Thessalonian letters "contain further instructions in Christian faith (e.g., 1 Thess 4:13–18; 2 Thess 2:1–12), implications that these (and formerly preached) cognitive facts had for upholding Christian faith and living (2 Thess 2:5–6, 14–17; 4:4), and for maintaining and further developing Christian practices in daily life, also in a time of persecution (1 Thess 2:13–16; 3:1–13; 2 Thess 1:4ff.)" (75). In short, Paul "spells out the standards that must continually guide their transformation. And, since conversion cannot be separated from their sanctification, he asks

---

3. For the unique role and key question concerning the function of Paul's epistles in regard to the apostolic ministry, see already Stuhlmacher, "Theologische Probleme."

God in prayer to bring this process to a good conclusion (1 Thess 5:23-24; 2 Thess 1:11-12; 2:13-17; 3:4-5)" (75).

In addition to the ethical standards Paul spells out, which were of particular relevance to the recent Gentile converts (76), central to the new worldview Paul wanted to communicate was the nature of the second coming of Christ and its preceding signs (4:13—5:1; 2 Thess 2:3—3:5). In particular, in 2 Thessalonians Paul combats a "millenarian fever" in the church, which, according to Jewett, is based on "the belief that the Parousia could be present while this evil age is still so clearly in evidence" (quoted, 76); that is, central to Paul's teaching is his desire to "demolish" this "millenarian worldview" (76), since it is not in harmony with the received Christian tradition he had taught them or they had received (2 Thess 2:2, 15; 3:6-7).

Here too, Strandenæs's perspective is exceedingly helpful. Clearly, both the conversion-sanctification of the Thessalonians and the future Parousia of Christ must be included together in the "salvation historical events" that form essential aspects of God's salvific work in history. Doing so breaks down the faith/obedience dichotomy that has plagued our reading of Paul, in which obedience must be added to faith as a second step in the Christian life rather than being conceived of as the organic expression of faith itself (cf. the "work of faith" in 1:3; 2 Thess 1:11).[4] It also retains the integral, future aspect of the gospel that is so often lost in current readings of Paul that focus almost exclusively on the first coming of Christ as the "fulfillment" of redemptive history. Indeed, Strandenæs rightly emphasizes the eschatological focus of 2 Thess 1:5. And in discussing Paul's references to Jesus, Strandenæs points out that the title "Son of God" is "particularly referring to his being sent on a divine mission into the world to die and resurrect, *a mission that will only be completed by his return from heaven* (1 Thess 1:10)" (91, emphasis mine). As the Son of God, Jesus "delivers us from the wrath to come" (1:10) (91).

ESCHATOLOGY AND THE EPISTLE

Strandenæs sees clearly that the focus of Paul's gospel is on the future. He also highlights the centrality of ethics within the gospel itself. But why does this dual focus exist in Paul's writings? And how within the framework of Paul's gospel is this eschatological emphasis to be integrated with its corresponding stress on the necessity of conforming to the ethical standards of the life of faith? Surely the content of the good news contains the assurance to a bewildered church that the Thessalonians "will 'obtain salvation

---

4. For a development of this point canonically, see my essay, "Covenant Relationship."

through Jesus Christ' (1 Thess 5:9) and 'live with him' whether they 'wake or sleep' (v. 10)" (89).[5] Yet why then does Paul also stress being delivered from the wrath *to come* (1:10)? What is the *relationship* between the current realities of the life of faith and the coming Parousia, both of which are consequences of God's past saving acts in Christ? Is it the case that the power for a continuing change in their worldview lies in the inextricable relationship between the Thessalonians' current lives as believers, as determined by the life, death, and resurrection of the Messiah, and the future return of (the) Christ as judge?

We may answer these questions raised by Strandenæs's observations by examining Paul's explicit statements regarding his *motivation* in writing his letters to the Thessalonians. As we will see, the structure of Paul's argument in these letters makes clear that the central consequence of knowing the "God of history" is to know that the history of this age ends in divine judgment. The second coming of Christ is *the* event that demonstrates that the living God is not remote, arbitrary, unpredictable, or of mixed character. As such, it is also the foundation and motivation for Paul's call to a transformed worldview and for his insistence on its corresponding ethical transformation. For Paul, eschatology drives ethics, since the Parousia, as the consummation of inaugurated eschatology, forms the core of the new, distinctively Christian, history-of-salvation worldview. Therefore, it is the centrality of eschatology that integrates the various aspects of Paul's continuing missionary mandate rightly highlighted by Strandenæs, while also providing a clear rationale both for Paul's insistence on the importance of his letters and for his own perseverance in ministry.

---

5. See now Nicholl, *From Hope to Despair*, who argues that the young Thessalonian church had moved from their initial hope to a hopeless grieving and dread in view of the unexpected deaths of members of their community, which they took to be an omen of God's wrath toward them, since they did not yet know or clearly understand the Christian doctrine of the resurrection of the dead saints in relationship to the Parousia. This despair was accentuated by their later belief that "the Day of the Lord had come" (2 Thess 2:2), so that they had missed salvation. Paul writes 1 Thessalonians "to reassure the Thessalonians regarding the salvific eschatological destiny of their deceased and the whole community" (111). Paul writes 2 Thessalonians to "assure them that God's judgment will indeed be just, consisting of a reversal of fortunes for them and their persecutors ... [and to] make it clear that when that just judgment will come, who will be its victims and what it will look like.... There was a lack of hope and insecurity among 'the Thessalonians' regarding their status before God and 'Paul'" (185). The question before us is the means by which this reassurance is obtained personally as well as doctrinally.

THE ESCHATOLOGICAL FOCUS OF PAUL'S MINISTRY IN WRITING

In 1:5, Paul is assured that the Thessalonians are among the elect because (ὅτι) the gospel did not come to them in word only, but in power and in the Holy Spirit, and (therefore) in much conviction. The reality of the power of the Spirit in their lives is evidenced by the fact that, as 1:6 puts it, the Thessalonians became imitators of (the faith of?) Paul (and his cohort?)[6] and of the (faith of the?) Lord. In particular, they received the gospel with joy in the midst of (and despite) much affliction, a response that can only be attributed to the power of the Spirit.

The Thessalonians' exemplary lives, characterized by their "work of faith and labor of love and steadfastness of hope" (1:3), consisted in their having turned back from idols in order to serve the living and true God and to wait for his resurrected Son to return from heaven (cf. the two purpose infinitives of vv. 9–10: δουλεύειν, ἀναμένειν), since Jesus is the one who will rescue them "from the coming wrath" (1:10c, taking the appositional participle, ['Ιησοῦν] τὸν ῥυόμενον, to function causally). For Paul these are not two distinct purposes. The Thessalonians serve the living God precisely *because* they are waiting for Christ to return. In other words, the Spirit-determined acceptance of Paul's gospel, testified to by its *joy in the midst of adversity* (1:6; cf. 2:14–16), only makes sense when the life of serving the living and true God produced by the gospel is inextricably linked to the certain return of Jesus to rescue his people from eschatological wrath. One's hope for future deliverance motivates perseverance through the suffering of the present—even with joy!

Paul's statements concerning the Thessalonians reflect the fact that the gospel receives its life-transforming power from its future orientation toward final judgment, since the certainty of "the wrath to come" (1:10c) creates the present life of "serving God" (1:9) in preparation for it (cf. 2 Thess 1:5–10). For this reason, Paul *defines* Jesus first and foremost eschatologically as the one who, by transforming their lives now (1:3, 9; 2:13–14; 3:7, 9; 4:1, 10), rescues his people from the wrath to come (1:10). Jesus does this by being not only the *object* of faith and hope (1:3), since Jesus is also defined in 5:10 as "the one who died on our behalf" (cf. the appositional participle ['Ιησοῦ Χριστοῦ] τοῦ ἀποθανόντος), but also the *model* of what it means to live by faith and hope (1:6; cf. 2 Thess 3:5: τὴν ὑπομονὴν τοῦ Χριστοῦ). In the same way, in 2:12a Paul exhorts the Thessalonians to walk worthy of God, who, like Jesus in 1:10, is also *defined* first and foremost eschatologically

---

6. Cf. the call to "imitate us" in 2 Thess 3:7–13.

in 2:12b as "the one who calls you into his own kingdom and glory" (note the use again of the appositional participle [τοῦ θεοῦ] τοῦ καλοῦντος]). This definition of who God is in terms of the eschatological orientation of what he does is unpacked in 2 Thess 2:16 as "the one who loved us and gave [us] eternal encouragement and good hope through grace" (again using an appositional phrase). As with (the) Christ, here too God's identity grounds the identity of the Thessalonians. Moreover, their life of faith is made possible by the fact that the God who calls his people into his kingdom eschatologically is also the God who has already given to them his Holy Spirit (4:8; yet again expressed in an appositional participle, [τὸν θεὸν] τὸν διδόντα).

Because of Paul's conviction concerning Jesus and God as eschatological savior and judge, the "negative" side of Paul's hope is equally clear: the deliverance of those who believe also entails the condemnation "on that day" of those who do not know God (cf. the simultaneous occurrence of the eschatological revelation of the glory of God and of judgment in 2 Thess 1:9-10). In 1 Thess 2:16 (eschatological) wrath (ἡ ὀργή) is therefore said to have already come upon those Jews who killed Jesus and continue to persecute believers "until the [eschatological] end" (εἰς τέλος).[7] And in 2 Thess 1:7-9, when Christ is revealed from heaven "in flaming fire" he will give "vengeance" and "punishment"/"justice" (ἐκδίκησις and δίκη, both from the δικ-stem) to those who do not know God and hence do not obey the gospel. At that time, those who afflict the faithful will be "recompensed" (ἀνταποδίδωμι) with affliction as the expression of what is "righteous" (δίκαιος) before God (2 Thess 1:6).

On the "positive" side, the Thessalonians, in imitating the other churches by their endurance of persecution (2:14), are Paul's eschatological hope, joy, crown of boasting, and glory "before our Lord Jesus at his coming" (2:19-20; cf. 2 Thess 1:4; cf. also Rom 15:17; 2 Cor 1:14; Phil 4:1). Inasmuch as the Thessalonians' faith and love are increasing, even as they endure in the midst of adversity, Paul is bound to give thanks to God for bringing it about and to boast of their endurance of faith among the other churches (2 Thess 1:3-4). Their faithful endurance in the midst of adversity is "evidence" or "proof" (ἔνδειγμα) of God's righteous (eschatological) judgment, since he has delivered them from unbelief "so that they may be made worthy of the kingdom of God, for which they are also suffering" (2 Thess 1:5). As a result, God will grant them (eschatological) "rest" at the revelation of the Lord Jesus in judgment (2 Thess 1:7). For those who are "awake" during the "day" of a redeemed life live sober lives of faith and love

---

7. This meaning is confirmed by the other NT uses of εἰς τέλος; cf. Matt 10:22; 24:13; and Mark 13:13 for the use of εἰς τέλος as a time reference to the end of the age, and Luke 18:5 and John 13:1 for its use to refer to a completed period of time.

in expectation of Christ's return. Salvation (ἡ σωτηρία) is their confident "hope" (ἡ ἐλπίς), since God has not appointed them for eschatological wrath (ἡ ὀργή), but for the attaining of salvation through Christ the Lord (5:8–10).

This is true, however, only if they "stand fast in the Lord" (3:8). If they were to give up, Paul's work would be in vain (3:5). For this reason, Paul's present joy over the Thessalonians' current life of faith does not satisfy him (cf. 4:1, 10); rather, he begs God more than ever to be able to see them again face to face in order to strengthen (καταρτίζω) what is still lacking in their faith (3:10). In the meantime and to this same end, Paul writes his epistles and sends Timothy in his place as the ongoing extension of his own missionary efforts *in his absence* (cf. στηρίζω, 3:2). He also prays for this same strengthening (στηρίζω) in holiness "before our God and Father [as judge], at the coming (παρουσία) of our Lord Jesus with all his saints" (3:13; cf. 5:23; 2 Thess 2:16–17; 3:3). The goal of his prayers is that on this "day" Christ will be glorified in them and they in him through their ongoing, grace-created "work of faith" (2 Thess 1:11–12). For God called them to salvation through Paul's gospel for the purpose of inheriting the glory of the Lord Jesus Christ (2 Thess 2:14).

The reason for the seriousness of Paul's ethical admonitions is thus clear: the Lord is an avenger (ἔκδικος) against all immorality, as Paul has already solemnly testified (4:6). Paul's warning, even to the believing Thessalonians, must therefore be taken seriously. Not to persevere or increase in their work of faith would not mean that they were saved, but had failed to respond sufficiently to the gospel, but that the gospel had in fact not taken root in their lives (cf. 3:12–13; 2 Thess 2:15). The Lord's gracious work is to cause his people to increase in their love for one another in order to establish them before his own righteous judgment (3:12–13); God has destined his people for salvation (5:9); the God who calls his people to sanctification and promises to keep them blameless at the coming of the Lord Jesus is faithful to do so (5:23–24). So there is no conversion that is not a "continuing conversion" (4:1, 10; 2 Thess 1:3; 2:11–12; see above). God's life-changing grace is expressed not only in the believers' calling and election, but also in their ongoing and increasing obedience to God's ensuing commands (cf., e.g., the "work of faith" to be accomplished "in the power" of God in 2 Thess 1:11).[8] Paul's commands and warnings simply reflect what God's calling and election look like in everyday life.

The return of Christ as savior and vindicating judge thus plays a foundational role both in Paul's own motivation for ministry and in the

---

8. This same point is at the heart of the argument of 2 Peter; see now my "(Un)Conditionality of Salvation," 248, 260.

Thessalonians' life of faith. This is why Paul is concerned to deal with any misunderstandings surrounding its universal applicability or its certain, but still future, reality (cf. 4:13—5:11; 2 Thess 2:1–12). Paul's letters are consequently an essential continuing means of his missionary activity since, as Strandenæs points out so well, the goal of the gospel Paul preaches, of the content of his prayer, and of the sending of Timothy is not a onetime act of conversion in the past (i.e., the historical prologue of the covenant relationship), but the continuing strengthening of the church's faith in the present (i.e., the stipulation of the covenant relationship), in anticipation of the future (i.e., the promise of the covenant relationship; cf. 1 Thess 3:2). In support of this point, Paul's theological motivation for his writing is not to underscore their acceptance of the gospel in the past, but to continue to minister this gospel in the present in order to prepare his churches for the judgment to come. It is because of the gospel's future focus on God's judgment that Paul sees the value of his own ministry at stake in the perseverance of his churches (1 Thess 2:19–20; 3:5; 2 Thess 1:4).

CONCLUSION

Strandenæs mentions the future judgment of God as an important part of the message Paul preached. I would make it *central* to that message, and hence to Paul's motivation for ministry as well. Eschatology drives not only Paul's ethics, but also Paul's missionary activity. Although the kingdom has been inaugurated (cf. the preaching of the "gospel of God," which is equated with "the gospel of Christ," in 1 Thess 2:8, 9; 3:2), the missionary period of repentance and of the corresponding endurance of the "work of faith" has been extended until Christ returns. In response, Paul's spoken "word" (λόγος) and his "letter" (ἐπιστολή) both serve the same end: to pass on the traditions of the gospel that will prepare them for the coming day of the Lord (2 Thess 2:15). In 2 Thess 3:14 Paul can therefore speak of being obedient to "our word through this letter," thereby equating obedience to the gospel (2 Thess 1:8) with obedience to Paul's preaching (2 Thess 2:15) with obedience to Paul's letter (2 Thess 3:14)—without which there will be no inheritance of God's glory on judgment day. It is no wonder, then, that Paul made them swear an oath to read his epistles (1 Thess 5:27), authenticating them with his own hand (2 Thess 3:17).

Strandenæs rightly concludes that "Paul's mission task toward the Thessalonians was not completed after his visit in Thessalonike"; rather, it continued on through the subsequent visits of Timothy and of Paul himself, and through Paul's letters, in order that the Thessalonians might "abide by the implicit and explicit values of the Christian faith to which they had converted and of which they were now taught to see more clearly the consequences" (94). For "the Thessalonians needed a more comprehensive understanding of the contents of faith as well as the ethos it required" (94). For Paul, however, the reason for this need is not only inherent (95), but also eschatological. The mission task is not complete until the judgment day of the Parousia, from which it receives its impetus and for which it prepares. Eschatology was such a priority to Paul and so problematic in Thessalonica precisely because eschatology, inaugurated but not yet consummated, stands at the heart of the gospel and of the life of faith it creates. As Strandenæs puts it, "this Son, Jesus Christ, would certainly return—but not yet. . . . Since not all the Thessalonian converts seem to have grasped this truth fully, nor its implications, Paul's mission was incomplete until all the brethren had come to believe and behave according to the standards of the new faith" (95).

At the center of the Christian worldview is the reality that salvation history—indeed, all of history—climaxes at the day of judgment, when Christ returns to establish God's righteous rule over his creation. This is the "deep" countercultural lens through which believers are to evaluate and live in this world and from which their life of faith derives. As 1 and 2 Thessalonians demonstrate, the common Christian, ethical tradition that Paul passes on (2 Thess 3:6!), like the focus of faith itself, both reflects and is driven by this eschatology. In turn, the gospel's focus on the future is the integrating center of Paul's missionary task. As such, the necessity of persevering in faith in light of the consummation of God's kingdom, both for himself and for his churches, is also the motivation for his missionary endeavors.

I offer these reflections on the eschatological motivation for Paul's ministry in honor of and thankfulness for Peter Kuzmič's own life and ministry, since he too shares Paul's profound confidence in the fact that God, in Christ, will have the last word over the evil and suffering of our world. Peter's faithfulness in the midst of adversity is a continuing testimony to the reality of the redemption and righteousness to be found in the first and second comings of Christ—and the need to persevere between the two. In many a hopeless situation, Peter, like the apostle Paul, has brought to others both the hope and the challenge of the same gospel that continues to motivate his own life and ministry.

13

The Sum of the Ministry
Challenges to Paul's Exclusive Gospel[1]

Due to our extreme isolation and homogeneity in the past, most Christians in the West have only recently been confronted personally with the problem of pluralism. Encountering sincere adherents of other faiths has caused many to rethink whether the exclusive claims of the gospel preached by Paul can be or should be maintained. This uncertainty is more a reflection of the sudden shock caused by our own cross-cultural myopia and provincialism than it is a discovery that Paul actually taught universalism. Indeed, the pluralism of the modern world is no more dramatic than that faced by Israel or Paul. In Paul's day, every Roman was born into a diverse nexus of personal religious affiliations and family household cults. Add to this milieu the Roman imperial cult, the Greco-Roman pantheon of deities descending down from Jupiter, and the mystery religions venerating gods from Greece, Anatolia, Egypt, Persia, and Syria, and our situation looks tame in comparison. In Corinth, for example, remains have been found of official temples and shrines to the emperor, to the Greek deities Apollo, Athena, Aphrodite, Asclepius, Tyche, Dionysus, Zeus, Neptune, Demeter and Kore, Palaimon, and Sisyphus, as well as to the Egyptian gods Isis and Sarapis. To assert the exclusive reality of the One God of Israel and of Jesus as his Messiah, *the* Son of God, was just as startling then as it is now (cf. 1 Cor 8:5–6; Phil 2:9–11).

Yet Paul plainly teaches the reality of eternal judgment for those who do not embrace (the) Christ (cf. 2 Thess 1:8–9; 2:8–12; Gal 6:7–8; Phil

[1]. From Scott J. Hafemann, "Challenges to Paul's Exclusive Gospel." *SBJT* 2/2 (1998) 55–58.

3:18-19; 1 Cor 6:9-10; 16:22; Rom 1:18—2:12, etc.). He holds no hope for those who remain in idolatry and its lifestyles, for he attributes the practice to demons (cf. Rom 1:25, 28-32; 1 Cor 6:9-10, 12-20; 8:4; 10:14-22; 12:2; Gal 4:8; 1 Thess 1:9; 4:5; Eph 2:12; Col 2:8, 15, etc.). Of course, many today simply reject these declarations as patently false or reinterpret them in view of some abstracted theological principle (such as "love," "justice," or a universal "election" in *the* elect one, Christ). These challenges are clear-cut, for they are related to questions of the authority of Scripture and of a proper theological method.

More challenging are the arguments of those who posit a universalism within Paul's own thought. Those who take this tact usually point to the parallels in Rom 5:15-18 (cf. 2 Cor 5:19; 1 Tim 4:10; Titus 2:11) between the consequences of Adam's sin and the incomparably greater consequences of Christ's act of righteousness (see esp. 5:17-18). They argue that while some people are justified by faith already in this life, Paul believes that the rest of humanity will be justified at the final judgment, when Christ's last, cosmic act of deliverance will bring eternal life to all creation (cf. Rom 8:21-25).

But it is clear from many passages that the terms "all" (Greek: πᾶς) and "world" (κόσμος) do not always mean "every single human being." The former is often limited by context (cf. Rom 8:32; 12:17-18; 14:2; 16:19). The latter often refers to the realm of rebellion under this evil age (1 Cor 6:2; 7:31, 33; 2 Cor 4:4; Rom 12:2; Gal 1:4; 6:14; Eph 2:2; 6:12; Col 2:8; 2 Tim 4:10), the inhabited earth generally or part of it (Rom 1:8; 10:18; Col 1:6; 1 Cor 4:9; 1 Tim 1:15; 6:7), or the diversity of those within the world as made up of Jews and Gentiles (Rom 11:12, 15). Context is king: we must determine the specific referent of these terms in their own respective contexts. Thus, Douglas Moo rightly observes that in Rom 5:15,

> "The many" refers simply to a great number; how inclusive that number might be can be determined only by context. In the protasis of this verse, "the many" clearly includes all people; for Paul has already said that "all died" with reference to the sin of Adam (v. 12). But in the apodosis ("how much more . . .") "the many" must be qualified by Paul's insistence in v. 17 that only those who "receive" the gift benefit from Christ's act. Here it refers to "a great number" of people (but not all of them) or to "all who respond to the gift of grace."[2]

In support of this limitation, Rom 5:17

---

2. Moo, *Romans*, 336-37.

reminds us—lest we have forgotten Romans 1–4!—that righteousness and life are for those who *respond* to God's grace in Christ and that they are *only* for those who respond. What appears at first sight to be a universalism on both sides of the Adam/Christ parallel is here, then, importantly qualified.³

Hence, Paul's point in 5:18 is not so much that the groups affected by Christ and Adam, respectively, are coextensive, but that Christ's act of righteousness on the cross affects those who belong to him just as certainly as Adam's trespass in the garden does those who take their identity from him. When we ask who belongs to Adam and Christ respectively, Paul makes his answer clear: every person, without exception, is "in Adam" (cf. vv. 12d–14), but only those who "receive the gift" (v. 17), i.e., "those who believe," according to Rom 1:16—5:11, are "in Christ."⁴ The attempt to argue exegetically that *Paul* taught an ultimate universalism will have difficulty convincing anyone who is not predisposed to that view.

The importance of one's predisposition regarding the question of Paul's view of the exclusivity of Christ can be seen most poignantly in the corollary question of the status for Paul of the Jews within salvation history. We may concede that Paul believed that Gentile pagans need Jesus. But do the Jews need to know Jesus as the Christ in order to belong to God's eschatological people? In the shadow of modern Zionism, the Holocaust, the reestablishment of the state of Israel, and the influence of dispensational theology, this question is filled with the intense emotion of an apparent anti-Semitism.

For almost forty years Krister Stendahl, longtime professor of New Testament at Harvard Divinity School and former Bishop of Stockholm, has argued that Paul's doctrine of justification by faith alone merely served the very narrowly defined purpose of defending the rights of Gentile converts to full participation in God's promises to Israel—that is, to be "honorary Jews"—without having to keep the law.⁵ Conversely, Stendahl argues that Paul's purpose in Rom 9–11 is to counter Gentile pride in the face of the Jewish rejection of Jesus and to affirm "a God-willed coexistence between Judaism and Christianity in which the missionary urge to convert Israel is held in check."⁶ God has a mysterious plan of salvation for Israel outside of Christ, just as he has deemed Gentiles to be saved in Christ. In short, there are two covenants: Sinai for the Jews and Jesus for the Gentiles. Stendahl's

---

3. Ibid., 340.

4. Ibid., 343. Here I take "in Adam" and "in Christ" to refer to being in or under the sphere of their respective dominions, with its consequences; see the Introduction.

5. See his *Paul*, esp. 2–9, 130.

6. Ibid., 4.

view has been immensely influential, and has since been widened out to embrace other religions as valid for Gentiles as well.[7]

The answer to Stendahl's thesis resides in a detailed exegesis of Rom 9–11, which forms the heart of his argument, against the backdrop of a nuanced reevaluation of Stendahl's understanding of Paul's "conversion" and the role of justification in Paul's thought.[8] In the space permitted here, let me simply call attention to two glaring facts and the fundamental issue that grounds them.

First, Paul feels great anguish over his fellow Jews' rejection of Jesus as the Messiah, since they above all are the ones to whom the covenant blessings and promises have been given. He would even give himself over to God's eternal curse if this could save them (Rom 9:2–3)! Second, Paul's concern that Israel's rejection of Jesus seems to call into question the covenant faithfulness of God *himself* (Rom 9:4–6) only makes sense if Paul regarded those among his covenant "kinsmen by race" who are rejecting Jesus to be outside of God's legitimate covenant people. It is this feeling of personal anguish and the fundamental theological question raised by "Israel's" rejection of the Messiah that drive Paul's argument in Rom 9–11.

The central issue underlying both matters is whether God's faithfulness to his promises is to be affirmed in spite of Israel's rejection of Jesus. This would be no problem at all if Paul thought that there was salvation for the Jews (or for anyone else for that matter) outside of Christ. Nor would Paul be concerned with Israel's future as an ethnic people in Rom 11:1–2 if her present rejection of Christ did not have salvific implications. Furthermore, faith (in Jesus Christ) is explicitly referred to as the way to salvation for both Jews and Gentiles in Rom 11:20 and 23. Paul's God-centered doxology in 11:33–36 is therefore not an attempt to downplay the centrality of Jesus (*contra* Stendahl), but is intended to show that all people, both Jews and Gentiles, will one day be worshipping the same Father for the same reason—namely, his sovereign, electing mercy in Christ (cf. 11:35 with 9:16). The parallel between Rom 9:30–33 and 11:5–7 indicates that Paul's doctrine of justification by faith alone through grace is to be applied equally to both Gentiles and Jews.

Gentiles and Jews alike stand before God only by faith in response to God's mercy and sovereign grace (Rom 11:17–24). Accordingly, those who preach to others must do so with humility and fear (Rom 11:20). Paul's missionary activity is not the expression of a colonial imperialism designed to conquer and exploit others for one's own aggrandizement. It is the heartfelt

---

7. See Stendahl, "Christ's Lordship," 233–44.
8. For my own earlier attempt to do so, see my essay, "The Salvation of Israel."

cry of one who was convinced that the gospel was God's one and final word of reconciliation for all, both Jews and Gentiles (Rom 1:16–17; 2 Cor 5:14–21).

Bibliography

Aland, Kurt, ed. *Vollständige Konkordanz zum griechischen Neuen Testament.* 2 vols. Berlin: de Gruyter, 1975–83.
Baasland, Ernst. "Persecution: A Neglected Feature in the Letter to the Galatians." *ST* 38/2 (1984) 135–50.
Barnett, Paul. *The Second Epistle to the Corinthians.* NICNT. Grand Rapids: Eerdmans, 1997.
Barrett, C. K. "Cephas and Corinth." In *Abraham unser Vater: Juden und Christen im Gespräch über die Bibel; Festschrift für Otto Michel zum 60. Geburtstag,* edited by Otto Betz et al., 1–12. Leiden: Brill, 1963.
———. "Paulus als Missionar und Theologe." *ZTK* 86/1 (1989) 18–32.
———. *The Second Epistle to the Corinthians.* HNTC. New York: Harper & Row, 1973.
Bauer, Walter, et al. *Griechisch-deutsches Wörterbuch zu den Schriften des Neuen Testaments und der frühchristlichen Literatur.* 6th ed. Berlin: de Gruyter, 1988.
Beale, G. K. "The Old Testament Background of Reconciliation in 2 Cor 5–7 and Its Bearing on the Literary Problem of 2 Cor 6:14—7:1." *NTS* 35 (1989) 550–81.
———. *The Temple and the Church's Mission: A Biblical Theology of the Dwelling Place of God.* NSBT 17. Downers Grove, IL: InterVarsity, 2004.
Begbie, Jeremy. "Room of One's Own?" In *Music, Modernity, and God: Essays in Listening,* 141–75. Oxford: Oxford University Press, 2013.
Beker, J. Christiaan. *Paulus: Der Apostel der Völker.* Tübingen: Mohr Siebeck, 1989.
———. *Paul the Apostle: The Triumph of God in Life and Thought.* Philadelphia: Fortress, 1980.
Belleville, Linda L. *Reflections of Glory: Paul's Polemical Use of the Moses-Doxa Tradition in 2 Corinthians 3.1–18.* JSNTSup 52. Sheffield, UK: JSOT, 1991.
Betz, Hans Dieter. *Galatians: A Commentary on Paul's Letter to the Churches in Galatia.* Hermeneia. Philadelphia: Fortress, 1979.
Black, David Alan. "Weakness Language in Galatians." *GTJ* 4/1 (1983) 15–36.
Block, Daniel I. "The Prophet of the Spirit: The Use of RWḤ in the Book of Ezekiel." *JETS* 32/1 (1989) 27–49.
Brichto, Herbert Chanan. "The Worship of the Golden Calf: A Literary Analysis of a Fable on Idolatry." *HUCA* 54 (1983) 1–44.
Bring, R. "Paul and the Old Testament: A Study of the Ideas of Election, Faith and Law in Paul, with Special Reference to Romans 9:30—10:30." *ST* 25 (1971) 21–60.
Burton, Ernest Dewitt. *A Critical and Exegetical Commentary on the Epistle to the Galatians.* ICC. Edinburgh: T. & T. Clark, 1921.

Campbell, Douglas. *The Deliverance of God: An Apocalyptic Rereading of Justification in Paul.* Grand Rapids: Eerdmans, 2009.

———. "The Faithfulness of Jesus Christ." In *The Faith of Jesus Christ: Exegetical, Biblical, and Theological Studies,* edited by Michael F. Bird and Preston M. Sprinkle, 57–71. Milton Keynes, UK: Paternoster, 2009.

Cassuto, Umberto. *A Commentary on the Book of Exodus.* Jerusalem: Magnes, 1968.

Childs, Brevard S. *The Book of Exodus: A Critical, Theological Commentary.* OTL. Louisville, KY: Westminster John Knox, 1974.

Clark, Kenneth Willis. "The Meaning of *ENERGEO* and *KATARGEO* in the New Testament." In *The Gentile Bias and Other Essays,* edited by John L. Sharpe III, 183–91. NovTSup 54. Leiden: Brill, 1980.

Colpe, C. *Die religionsgeschichtliche Schule: Darstellung und Kritik ihres Bildes vom gnostischen Erlösermythus.* Göttingen: Vandenhoeck & Ruprecht, 1961.

Coats, George W. "The King's Loyal Opposition: Obedience and Authority in Exodus 32–34." In *Canon and Authority: Essays in Old Testament Religion and Theology,* edited by George W. Coats and Burke O. Long, 91–109. Philadelphia: Fortress, 1977.

———. *Moses: Heroic Man, Man of God.* JSOTSup 57. Sheffield, UK: JSOT, 1988.

Cranfield, C. E. B. "Changes of Person and Number in Paul's Epistles." In *Paul and Paulinism: Festschrift for C. K. Barrett,* edited by M. D. Hooker and S. G. Wilson, 280–89. London: SPCK, 1982.

———. *The Epistle to the Romans.* 2 vols. ICC. Edinburgh: T. & T. Clark, 1975, 1979.

———. "'The Works of the Law' in the Epistle to the Romans." *JSNT* 43 (1991) 89–101.

Cross, F. M. "Kinship and Covenant in Ancient Israel." In *From Epic to Canon,* 3–21. Baltimore: Johns Hopkins, 1998.

Cullmann, Oscar. *Heil als Geschichte: Heilsgeschichtliche Existenz im Neuen Testament.* 2nd ed. Tübingen: Mohr Siebeck, 1967.

Davies, W. D. *Paul and Rabbinic Judaism: Some Rabbinic Elements in Pauline Theology.* 4th ed. Philadelphia: Fortress, 1980.

De Boer, Martinus C. *Galatians: A Commentary.* Louisville, KY: Westminster John Knox, 2011.

Dempster, Stephen G. *Dominion and Dynasty: A Theology of the Hebrew Bible.* NSBT 15. Downers Grove, IL: InterVarsity, 2003.

Dumbrell, William J. *The End of the Beginning: Revelation 21–22 and the Old Testament.* Grand Rapids: Baker Book House, 1985.

———. "Paul's Use of Exodus 34 in 2 Corinthians 3." In *God Who Is Rich in Mercy: Essays Presented to Dr. D. B. Knox,* edited by Peter T. O'Brien and David G. Peterson, 179–94. Grand Rapids: Baker, 1986.

Dunn, James D. G. "The New Perspective on Paul." *BJRL* 65 (1983) 95–122.

———. "The New Perspective on Paul: Whence, What, Whither?" In *The New Perspective on Paul: Collected Essays,* 1–88. WUNT 185. Mohr Siebeck, 2005.

———. *Romans 9–16.* WBC 38B. Dallas: Word, 1988.

Eissfeldt, Otto. "Das Gesetz ist zwischeneingekommen: Ein Beitrag zur Analyse der Sinai-Erzählung Ex. 19–34." In *Kleine Schriften IV,* 209–14. Tübingen: Mohr Siebeck, 1968.

Ellis, E. E. "Paul and His Opponents: Trends in Research." In *Prophecy and Hermeneutic in Early Christianity: New Testament Essays,* 80–115. WUNT 18. Tübingen: Mohr Siebeck, 1978.

———. *Paul and His Recent Interpreters.* Grand Rapids: Eerdmans, 1961.

Epp, E. J., and G. W. MacRae, eds. *The New Testament and Its Modern Interpreters.* Philadelphia: Fortress, 1989.
Fee, Gordon D. *The First Epistle to the Corinthians.* NICNT. Grand Rapid: Eerdmans, 1987.
———. *God's Empowering Presence: The Holy Spirit in the Letters of Paul.* Peabody, MA: Hendrickson, 1994.
———. "II Corinthians vi.14—vii. 1 and Food Offered to Idols." *NTS* 23 (1977) 140–67.
Fuller, Daniel P. *Gospel and Law: Contrast or Continuum?* Grand Rapids: Eerdmans, 1980.
———. *The Unity of the Bible: Unfolding God's Plan for Humanity.* Grand Rapids: Zondervan, 1990.
Furnish, Victor Paul. *II Corinthians.* AB 32A. Garden City, NY: Doubleday, 1984.
Garland, David E. *1 Corinthians.* BECNT. Grand Rapids: Baker Academic, 2003.
Goddard, A. J., and S. A. Cummins. "Ill or Ill-Treated?: Conflict and Persecution as the Context of Paul's Original Ministry in Galatia (Galatians 4:12–20)." *JSNT* 52 (1993) 93–126.
Gorman, Michael J. *Apostle of the Crucified Lord: A Theological Introduction to Paul & His Letters.* Grand Rapids: Eerdmans, 2004.
———. *Cruciformity: Paul's Narrative Spirituality of the Cross.* Grand Rapids: Eerdmans, 2001.
———. *Inhabiting the Cruciform God: Kenosis, Justification, and Theosis in Paul's Narrative Soteriology.* Grand Rapids: Eerdmans, 2009.
Greenberg, Moshe. "נסה in Exodus 20:20 and the Purpose of the Sinaitic Theophany." *JBL* 79 (1960) 273–76.
Gundry Volf, J. M. *Paul and Perseverance.* WUNT 2/37. Tübingen: Mohr Siebeck, 1990.
Gunther, J. J. *St. Paul's Opponents and Their Background: A Study of Apocalyptic and Jewish Sectarian Teachings.* NovTSup 30. Leiden: Brill, 1973.
Hafemann, Scott J. "The Covenant Relationship." In *Central Themes in Biblical Theology: Mapping Unity in Diversity,* edited by Scott J. Hafemann and Paul R. House, 20–65. Grand Rapids: Baker, 2007.
———. "Eschatology and Ethics: The Future of Israel and the Nations in Romans 15:1–13." *TynB* 51 (2000) 161–92.
———. *The God of Promise and the Life of Faith: Understanding the Heart of the Bible.* Wheaton, IL: Crossway, 2001.
———. "Paul and the Exile of Israel in Galatians 3–4." In *Exile,* edited by James M. Scott, 329–71. Leiden: Brill, 1997.
———. *Paul, Moses, and the History of Israel: The Letter/Spirit Contrast and the Argument from Scripture in 2 Corinthians 3.* WUNT 81. Tübingen: Mohr Siebeck, 1995. Reprinted, Milton Keynes, UK: Paternoster, 2005.
———. "Paul's Argument from the Old Testament and Christology in 2 Cor 1–9." In *The Corinthian Correspondence,* edited by R. Bieringer, 277–303. BETL 125. Leuven: Leuven University Press, 1996.
———. "The 'Righteousness of God': An Introduction to the Theological and Historical Foundation of Peter Stuhlmacher's *Biblical Theology of the New Testament.*" Introduction to *How to Do Biblical Theology,* by Peter Stuhlmacher, xv–xli. Allison Park, PA: Pickwick, 1995.

———. "The Role of Suffering in the Mission of Paul." In *The Mission of the Early Church to Jews and Gentiles*, edited by Jöstein Ådna and Hans Kvalbein, 113–32. WUNT 127. Tübingen: Mohr Siebeck, 2000.

———. *2 Corinthians*. NIVAC. Grand Rapids: Zondervan, 2000.

———. "'Self-Commendation' and Apostolic Legitimacy in 2 Corinthians: A Pauline Dialectic?" *NTS* 36 (1990) 66–88.

———. "The Salvation of Israel in Romans 11:25–32: A Response to Krister Stendahl." *Ex Auditu* 4 (1988) 38–58.

———. *Suffering and Ministry in the Spirit: Paul's Defense of His Ministry in 2 Corinthians 2:14—3:3*. Grand Rapids: Eerdmans: 1990. Reprinted, Milton Keynes, UK: Paternoster, 2000.

———. *Suffering and the Spirit: An Exegetical Study of 2 Corinthians 2:14—3:3 within the Context of the Corinthian Correspondence*. WUNT. Second Series 19. Tübingen: Mohr Siebeck, 1986. Reprinted, Eugene, OR: Wipf & Stock, 2011.

———. "The (Un)Conditionality of Salvation: The Theological Logic of 2 Peter 1:8a–10a." In *Staying In*, edited by Charles H. Talbert and Jason A. Whitlark, 240–62. Grand Rapids: Eerdmans, 2011.

Haran, Menahem. "The Shining of Moses' Face: A Case Study in Biblical and Ancient Near Eastern Iconography." In *In the Shelter of Elyon: Essays on Ancient Palestinian Literature in Honor of G. W. Ahlström*, edited by W. Boyd Barrick and John R. Spencer, 159–73. JSOTSup 31. Sheffield, UK: JSOT, 1984.

———. *Temples and Temple-Service in Ancient Israel*. Oxford: Clarendon, 1977.

Harris, Horton. *The Tübingen School: A Historical and Theological Investigation of the School of F. C. Baur*. Grand Rapids: Baker, 1990.

Harris, Murray J. *The Second Epistle to the Corinthians*. NIGTC. Grand Rapids: Eerdmans, 2005.

Harrison, James R. *Paul and the Imperial Authorities at Thessalonica and Rome: A Study in the Conflict of Ideology*. WUNT 273. Tübingen: Mohr Siebeck, 2011.

Harvey, A. E. "Forty Strokes Save One: Social Aspects of Judaizing and Apostasy." In *Alternative Approaches to New Testament Study*, edited by A. E. Harvey, 79–96. London: SPCK, 1985.

Hauerwas, Stanley, and William H. Willimon. *Resident Aliens: Life in the Christian Colony*. Nashville: Abingdon, 1989.

Hays, Richard B. *Echoes of Scripture in the Letters of Paul*. New Haven, CT: Yale University Press, 1989.

Heckel, Ulrich. "Der Dorn im Fleisch: Die Krankheit des Paulus in 2 Kor 12,7 und Gal 4,13f." *ZNW* 84 (1993) 65–92.

———. *Kraft in Schwachheit: Untersuchungen zu 2. Kor 10–13*. WUNT. Second Series 56. Tübingen: Mohr Siebeck, 1993.

Heinrici. C. F. Georg. *Der zweite Brief an die Korinther*. KEK 8. Göttingen: Vandenhoeck and Ruprecht, 1900.

Héring, Jean. *The Second Epistle of Saint Paul to the Corinthians*. London: Epworth, 1967.

Hock, Ronald F. *The Social Context of Paul's Ministry, Tentmaking and Apostleship*. Philadelphia: Fortress, 1980.

Hodge, Charles. *An Exposition of the Second Epistle to the Corinthians*. Reprint. Grand Rapids: Eerdmans, 1959.

Hofius, Otfried. "'Der Gott allen Trostes': *Paraklesis* und *Parakalein* in 2 Kor 1,3–7." *TBei* 14 (1983) 217–27.
———. "Gesetz und Evangelium nach 2. Korinther 3." In *Paulusstudien*, 75–120. WUNT 51. Tübingen: Mohr Siebeck, 1989.
Hooker, Morna. "Beyond the Things That Are Written? St. Paul's Use of Scripture." *NTS* 27 (1981) 295–309.
Hübner, H. "Paulusforschung seit 1945: Ein kritischer Literaturbericht," *ANRW* 25.4:2649–840
Hunter, Archibald M. *The Unity of the New Testament*. London: SCM, 1943.
Jaros, Karl. "Des Mose 'Strahlende Haut': Ein Notiz zu Exod. 34:29; 30:35." *ZAW* 88 (1976) 275–80.
Jirku, Anton. "Die Gesichtsmaske des Mose." In *Von Jerusalem nach Ugarit: Gesammelte Schriften*, 347–49. Graz, Austria: Akademische Druck, 1966.
Käsemann, Ernst. "On the Subject of Primitive Christian Apocalyptic." In *New Testament Questions of Today*, 108–37. Philadelphia: Fortress, 1969. English translation of "Zum Thema der urchristlichen Apokalyptik." *ZTK* 59 (1962) 257–84.
Kearney, Peter J. "Creation and Liturgy: The P Redaction of Ex. 25–40." *ZAW* 89 (1977) 375–87.
Kim, Seyoon. *The Origin of Paul's Gospel*. Grand Rapids: Eerdmans, 1982.
Kleinknecht, Karl Theodor. *Der leidende Gerechtfertigte: Die alttestamentlich-jüdische Tradition vom 'leidenden Gerechten' und ihre Rezeption bei Paulus*. WUNT. Second Series 13. Tübingen: Mohr Siebeck, 1984.
Knibb, Michael A. "Martyrdom and Ascension of Isaiah." In *The Old Testament Pseudepigrapha*, vol. 2, edited by James Charlesworth, 143–76. New York: Doubleday, 1985.
Kruse, Colin G. "The Offender and the Offence in 2 Corinthians 2:5 and 7:12." *EvQ* 88 (1988) 129–39.
Kümmel, W. G. *The New Testament: The History of the Investigation of Its Problems*. Nashville: Abingdon, 1972.
Ladd, George Eldon. *The Gospel of the Kingdom: Scriptural Studies in the Kingdom of God*. Grand Rapids: Eerdmans, 1959.
Lane, William L. "Covenant: The Key to Paul's Conflict with Corinth." *TynB* 33 (1982) 3–29.
Lightfoot, J. B. *St. Paul's Epistle to the Galatians*. 2nd ed. Andover, UK: Draper, 1885.
Macchia, Frank D. "Justification through New Creation: The Holy Spirit and the Doctrine by which the Church Stands or Falls." *ThTo* 58/2 (2001) 202–17.
Martens, Elmer A. "The People of God." In *Central Themes in Biblical Theology: Mapping Unity in Diversity*, edited by Scott J. Hafemann and Paul R. House, 225–53. Grand Rapids: Baker, 2007.
Martin, Ralph P. *2 Corinthians*. WBC 40. Waco, TX: Word: 1986.
Martin, Troy W. "Apostasy to Paganism: The Rhetorical Stasis of the Galatian Controversy." *JBL* 114/3 (1995) 437–61.
———. "Whose Flesh? What Temptation? (Galatians 4:13–14)." *JSNT* 74 (1999) 65–91.
Martyn, J. Louis. *Theological Issues in the Letters of Paul*. Edinburgh: T. & T. Clark, 1997.
Meyer, Heinrich A. W. *Kritisch Exegetisches Handbuch über den zweiten Brief an die Korinther*. KEK 6. 5th ed. Göttingen: Vandenhoeck und Ruprecht, 1870.
Mitchell, Margaret M. *Paul, the Corinthians and the Birth of Christian Hermeneutics*. Cambridge: Cambridge University Press, 2010.

Moberly, R. W. L. *At the Mountain of God: Story and Theology in Exodus 32–34*. JSOTSup 22. Sheffield, UK: JSOT, 1983.
Moo, Douglas J. *The Epistle to the Romans*. NICNT. Grand Rapids: Eerdmans, 1996.
———. "Paul and the Law in the Last Ten Years." *SJT* 40 (1987) 287–307.
Morgenstern, J. "Moses with the Shining Face." *HUCA* 2 (1925) 1–27.
Moule, C. F. D. "Obligation in the Ethic of Paul." In *Christian History and Interpretation: Studies Presented to John Knox*, edited by W. F. Farmer et al., 313–35. Cambridge: Cambridge University Press, 1976.
Murphy-O'Connor, Jerome. "Paul and Macedonia: The Connection between 2 Corinthians 2:13 and 2:14." *JSNT* 25 (1985) 99–103.
Neill, S., and N. T. Wright. *The Interpretation of the New Testament 1861–1986*. 2nd ed. New York: Oxford University Press, 1988.
Nicholl, Colin. *From Hope to Despair in Thessalonica*. SNTSMS 126. Cambridge: Cambridge University Press, 2004.
Nock, A. D. *St. Paul*. London: Butterworth, 1938.
Novenson, Matthew V. *Christ among the Messiahs: Christ Language in Paul and Messiah Language in Ancient Judaism*. Oxford: Oxford University Press, 2012.
O'Brien, Peter T. *Consumed by Passion: Paul and the Dynamics of the Gospel*. Annual Moore College Lectures 1992. Homebush West, NSW: Lancer, 1993.
———. *Introductory Thanksgivings in the Letters of Paul*. NovTSup 49. Leiden: Brill, 1977.
Osten-Sacken, Peter von der. "Die Decke des Moses: Zur Exegese und Hermeneutik von Geist und Buchstabe in 2 Korinther 3." In *Die Heiligkeit der Tora: Studien zum Gesetz bei Paulus*, 87–115. München: Kaiser, 1989.
Pate, C. Marvin. *Adam Christology as the Exegetical and Theological Substructure of 2 Corinthians 4:7—5:21*. Lanham, MD: University Press of America, 1991.
Piper, John. *The Justification of God: An Exegetical and Theological Study of Romans 9:1–23*. Grand Rapids: Baker, 1983.
Plank, Karl A. *Paul and the Irony of Affliction*. SemeiaSt. Atlanta: Scholars, 1987.
Plummer, Alfred. *Second Epistle of St. Paul to the Corinthians*. ICC. 1915. Reprint. Edinburgh: T. & T. Clark, 1978.
Porter, Stanley E. *Idioms of the Greek New Testament*. Biblical Languages: Greek 2. 2nd ed. Sheffield, UK: JSOT, 1994.
Propp, William H. "The Skin of Moses' Face—Transfigured or Disfigured?" *CBQ* 49 (1987) 375–86.
Ridderbos, Herman. *Paul: An Outline of His Theology*. Grand Rapids: Eerdmans, 1975.
Sanders, E. P. *Paul and Palestinian Judaism: A Comparison of Patterns of Religion*. Philadelphia: Fortress, 1977.
Sandnes, Karl Olav. *Paul—One of the Prophets?: A Contribution to the Apostle's Self-Understanding*. WUNT. Second Series 43. Mohr Siebeck, 1991.
Satake, Akira. "Apostolat und Gnade bei Paulus." *NTS* 15 (1968) 96–107.
Savage, Timothy B. *Power through Weakness: Paul's Understanding of the Christian Ministry in 2 Corinthians*. SNTSMS 86. Cambridge: Cambridge University Press, 1996.
Schlatter, Adolf. *Paulus, der Bote Jesu: Eine Deutung seiner Briefe an die Korinther*. 1934. Reprint. Stuttgart: Calwer Verlag, 1969.
Schlier, Heinrich. *Der Brief an die Galater*. 5th ed. Göttingen: Vandenhoeck & Ruprecht, 1971.
———. "ἐκπτύω." In *TDNT* 2:448–49.

Schröter, Jens. *Der versöhnte Versöhner: Paulus als unentbehrlicher Mittler im Heilsvorgang zwischen Gott und Gemeinde nach 2. Kor 2:14—7:4.* TANTZ 10. Tübingen/Basel: Francke, 1993.
Schulz, Siegfried. "Die Decke des Moses: Untersuchungen zu einer vorpaulinischen Überlieferung." *ZNW* 49 (1958) 1–30.
Schweitzer, A. *The Mysticism of Paul the Apostle.* New York: Holt, 1931.
———. *Paul and His Interpreters: A Critical History.* 1912. Reprint. London: A. & C. Black, 1948.
Scott, James M. *2 Corinthians.* NIBC 8. Peabody, MA: Hendrickson, 1998.
———. "The Triumph of God in 2 Cor 2.14: Additional Evidence of Merkabah Mysticism in Paul." *NTS* 42/2 (1996) 260–81.
———. "The Use of Scripture in 2 Corinthians 6:16c–18 and Paul's Restoration Theology." *JSNT* 56 (1994) 73–99.
Scullion, J. J. "Righteousness (OT)." In *ABD* 5:724–36.
Stendahl, Krister. "Call Rather than Conversion." In *Paul among Jews and Gentiles and Other Essays*, 7–23. Philadelphia: Fortress, 1976.
———. "Christ's Lordship and Religious Pluralism." In *Meanings: The Bible as Document and as Guide*, 233–44. Philadelphia: Fortress, 1984.
———. *Paul among Jews and Gentiles and Other Essays.* Philadelphia: Fortress, 1976.
Stockhausen, Carol Kern. *Moses' Veil and the Glory of the New Covenant: The Exegetical Substructure of II Cor. 3:1—4:6.* AnBib 116. Rome: Pontifical Biblical Institute, 1989.
Strandenæs, Thor. "Completing the Mission: Paul's Application of the Gospel to the Faith and Life of the Thessalonian Converts in 1 and 2 Thessalonians." *SMT* 98 (2010) 69–98.
Stuhlmacher, Peter. *Biblische Theologie des Neuen Testaments: Vol. 1; Grundlegung. Von Jesus zu Paulus.* 3rd ed. Göttingen: Vandenhoeck & Ruprecht, 2005.
———. "'He is our Peace' (Eph 2:14): On the Exegesis and Significance of Ephesians 2:14–18." In *Reconciliation, Law, and Righteousness: Essays in Biblical Theology*, 182–200. Philadelphia: Fortress, 1986.
———. *Paul's Letter to the Romans: A Commentary.* Translated by Scott J. Hafemann. Louisville, KY: Westminster/John Knox, 1994.
———. "Theologische Probleme des Römerbriefpräskripts." *EvT* 27 (1967) 374–89.
Sumney, J. L. *Identifying Paul's Opponents: The Question of Method in 2 Corinthians.* JSNTSup 40. Sheffield, UK: Sheffield Academic Press, 1990.
Tasker, R. V. G. *The Second Epistle to the Corinthians.* TNTC 8. Grand Rapids: Eerdmans, 1958.
Taylor, Bernard A. "Deponency and Greek Lexicography." In *Biblical Greek Language and Lexicography: Essays in Honor of Frederick W. Danker*, edited by B. A. Taylor et al., 167–76. Grand Rapids: Eerdmans, 2004.
Thiselton, Anthony C. *Hermeneutics of Doctrine.* Grand Rapids: Eerdmans, 2007.
Versnel, Hendrik Simon. *Triumphus: An Inquiry into the Origin, Development and Meaning of the Roman Triumph.* Leiden: Brill, 1970.
Walton, John H. *Ancient Near Eastern Thought and the Old Testament: Introducing the Conceptual World of the Hebrew Bible.* Grand Rapids: Baker Academic, 2006.
Watson, Nigel M. "'. . . To Make Us Rely Not on Ourselves But on God Who Raises the Dead': 2 Corinthians 1,9b as the Heart of Paul's Theology." In *Die Mitte des Neuen Testaments: Einheit und Vielfalt neutestamentlicher Theologie*, edited by Ulrich Luz and Hans Weder, 384–98. Göttingen: Vandenhoeck & Ruprecht, 1983.

Way, D. V. *The Lordship of Christ: Ernst Käsemann's Interpretation of Paul's Theology.* Oxford: Clarendon, 1991.
Webb, William J. *Returning Home: New Covenant and Second Exodus as the Context for 2 Corinthians 6:14—7:1.* JSNTSup 85. Sheffield, UK: Sheffield Academic Press, 1993.
Wells, David. *God in the Wasteland: The Reality of Truth in a World of Fading Dreams.* Grand Rapids: Eerdmans, 1994.
Wendland, H. D. *Die Briefe an die Korinther.* NTD 7. Göttingen: Vandenhoeck & Ruprecht, 1972.
Wenham, David. "2 Corinthians 1:17, 18: Echo of a Dominical Logion." *NovT* 28 (1986) 271–79.
Westerholm, Stephen. *Israel's Law and the Church's Faith: Paul and His Recent Interpreters.* Grand Rapids: Eerdmans, 1988.
White, Joel R. "'Baptized on Account of the Dead': The Meaning of 1 Corinthians 15:29 in Its Context." *JBL* 116/3 (1997) 487–99.
Wilms, Frank Elmar. *Das Jahwistische Bundesbuch in Exodus 34.* Munich: Kösel, 1973.
Wilson, Todd A. *The Curse of the Law and the Crisis in Galatia.* WUNT. Second Series 225. Tübingen: Mohr Siebeck, 2007.
Windisch, Hans. *Der Zweite Korintherbrief.* KEK 6. Göttingen: Vandenhoeck & Ruprecht, 1924. Edited as the 9th ed. in 1970 by G. Strecker.
Wright, N. T. *The Climax of the Covenant: Christ and the Law in Pauline Theology.* Minneapolis: Fortress, 1991.
———. *The Letter to the Romans.* In *The New Interpreter's Bible: Vol. 10; The Acts of the Apostles, Introduction to Epistolary Literature, The Letter to the Romans, The First Letter to the Corinthians*, 393–770. Nashville: Abingdon, 2002.
———. *Paul and the Faithfulness of God.* 2 vols. London: SPCK, 2013.
———. *What Saint Paul Really Said: Was Paul of Tarsus the Real Founder of Christianity?* Grand Rapids: Eerdmans, 1997.
Yarbrough, Robert W. *The Salvation Historical Fallacy? Reassessing the History of New Testament Theology.* Leiden: Deo, 2004.

www.ingramcontent.com/pod-product-compliance
Lightning Source LLC
Chambersburg PA
CBHW022016220426
43663CB00007B/1107